First edition published by Putnam & Company Limited, 1961.

Republished by Peacock Press, 2019.

© Peacock Press, Scout Bottom Farm, Mytholmroyd, West Yorkshire, HX7 5JS, UK.

Cover photos: 'The Albion' in colour by Tim Groves; mono photo courtesy of the Roy Clark Archive

www.northernbeebooks.co.uk

ISBN: 978-1-912271-44-3

BLACK-SAILED TRADERS

The Keels and Wherries of Norfolk and Suffolk

by

Roy Clark

Last of the black-sailed traders—*Albion* sails into Lowestoft, 8th August, 1951

CONTENTS

CHAPTER		PAGE
I.	Now and Then	7
II.	The Fleeing Dutchmen	34
III.	Made to Measure	52
IV.	Shrouds, Topsails and Spinnakers	72
V.	Marl, Mud and Merchandise	88
VI.	Southwold Harbour and the Blyth Navigation	110
VII.	Blue Water Wherries and Far-away Havens	130
VIII.	Clippers of the Tideway	143
IX.	Tavern Tales and Spun Yarns	168
	Appendix One	201
	Appendix Two	238
	Appendix Three	240
	Appendix Four	242
	Appendix Five	244
	Bibliography	255
	Index	257

LIST OF ILLUSTRATIONS

Last of the black-sailed traders	*frontispiece*
	FACING PAGE
Three photographs of *Albion*	32
Norfolk as it used to be	33
Postwick Reach	33
Wherries in Yarmouth Roads	48
Wherries racing at sea	48
The river at Norwich	49
Fore and aft rig in Holland in the 1570s	49
The fore and aft rig comes to Norfolk	80
Burgh Castle water frolic, 1830s	81
Entrance to Yarmouth Harbour, 1830	81
Norwich about 1900	96
Down river from Bishop's Bridge	96
Two more photographs of *Albion*	97
Wherry inn signs	128
The New Cut, Haddiscoe	129
Jack Cates tending the *Albion*'s sheet	129
Three wherry skippers	144
The *Elizabeth* and *Dora*	145
Barton Regatta	176
The Breydon Wherry Race	177
Wherry-building on the River Wensum	192
A wherry woman at the tiller	192
Lowestoft in the Golden Age of sail	193

PLANS

Sail plan of the wherry *Gleaner*	57
Hull plan of the wherry *Gleaner*	69

CHAPTER ONE

Now and Then

Big logs for Beccles—the effects of women and drink—Albion sails down the Yare—ploughing a way through the New Cut—the 'market wherry'—the phantom on the Waveney—'shooting' a bridge—safe moorings in Beccles.

There was a raw edge to the wind as Jack Cates and I got off the train at Buckenham Halt. It was seven o'clock of a blustery March morning. Heaps of tousled, purple-grey clouds swept down on us from the north.

"Bit chilly," said the chap on the platform, taking our tickets into his numbed hands.

"It is that and no mistake, reckon we'll be making snowballs afore it's dark," answered Jack, striking a match and lighting the stub of his hand-rolled fag for the umpteenth time since we left Norwich.

"Where are you for this time?"

"Beccles, old partner, got forty tons of logs on board; brought 'em from Whitlingham off the Crown Point estate." We moved off towards the driftway leading down to the river when the railway chap called out to Jack, "Where's your mate?"

"He's here."

"Thought your brother went with you?"

"He's abed, bit poorly in the chest, so I've brought a substitute."

I was given a short, but all-embracing, glance.

"Does he know the job?"

"He can learn!" called out Jack over his shoulder, and giving me a broad wink we strode away down to the river.

It was a straight track we passed along, flanked on either side by alders and poplars. For about half a mile it crossed the belt of grazing marsh which made up the land between the railway and the river. But being early in the year no cattle had yet been put out to feed.

Jack cocked an eye at the banks of cloud galloping away to the south-west.

"Be some shovin' to do if it don't back a bit," he murmured. As he spoke I caught a glimpse of red bunting through the bare branches of the alders and poplars. It was the *Albion*'s weather-vane whipping and straining in the stiff breeze. And from its direction it certainly looked as if we were in for 'some shovin' ', a delightful understatement for the back-aching grind of quanting when the wind comes foul.

We clambered up on to the stretch of rough planking which served as landing-place and where the *Albion* was secured. In the cold, grey morning light the gleaming vermilion, white, blue and yellow of her deck works would have cheered the dullest heart. The rich amber-red of her forty-foot pitch-pine mast, glinting through its many coats of linseed oil, carried the eye instinctively to the top where the gaudy, gold-leafed vane, trailing its fathom of bunting, put a blob of welcome colour into the lowering sky.

We were surprised to find the village constable leaning on his bicycle looking at her.

"Morning," said Jack, " 'bout early, aren't yer?"

"Always on the job, that's us you know!" answered the constable with a broad grin for that hour of the morning, his cheeks red to blushing from the keen wind. "But just going off duty I'm glad to say. Came along to get a few eggs from the farm yonder and thought I'd have a decko at the old girl we all read so much about in the papers. Gets photographed like a film-star, doesn't she?"

We had to agree. Ever since she had been converted back into a trading wherry under canvas, the *Albion* had received her full share of publicity. Now, wherever she went, people stopped and looked at her, because she was the last of her kind, rigged out and painted as a wherry should be, and doing the work such craft have done on the rivers of Norfolk and Suffolk for centuries past.

We had a good hour to go before the tide would serve; with the scant wind blowing there was nothing to gain by trying to punch it. If we waited for the ebb there would not be so much 'shovin' ' to do in the middle reaches.

"Better put the kettle on," said Jack, examining carefully the half-inch butt of his fag. Deciding, rather reluctantly, that it did not merit the expenditure of still another match, he flicked it deftly into the river, took a rusty, battered tin from his pocket that once contained throat pastilles but now held his tobacco, and rolled himself a replacement with the rank, black shag he so greatly favoured. Only when reduced to desperate straits did I ever avail myself of his oft repeated invitation to "roll yourself one and have a decent smoke!"

I took the cabin key and left Jack and the constable yarning. Before we could put the kettle, on the fire had to be lit and as I was mate for the trip it was up to me to make a move.

A wherry's cabin is right aft, small but comfortable, about ten feet fore and aft. Against the bulkhead forward is the tiny, coal-fired stove and on either side a bunk for the skipper and mate. Under these bunks are lockers for coal, kindling and groceries and, above them, at each end, storage spaces for food, crockery and the like. There is no room for a table between the bunks, you eat sitting down with the plate on your knees.

I soon had the fire drawing and the kettle on, but before it got through I dabbed away some rust marks on the stove with the black-lead brush, just to show I knew my job. No wherryman can abide the slightest blemish on his stove, it has to be done and re-done till it shimmers like a piece of black velvet.

I squared up the cabin while the kettle boiled, got out the mugs and spoons, and the tin of Dutch condensed milk with the happy little inscription UNFIT FOR BABIES, and set the great brown teapot on the stove to warm. It held the best part of a gallon, was always kept simmering, and with frequent toppings up from the tea-tin and the kettle would keep us supplied until we got to Beccles. By then a spoon would stand up in it, which was all to the good, for the longer the day wore on the stronger you seemed to want your tea. He was a pretty poor mate who couldn't respond to the skipper's age-old call of "How's the pot?" with a piping hot mugful strong enough to put paid to the chatter of maiden ladies at a tea-party for the next month.

I gave the pot a good start with ten heaped-up teaspoonfuls and filled it to within an inch of the lid.

"Tea up!" I shouted, and looking out saw Jack had found a good listener in the constable. He was telling him about all the twists and turns in the river between Norwich and Yarmouth.

"Why, from Norwich to Reedham there are no less than forty reaches, each of 'em has a name, and there's a tale for the telling about everyone of 'em."

"What reach is this, then?" asked the constable.

"Where we are now is Buckenham Reach, the next one above us is Buckenham Horse Shoes, and that round the corner there, below us, is Hassingham Hubs, but don't ask me why. They mostly got their names from queer old characters who used to live nearby or had things happen to 'em, but what Hassingham Hubs stands for I never did figure out. But, as I said, there's a yarn could be told about all of 'em, take this one for instance, Buckenham Reach."

"What happened here?" asked the constable, who was now, like many more before him, completely under the spell of Jack's yarn-spinning.

"Something in your line of business, I reckon," said Jack, "though it was a long time ago. A wherry brought up for the night just where we're standing now. The mate lived handy so the skipper told him he could go home and bring up in the lee of something warm. They agreed to muster at six in the morning and make the best of the tide down to Yarmouth. Well, the mate turned up all right, but the skipper wasn't much use to him. He was hanging in the forepeak with the halliard fast round his neck."

"Lor'," muttered the constable, "must have had plenty on his mind to do a thing like that."

"Oh, women, I suppose, or beer, usually one or t'other when a chap hangs himself. Tea, now, that'll keep you on the straight and narrow. Come aboard and have a mug, it's cold standing here."

Jack led the way, and in a few minutes we were all settled down warming our noses over pint pots, which in a wherry serve as teacups. Both the polish on the stove, and the tea, must have come up to scratch, for they passed without comment. Jack swigged at the one and looked at the other but said nothing. That's the way with skippers. They don't say a word when things are as they should be, but blow their top when they aren't. Which is really very sensible when you come to think of it.

The constable was impressed with the warmth and comfort of our quarters. His helmet dangled from the catch on one of the locker doors and he seemed in no hurry to sign off and go for his breakfast. He told us he was just out of the Navy and how he missed the life aboard ship. Like a good many others he was finding it a struggle to settle down in civvy street. Both Jack and I had been in the Navy, too, so there was plenty to talk about. But at last Jack slid himself off the bunk into the sternsheets, took a look at the water along the banks, and said, "Tide's just about away. Better be moving."

"Ah, well, suppose I'll have to be getting along," said our sailor-cum-policeman, finishing his tea and reaching out for his helmet. Very reluctantly he got to his feet and went on deck, followed by Jack and myself.

"Wish I were coming with you," he called as he hopped ashore and watched our preparations for sailing. "You can give us our ropes when we get the sail up," added Jack by way of consolation, stepping on to the hatches to take off the sail lashings.

Size for size there is no craft in the world easier to get under way than a Norfolk wherry, for her rig is the essence of simplicity. The mast, despite its height and weight, is counterbalanced for easy lowering and is supported by a single stay only, leading to the stem-head. There are no shrouds and the one great black sail is hoisted by a single halliard brought to a small barrel-winch at the foot of the mast.

In less than five minutes we had got it up and everything on deck was shipshape for the day's run. This was to take us down the Yare as far as Reedham, south-eastward through the Cut to Haddiscoe, then south and south-west up the Waveney to Beccles, a distance all told of twenty miles or so.

It was the second leg of the passage which had begun a few days before at Whitlingham, two miles down-river from Norwich, where the *Albion* had loaded forty tons of big logs from a riverside plantation. Wherrymen call them big logs because they really are big and often weigh two or three tons each. If you imagine a good-sized tree trunk, two to three feet in diameter, sawn into about four lengths, you will get a good idea what they are like.

Forty tons is full lading for the *Albion* and she was deep in the water, or 'down to her bins' as they say, when she set off for Beccles. The wind was northerly in the early part of the day and she made fair progress. But gradually it began edging ahead so that by nightfall she had only managed to fetch Buckenham where Jack Cates brought her alongside and called it a day.

Now one advantage of the wherryman's life over the sailor's is that when he brings up for the night he is never at anchor, but comfortably and safely tied up to a river bank. All he need do is turn the key in his cabin door and go home. Nine times out of ten a short walk will bring him to a railway station or a road and within the hour he is generally sitting round his own tea-table. To make doubly sure the skipper and mate often take their bicycles, which you can see propped up against the tabernacle or lying on the hatches.

On this first stage of the trip the *Albion* had had her regular crew of two, Jack Cates, skipper, and, along with him for mate, his brother George, 'Snowball' to all and sundry, because he was born on Christmas Day. They had caught the train at Buckenham Halt and gone home to Norwich intending to muster first thing, or rather first train, in the morning, and carry on for Beccles. But the wind held easterly, blew half a gale, and they could not move. Then George had a nasty touch of bronchitis, the doctor sent him to bed for a spell, and when the wind freed into the north-west a couple of days later, the *Albion* had no mate.

That is how I came to be on board though, to be sure, I felt Jack's invitation was more a kindly gesture than an expression of his faith in me as a wherryman. For wherrymen, he used to say, were born and not made. The more I came to sail in the *Albion* the more I came to agree with him, because although I have knocked about in boats all my life and reckon myself a passable seaman, I always had the feeling when he sang out an order that had I been a proper wherryman, firstly, he would have had no need to give an order at all, and, secondly, that I should have carried it out in much better fashion than I did. I do not think this is to be wondered at because in every specialized trade there is an accumulation of skills which are handed down from generation to generation, modified, perhaps, from time to time, and improved upon, but which always remain the hallmark of the master-craftsman. I believe that is why so many of the skilled trades run in families. From father to son, down the years, knowledge and the ability to use it, are passed on, and you could look for no better example of this than amongst the families of wherrymen who, up to thirty years ago, traded on the rivers of Norfolk and Suffolk.

But wherryman or no, I hopped ashore at a nod from Jack and stood by the stern rope. With the wind right across the river as it was here the *Albion* was snubbing at her moorings as if impatient to be off.

"Right-o," said Jack, and as he slacked up I threw off the bowline and jumped aboard with it.

"Slack up for'ard and let go," was the next order which sent me hurrying on to the forepeak. As I took off the turns our constable lifted his end from the tree-stump, serving for a bollard, and in best wherryman style brought it to me to save it getting wet.

"Good sailing," he called out, and quite forgetting the uniform he was then wearing, saluted in a manner that would have done credit to the quarterdeck of a battleship.

"And don't break them eggs of yours!" sang out Jack. With a wave of the hand and a "see you again next time we're up this way", he gave the *Albion* her head.

The wind was fresh but true and for all her fifty years she picked up her skirts and sped away like a witch. With an eye continually cocked aloft at the vane, haunches against the tiller, Jack tended the sheet at every turn of the river to keep her doing her best, coaxing and encouraging as a jockey might some fine thoroughbred on Newmarket Heath.

The heavy load she was carrying made her stiff but the little she did heel over was enough to put her lee plankway under the water. I remembered then what I had been told many a time, that a wherry was not properly loaded unless a robin could drink off her decks. A flock of them might have quenched their thirst this morning.

With all this water around for the asking I gave the decks a good scrubbing and then cheesed down our mooring ropes, saw that the quants were in their right place inboard of the timber heads and laid a couple of cork fenders handy in case of emergency.

All the time Jack kept her hugging the weather bank except where a turn in the river brought her a bit too close to the wind, forcing him to cut the corner to leeward into the next reach. But once round up he would bring her towards the weather bank again. Jack, of course, knew every reach, every twist and turn by heart. He had learned them through years of experience and could look out of his bedroom window, back home in Norwich, at the crack of dawn, take one glance at the way the clouds were blowing, and tell you just which reaches you would be able to sail and those you would not. And there were more than fifty of them between Norwich and Yarmouth.

We were romping along in Langley Middle Short Reach when I came aft and stood in the sternsheets with him. The rusty pastille tin lay handy on the cabin top, the inevitable burnt out stub of a cigarette hung in his mouth.

"You might take her a minute while I go and see that chap about a dog," he said looking up at the vane, "keep her as she goes."

I braced my haunches against the tiller as Jack ambled into the lee of the sail for the particular bit of business he had in hand. I had never sailed the *Albion* in a wind like this before, it was a new, exhilarating experience. Here was no docile creation of canvas and wood, but something alive, something with a will and purpose of her own that could be led, but never driven; her whole frame trembled to the press of wind on her canvas.

The six-foot long tiller seared into my hip and I jammed my boot against the footrest to get a better purchase. In that contact was the feel of the very wind itself, that sense of exultation man gains from taming the elements to carry himself and his goods from place to place. The free winds of heaven were urging forty tons of timber on their way to Beccles and there would be no fuel bills to pay when we got there.

But for me at that moment it did not matter about the cargo or the fuel bills; all that counted was the thrill of sailing the veteran *Albion* over the tideway she knew so well. There was the added excitement, too, of knowing that a wherry's black sail had not been seen on the river for more than ten years. Between the wars most of these craft had slowly given ground to diesel engines, and steam tugs towing lighters, till, in 1939, only three were left. When the war ended, the *Albion* was the sole survivor, and she had been stripped of her gear and put to lightering.

It was a menial job for so fair a lady and with the help of a few enthusiasts as keen as myself I set about getting her a reprieve. With letters to the papers, handbills, public meetings in riverside towns which once had been strongholds of the wherries, we appealed to people's local patriotism to help preserve one of these unique craft. As a result, the Norfolk Wherry Trust was formed, and sufficient funds were subscribed to buy the *Albion* and refit her.

Right at the start Jack Crates had offered himself as skipper and a tower of strength he proved to be. His help was invaluable in fitting out and rigging her, and her rapid transformation from a woebegone hulk to a smart sailing craft owed a very great deal to his advice and enthusiasm.

So, from the beginning of this venture, he and I had worked closely together. There was little enough cash available for all the repairs needed and it was one long headache deciding between what ought to be done and what we could afford to do. In the end, for all our shoestring budget, we made her staunch and fit to trade. In one or two places where her timbers were weak we had them doubled; several badly worn strakes between wind and water were replaced; the tabernacle was strengthened with new knees; and she was given a new ceiling.

The brand-new mast and sail ran away with a lot of our hard-won money, but when she came out of dock, we had every reason to be proud of her. Wherever she went, crowds collected, the youngsters marvelling at something they had heard about but never seen, the older ones nodding their heads and murmuring approval as she kindled memories of the old days. The village constable at Buckenham had come to fetch eggs, but stayed to admire, and then drink tea aboard, the *Albion*; it was typical of her reception up and down the rivers. It was, too, ample reward for all the hard work we had put in.

The good wind held strong and true setting the reeds and the slim willow branches into a merry caper along the banks. They danced and curtsied as we skimmed by; a lordly swan paused for a moment from his grubbing amongst the ooze and pointed a yellow, inquiring beak at us; the sun found a crack in the clouds and flashed a trail of golden warmth over the marshes.

I heard the clump of Jack's boots as he came back aft. He had been trying the pump up forward and I was a bit anxious to know if we were making much water with all this weight aboard.

"Not a lot," he said, in answer to my question, "and what there is is coming in under the bins and through the plankways. Doesn't matter, of course, with a freight like this, but we'll have to watch it when we've got wheat or anything perishable like that." It was a weakness we both knew about only too well, but it was a major job to put right, and we just had not got enough in the kitty to do anything about it at present. But to wet a cargo of perishable goods was a serious matter and to avoid that we did not intend to load more than thirty-five tons. We knew her hull was tight enough and she only made water when her decks, or plankways as they are called, were awash. It would not happen if we did not load her so deeply.

Jack was in no hurry to take over again but sat down on the cabin top and rolled himself a smoke. I listened to the water gurgling and chuckling past the rudder, and the gentle singing of the kettle coming up through the open cabin door. The wind did its work so quietly that these were the only sounds, except when we disturbed a heron at his breakfast, and sent him away krawking protests at the instrusion.

The river now began its wide sweep round to the north-east leading to Cantley and as we brought the wind more and more ahead it took a good, honest pull to haul in the sheet. We gradually opened out the tall buildings and tapering chimney of the sugar-beet factory and saw a couple of London coasters loading sacks of the new season's crop.

This was the reach we knew we should not be able to sail.

"Might go and help her round," said Jack, as he slipped into the sternsheets and took over the tiller, "one board should do us."

I put a match to my pipe and went forward down the weather plankway, to keep my feet dry. We were doing better than I had expected, for one tack across the river, which hereabouts is fairly wide, would give us enough offing to weather the bend into Devil's House Reach. Slowly we closed the starboard bank and my job was now, as she began turning on to the other tack, to plunge a quant into the bed of reeds, and bring all my weight to bear on it, so that I not only helped to force her head round, but also kept way on her. It needs nice judgment to place the quant at just the right angle; if it's too square you tend to stop her, and if it's too fine you do not get enough purchase to do any good.

Luck was with me on the first turn and she came round as sweet as a nut, filling away in fine style for the opposite bank. The second time I did not do so well, took quite a bit of way off her and hung her up. But an extra hard shove remedied matters and away we went with the rest plain sailing, we hoped, as far as Beccles.

But wind and tide were not our only concern; we should soon be approaching the railway bridge at Reedham, the first of five such obstacles across our path, and in a sailing craft, where you cannot just ring a bell and go astern, they present a very real hazard. Usually the bridgemen are pretty good, they realize you cannot put on your brakes like a motor car, and flag you in good time if you have got to wait for a train. When that happens, you can either ease your sheet and let her fall into the reeds, or round to and dodge into the tide till you get the all-clear. You can, of course, lower sail and mast and shoot through, but the extra work involved is usually reserved for fixed bridges.

Today our luck was in; as we came down Black House Reach, a half a mile or so above the bridge, we saw a plume of smoke across the marshes.

"That'll be the Lowestoft train coming up," said Jack, "we couldn't have timed things better. Get her out of the way and they ought to give us the bridge."

"And what shall we do with it, I wonder, put it on top of the logs and take it to Beccles?"

Jack winced at this un-wherrymanlike sally and in despair picked up his mug and looked ruefully at the dregs in the bottom.

"What's more to the point," he answered, "is what I'm going to do with this here pot o' mine? Fill it with river water and drink that?"

I took the hint and dived down into the cabin. In a minute or two I was back with a couple of flaming hot mugs of real strongers. He took a long, approving pull at the steaming dark fluid; I did the same, and grinned. The mate's honour was preserved, he had been weighed in the balance and was not yet found wanting.

As we got abreast of the Lord Nelson pub the bridge began to swing. A burst of sunshine sent the shadow of our sail scurrying past the windows of the waterside cottages which acted like magic on those within. We saw a succession of doors open and old men peer forth, their wives craning their necks behind them, to feast their eyes once more upon a wherry under sail. The sight of her must have taken their minds back to the days when Reedham wherries were the cocks of the river, when whole fleets were owned in the village and when they boasted one of the best yards in the two counties. Most Reedham men were connected in some way or other with the river and a great many were either owners, skippers or mates.

All that is going back thirty or forty years but even now a few of the old-timers are left and it cheered us to see them coming to their doors and waving a gnarled fist in greeting

"Ahoy, there, Jack boy," shouted one blue-jerseyed old fellow in carpet slippers. "how's Pinwire these days?"

"He's a-doing," called back Jack. Pinwire is his brother Walter.

"And Snowball?"

"Bit poorly, touch of bronchial."

"Ah! that's bad."

The distance between us grew till we were nearly out of earshot, then came the inevitable question, "Where're you for, Beccles?"

Jack raised a hand and nodded.

"Thought so when I see them logs. Mind how you go, young Jack," and we felt his keen eyes follow our every movement as we made down to the bridge. The single span had swung open and from the forepeak I could see the rip of the tide round the protecting dolphins.

I had a fender ready just in case, but there was no need of it. Jack slipped her through as cleanly as if he had been threading a needle and with as little fuss. As the bridge swung to behind us the New Cut opened out ahead and in five minutes we were out of the River Yare and sailing with a free sheet on the canal which had been made a hundred years before with the aim of turning the city of Norwich into a port. It was a well-intentioned but ill-fated venture which almost from the moment it was finished began to fall into decay. The first two ships to use it passed through on the last day of September 1833. They were the *Squire* and the *City of Norwich* belonging to the newly formed Norwich, Lowestoft and London Shipping Company, and they had a draught of about nine feet each.

When they reached Norwich, which they did to scenes of great rejoicing, they reported not having touched the ground once since leaving Lowestoft. We had less cause to rejoice for with about half that draught we were scraping the bottom all the way to Haddiscoe. If we had been any later on the tide we should have come up solid.

But with a quant over the side every now and again to help her through the worst bits, we passed under the rickety span of Haddiscoe road bridge, obligingly raised for us in exchange for a two-shilling piece, lowered the sail and brought up just where the Cut enters the River Waveney.

The tide would be down here for another two hours, and the wind, though still fair, had dropped a lot since we started, so there was no particular object in plugging on.

"We'll be there just as soon if we lay up till the tide makes," was Jack's summing up, "and I don't know about you, but I've got a bit of grub I'd like to warm up in the oven."

I had not forgotten the inner man either and as soon as Jack's meat patty was stowed away in the oven I shovelled on some small coal, pulled out the damper, and got to work with the frying-pan.

"Cor! big eats, and no mistake!" murmured Jack, as I set a pair of gammon rashes to sizzle, "didn't you have any breakfast?"

"About as much as you did, I shouldn't be surprised," said I, "a cup of tea and a bite of toast. Can't stomach a lot first thing in the morning. But I must say that quanting has given me a new interest in food," and to emphasize the needs of the moment I broke two eggs into the crackling fat alongside the rashers and began getting out the knives and forks, pepper and salt and mustard.

I always find a pleasant peacefulness about meals aboard ship when you are safely at anchor or moored up, a delightful sense of rest which makes you want to start telling tales and spinning yarns. You have no worries about your vessel, and because of that your digestion is good, and your mind that bit more receptive to the glow of romance which always seems to hover more closely then round stories of bygone days.

I knocked my pipe out in the grate and filled it again as Jack put his head out of the door for a glance up and down the Cut. Satisfied that the tide would keep us here a while longer he settled himself once more. I watched four curlew pipe their way northward across the small square of sky made by the door frame and hoped they would find as good a meal on the flats round Breydon Water as I had just had. Jack took up a point he had been making earlier.

"The trouble with wherrying today, with only the one of us at it, is the loneliness," he went on. "Take this morning, for instance, here we are come all the way from Buckenham to Haddiscoe and haven't seen another craft of any description, nor another soul on the water except ourselves. You don't always want to be mardling when you've got a job to do but you do miss a bit of company, like we used to have years ago, wherries here, there and everywhere, always someone to pass the time of day with as you sailed past. Nowadays everything is deserted and dead in comparison with what it used to be, staithes and moorings all broken down and dilapidated, weeds growing so thick there's hardly enough water to float in, trees grown up so you can hardly sail, and on top of all that," continued Jack, taking a long and satisfying pull from his mug, "you can't even get a bag full of mushrooms off the marshes here like you could in days gone by. They just don't grow as they used to."

The dearth of mushrooms is a sore point with chaps along the rivers and no one really knows where they have gone to. The few that manage to struggle up are small and tasteless, you never clap eyes now on those thick, fat, juicy monsters, the size of a dinner plate, that filled your pan half full with delicate brown gravy when they were fried, and made a marshland breakfast something to remember all your life. Perhaps it is that nature thrives better on the raw materials of horse and bullock than she does on the contaminating discharge of tractor exhaust pipes.

But this grumble of Jack's about mushrooms was thrown in as a sort of makeweight in criticizing present day life on the river. I am not really sure that 'criticizing' is the right word, 'comparing' would probably be better; it was inevitable he should always be comparing and contrasting things now with what they were when he was a youngster forty years ago.

"I don't know if I ever told you about George Harrod and Billy Thurgar," he went on, "but about 1890 they had a wherry called the *Test*. Along with a lot more they were down in Yarmouth loading up when it came on to blow a breeze of wind westerly, well, you know what that meant, they all had to stay there. It held like that for three days before it freed and when it did, the *Test* was the first of the bunch to get away. When they'd sailed to the top of Breydon Water George asked Billy to have a good look astern and count the wherries following them."

"Ah!" I said, "I bet there was a good thirty of 'em."

"Thirty, fiddlesticks," said Jack, "it took Billy all of ten minutes to work through them so thick were they, but when he'd finished he told George Harrod he made it sixty-one sail! Imagine that lot stretching away up the Waveney here to Beccles, and up the Yare to Norwich. When it got dark a few of them would keep going to make sure of hoisting in their freight money while the wind held, but the rest would bring up at a handy pub, all the riverside pubs had moorings where they could lie for the night, and by first light in the morning, when they would all be under way again, you could reckon on meeting a sail the whole length of the river from Norwich down to Yarmouth. And as you went by it would be, "Where bound?", "Seen *King Henry* lately?", "Two timber boats due Lowestoft tomorrow", "Bin a-bed with Liza lately?" and so on, all the latest news and gossip, bantering and chaffing each other, and you always knew if you got into a bit of a frap there'd soon be someone along to give you a hand, a pluck off the mud, maybe, or a boil-up of spuds if your locker was empty. There must have been a hundred or more more wherries then on the three rivers, and work to do for all of them. Pay wasn't much, of course, but things didn't cost the earth as they do now, and when a youngster got married he'd think himself well off if he and his wife had fifteen bob a week. And they were happy on it, too, leastways, judging by all the children they had, ten or twelve was nothing. Still, there wasn't much other entertainments of nights then, I suppose," ended Jack, with a twinkle in his eye.

I grinned back, wondering mildly what effect our addiction for television may have on the future birthrate, and asked him if he would like some more tea. He nodded, and as I stretched out for the pot, said you could not help missing all the old characters, the men and women of queer dress and strange habits who, for all that, took a real pride in their craft and their job, had a language all their own, were uncouth and rough of tongue, perhaps, but whose vitality and zest for life were infectious.

I knew just what he meant for I have been lucky to know some of them, to sit round their small fires with a cup of tea on my knee listening to their stories. They like talking about themselves because now they dwell in the past rather than the present. Their values are the values of yesterday, and there could be no better summing up of what those values were than the words of one fine old eighty-year-old who said to me, "We spent our life watching the tides so that we could get work, not watching the clock so that we could get out of it."

"Ah, yes," said Jack, "times change and people change with them, whether for better or worse, though, I wouldn't like to say. Lying like we are now in Haddiscoe Cut I've been kind o' wondering if we make 'em on the same pattern nowadays as old 'Tip' Hellesdon, who used to ply this way a fair bit. Had a gut like leather, he did."

"Sounds a tough'n," I chipped in.

"He was tough all right. See the pub there, by the road? Well, Tip has been known to drink seventeen pints in there before breakfast, and when the wind came foul down the Cut, to get out a rope and tow his wherry the four miles to Reedham. Now I reckon I can drink beer with the best of 'em and I'm not exactly what you'd call a weakling, but I'm damned if I could do that, not for a pension, and I don't know anyone else as could."

"Try drinking seventeen pints anyway in a public house before breakfast these days, and you'd soon find yourself in clink!"

"You're right! And that's another bit of tomfoolery that's changed things on the river. Didn't your working chap always have beer with his breakfast? And with a nice chunk of red meat if he could get it? I'll lay that did 'em a sight more good than what they get nowadays, a lot of wood shavings piled into a cardboard box and labelled 'corn flakes'. Might as well eat sawdust for all the good it does you. Get a pint of two of good ale into you, like in the old days, and you felt you'd had something. But I suppose because it did you good and put back some of the sweat you'd lost shovin' and heavin' the day afore, the government thought they'd stop it, make you a criminal for drinkin' it. It's all a rum do and no mistake. But if I tried to do what Tip Hellesdon did, tow all along here to Reedham, my biggest worry would be the tow-path. Did you see it as we came through? You'd be up to your armpits in thistles trying to get by there now."

Wherries were never towed, or trekked, to the same extent that canal barges were, because only rarely was there any need of it. A wherry could sail almost into the eye of the wind, the rivers were reasonably wide, and because they twisted and turned only a proportion of the reaches brought the wind dead ahead. With room to beat there was no need to send anyone ashore with a line, and it was only on a few stretches, such as Haddiscoe Cut, where a bit of hauling was resorted to. Horses were never used for towing as they were on the canals, though one old chap came very close to it. He owned a very small wherry, which he sailed single-handed, and being well on in years found baffling winds rather a trial on his strength. So he bought a small donkey which he kept in the hold and it must have had a very pleasant and peaceful life, for its sole duty was to go ashore at the beginning of a reach where the wind was a bit scant, and amble along towing the wherry till a bend brought the wind fair again! Then presumably, while the owner sat on the cabin top congratulating himself on such easy progress and enjoying a well earned pipe, the 'dickie' would nibble contentedly at the lush, green grass, and count his blessings! After that, in due course, he would trot down the plank into the hold followed by his master with a tub of cool, clear river water for him to drink. Then, patting the donkey appreciatively on the head, he would put the hatch covers back in place, and continue the voyage.

Slow, you may say? To be sure, but who would not like to think their groceries had arrived at the village store by such a romantic and friendly combination of forces?

This little craft was soon dubbed the 'Dickie' wherry; anyone who did something a bit out of the ordinary was not long in getting a nickname either for himself or his vessel. One I always liked hearing about was the *Rob Roy*, though she seldom went by her proper name; she was known everywhere as the 'Market' wherry because each Wednesday and Saturday morning, rain, blow or snow, she took aboard the market women from the district around Reedham and sailed them to Yarmouth. They carried with them great peds of vegetables, baskets of fine farm butter, eggs and poultry, and of course, hordes of children. Going to school did not count for much ninety years ago and these twice-weekly sprees in Yarmouth were not to be missed at any price.

They settled themselves wherever they could find room, most in the hold, sitting and lying among the produce, some on deck, and a few privileged ones in the cabin. When it rained or snowed they sheltered under the massive market umbrellas which every woman carried, for not one of them would have considered bad weather sufficient excuse for not taking their goods to market. Yet to reach Yarmouth they had to cross Breydon Water, anything but a cakewalk in a blow with the wind against the tide. Plenty of craft have come to grief there in the past and plenty will again. As long ago as 1712, twenty passengers in a wherry bound for Norwich were thrown out and drowned when she was capsized in a squall.

But John Anderson, who owned this market wherry and lived at Reedham, knew every inch of the eight miles to Yarmouth. And though hampered and harassed, as he must have been, by the swarms of young nippers scrambling all over the place, he never had a mishap and always landed his passengers on the dot. They went ashore at The Waterman's Arms, where everyone downed a tot or two, then made their way through the narrow Rows leading from the quayside to the market-place. When they had sold all there was to sell they would buy what things they wanted to take home, tea, sugar, pots, pans, candles and so on, and return to The Waterman's Arms, which at that time was kept by Benjamin Burton. Of course there were always stragglers to wait for and that meant there was ample opportunity for the others to sample Benjamin's brew. They found this no hardship and poor John Anderson had the double task on the way back of keeping the *Rob Roy* on her course and the women from falling overboard. As he groped his way through the darkness the night air echoed to the babble of lewd and earthy female chatter. The children slept soundly on their measure of small beer and hot meat pies, and for an hour or two it was a woman's world down in the hold. How fortunate John Anderson was a married man who had no cause to blush; and that he was so good a wherryman he could stand vigilant and wakeful at the tiller, faithful guardian of this little world of female intimacy.

In the snug warmth of the *Albion*'s cabin both Jack and I must have dozed off for a spell. I came to at last out of a strange reverie in which I had seen a white donkey sitting on our forepeak under a large black umbrella, drinking bucket after bucket of beer which Tip Hellesdon kept getting for it, out of the river. I heard Jack's voice float across to me, "Come on, Roy, the Beccles girls have got hold of the tow-rope, the tide's up, time we got a move on."

I pulled on my cap and went up top where Jack was already shipping the handles in the winch to hoist the sail. I glanced up at the vane which showed the wind had veered a trifle. It was all in our favour and meant a flowing sheet right the way to Beccles. A couple of locals had come to have a look at us and were promptly signed up to let go our ropes.

We took a handle apiece and began cranking; hoisting a wherry's sail is not like the grinding toil of getting the anchor in a Thames barge, but it's enough to put some colour in your cheeks and make you vow you will give up smoking for a week at least. The two onlookers watched our black canvas climb slowly up into the sky, a little astonished at the size of it.

"That'll do nicely," said Jack, with a quick, critical look aloft, "hope they've seen us at the bridge and don't keep us hanging about."

We had three more bridges to deal with before we got to Beccles. The last one we knew we should have to lower for, so we kept our fingers crossed that the others would open. As we nosed out of the Cut into the main stream of the Waveney we could see that the first of them, St. Olave's, was already beginning to swing. We gathered way quickly, passed through as clean as a whistle and stood on for the next one, Somerleyton, three miles away.

The country in these parts is quite flat and you can see for such great distances that vessels often seem to be sailing over the dry land. We knew the bridge-keeper would have spotted us long ago, probably ever since we left Reedham, and would do his best to let us through without any hold-ups. But our hopes were dashed when we saw a hand waving us down from the box and next instant I picked out the smoke of a train two miles off coming from Lowestoft. We should have to bring up.

The bank was soft and yielding enough for Jack to ease the *Albion* into; he hauled the sheet taut and spilled the wind out of the sail while I hopped ashore and took a turn with the stern rope.

We waited about ten minutes for the train. It appeared to be doing a good business in milk cans at Somerleyton station. At last it hove into sight, puffing delicate grey smoke-rings into the air which the wind caught eagerly and sent swirling away over the glistening brown backs of some Suffolk punches grazing down by the river.

Then, with a hollow, muffled rumbling, engine and carriages crossed the bridge, the fireman raised a grimy hand to us by way of greeting, and I went forward to shove the *Albion*'s head out into the stream. We had let go the stern rope and as the sail filled all I had to do was prod her clear of the bank with a quant. She would have sailed off herself quite easily but we wanted to save carrying away too much mud on her freshly tarred sides.

I was giving one final heave, shoulder to quant and really putting some weight into it, when the thick and rather clumsy boots I was wearing played me false. The studs slipped on the damp deck, I fell flat on my stomach, and with nothing to hang on to, lurched over the side chest deep in the icy water. As the wherry moved away from me I shot out a hand and took a precarious finger grip on the plancea; as I did so I saw Jack out of the corner of my eye bend down and salvage the quant and almost in the same movement grip my free wrist.

"Come on, old partner," I heard him say, "you can't go deserting the old ship like that," and getting a hold under my arms, yanked me inboard and bundled me on the hatches.

I sat there for a moment dazed, catching my breath, a soggy, sorry and very unhappy mess. Pools of stinking mud and water oozed out on to the bright new paintwork, thick, clinging slime covered me from toe to midriff.

Before I could start moaning Jack was back at the tiller and deftly poking the cause of all my woes through the bridge-hole. My humiliation was complete when the bridge-keeper called out to Jack, "Bit early in the year for your mate to start swimming, isn't it?" I was beginning to feel so numb with cold I could only shake a not very belligerent fist at him and start shedding my wet clobber.

"There's a spare pair of khaki trousers you can have on my bunk," called out Jack, "and an old guernsey. Leave that lot there and get below and dry out what you can. 'Tain't really sunbathing weather yet."

It was not, by any means, and I lost no time making for the warmth of the stove. I gave shirt and vest a good wringing and they were soon steaming away merrily on the rack. I rummaged around and found a nice clean deck cloth which served for a towel, then I dug out a pair of old, and rather holey socks, next the trousers, then the guernsey, a swig of tea and a pipe of baccy, and things began to brighten up quite a lot.

I filled Jack's mug for him and we were soon joking about the whole affair.

"Oh, well," he said, "you aren't the first whose fallen overboard and it's a sure thing you won't be the last. Anyway, that'll be something to remind you of your first trip as mate in the *Albion*!"

I set to wringing out the rest of my wet clothes and strung them up to dry; then I washed off the mud from the hatches and tidied up generally before coming aft to give Jack a spell at the tiller. The wind had gone down to a gentle breeze now, the sun was dropping away, and the old *Albion* steered as docile as a lamb as if repenting of the way she had handled me.

As darkness fell we watched heavy banks of cloud form up astern of us, the sort of clouds you feel instinctively are full of snow. But the cold was not unpleasant, just enough nip in the air to keep you on the move.

When it was quite dark Jack took over and I went forward. Back against the winch barrel, hands dug deep into my borrowed trousers, I kept an eye open for anything on the move. Not that there was likely to be, at night, and at this time of the year. I sang out the trend of each reach as we came to it more to let Jack know I was still awake than to guide him, as he could have sailed to Beccles blindfolded. A snatch of an old song kept running through my mind as we floated along over the black waters, telling of love and intimacy long ago on the banks of this selfsame river. Who, I wondered, was the young maiden who pleaded so earnestly not to be left in the lurch, and who the young lover who could sing:

> *Then 'twas I kissed her ruby lips*
> *As she laid upon the grass,*
> *And coming to herself again*
> *She did cry out, "Alas,*
> *Since you have had your will of me,*
> *Make me your lawful bride,*
> *And do not leave me here to mourn*
> *Down by the Wav'ney's side."*

I found no answer from the whispering reed-ronds, and gazing into the shadowy distances ahead I began wondering if, perchance, I should see the unearthly radiance of the Phantom Wherry, gliding silently towards me on her strange and terrible passage down to the sea. Others have sworn to seeing her in these parts, and they say her ghostly voyagings are doomed to go on like the *Flying Dutchman*'s for ever.

What appalling crime of violence or passion, you may ask, what scenes of fury and conflict occurred to demand such awful expiation? Was it the love of a man for a maid, of swift pursuing vengeance and sudden death? What was the devilish thing that needs eternity for atonement?

I can answer these questions only from hearsay and gossip, from scraps of conversations in waterside pubs and wherries' cabins, told by people who would never admit believing what they were saying but who, you felt instinctively, did not doubt for one moment the truth of it all. I will tell you the tale as I have come to know it; you must believe it or not according to your fancy.

Once upon a time a wherryman plied his craft carrying wheat from Lowestoft and Yarmouth up to Beccles. He always delivered it to the same mill and was soon aware that the miller had a very beautiful daughter who, from the first, he desired with a passion that grew and grew every time he saw her. The daughter was young, virtuous and deeply attached to her father, so much so that she had no inkling of the wherryman's feelings for her. She talked with him, modestly but without reserve, freely went aboard when he was unloading, and in general regarded him as a friend.

But these pleasant chats and visits to the wherry only inflamed his passion till he felt himself being consumed by his desire to possess her. Inevitably he began plotting her downfall and at last hit on the plan of inviting her to sail with him down to Yarmouth. Suspecting nothing of the dark scheme he was harbouring both she and her father readily agreed.

So one fine summer's afternoon the maid and the wherryman set sail down the Waveney, but had the black thoughts in his mind been given utterance they would have made a mockery of the warm sunshine glinting on the green marshlands.

The wind was fair and sent them scurrying over Breydon and when they reached Yarmouth both bridges were flung open to let them pass. The maid had never before been to such far-off places and she gazed about her in wonderment as they sailed down the harbour. It was then the wherryman asked her to go down into the cabin and make tea saying they would soon be at their destination and then he would join her.

Innocently she went below, brought the kettle to the boil, made the tea and fetched a large cake from her basket, the gift of her father for the trip.

Footsteps sounded on the deck above. She took the long, sharp carving knife and began cutting up the cake, then filled the mugs with tea. The bulk of the wherryman appeared in the doorway, blocking out the light. With fiery eyes he peered around him, but not at the food and drink prepared for his enjoyment; his every thought, his whole being had, at that moment, but one crying, overpowering need, to possess, consume, devour her, to make for ever his own that fair form he now had at his mercy. No barrier now, he swore to himself, not even virtue itself, should curb his wild and elemental craving, and with demon hands he fell to stripping her of every shred of raiment she possessed, to cast away at last the final torture to his desire.

But virtue is not so lightly trodden down; if honour be worth fighting for, as she had been taught it was, then she would fight. With an effort born of the spirit more than the body, the maiden wrenched herself free from his embrace and gathering the knife as she went, leapt upon the deck. Baffled and enraged by her escape the wherryman sprang after her. He found her standing on the plankway leaning with one hand on the cabin top, panting like an animal at bay. The wherryman lurched towards her, his face contorted with fury; then, with a sudden movement his arms came out and he made to press her down upon the cabin, to have his will of her under the blue skies and the sunshine.

But as he closed with her the hand she had been holding behind her back shot upwards, the point of the sharp carver pierced the thin wall of his stomach beneath the ribs, and came to rest deep within his black and evil heart. Blood spurted from the ghastly wound, he stumbled backwards, raised one hand feebly to his head and with a hollow, soul-searing scream, pitched over the side. The engulfing waters stifled his cry, and the last thing the maiden saw was a shaft of evening sunlight reflected for a second like a blob of gold on the handle of the knife.

Exhausted, sick in mind and body, despairing and alone she lay upon the cabin top, unseeing, unhearing, aware only of the crime she had committed. Not till darkness began to fall did she summon strength or interest to look around; not till then did the horror of her situation break in upon her. For the wherry was out upon the high seas, a great wind was blowing from the land and the sail was set.

Watchers on the shore saw the sail grow smaller till at last it disappeared over the darkening horizon; then, from where it had been, they saw a tongue of flame leap skywards, hover for a moment or two, and then slowly go out.

Night threw its black pall over the sea; the watchers, mystified, returned home; but neither the maid nor the wherry were ever seen again.

Not, that is, in human or material form. But on the exact anniversary of the events I have recounted, the phantom vessel, with her phantom crew, sails once more down the winding reaches of the Waveney. Brave souls have borne witness to her passing; and you may still find those who do. But it is no ordinary wherry they see.

Her hull is no longer its erstwhile black but a radiant, shimmering white, nor is her sail as it used to be; it floats now through the night a dazzling, terrifying expanse of rippling flame; there is no sound, no sense of movement, but a feeling of gradual enlargement as if the whole fearful scene were being slowly magnified through a giant glass. The intensity and brilliance blinds the eyes till they can bear to look no more.

But when at last they are opened again all is darkness, save for the stars reflected like glittering pin-heads in the smooth, unruffled surface of the river. Yet for a while there lingers in the air a strange, mysterious smell of burning.

Whatever hopes, or fears, I may have had of seeing this ghostly craft were ended by a hail from Jack.

"Can you see the bridge yet? We ought to be getting near it pretty soon."

I screwed up my eyes and followed the bend of the river round to the south and there, sure enough, I could just make out its shape. To 'shoot' through, as we should have to do, always called for nice judgment. It meant lowering the sail and mast at just the right distance from the bridge to keep enough steerage way through it and while everything was being raised again.

I went aft for final instructions from Jack. Conditions were perfect, a nice breeze on the starboard quarter and what little tide was left still nudging us upstream.

I filled my pipe, borrowed a match off Jack to light it, and went forward. I removed the carling board, the small hatch covering the space where the foot of the mast, and its counterbalance swings, cleared the spring stay fall and shipped the winch handle.

The bridge was now about two hundred yards away and I stood ready at the brake while from aft the gentle rattle of the mainsheet told me Jack was beginning to gather in the sail ready for lowering.

A hundred yards, seventy-five yards, fifty yards; the black outline of the bridge loomed threateningly ahead, my heart skipped a beat; I had hair-raising visions of the *Albion* running slap into that menacing mass of steel and ripping all the gear out of her; I cursed Jack for a damned fool standing on like this; had I been skipper we should have lowered down ages ago; what in heaven's name was he up to?

I was in a cold sweat. Then casually I heard him call, "Right-o, let her come."

Almost in panic I thrust my weight on to the winch handle, gained a vital inch and threw out the pawl, at the same time pressing with all my might on the brake lever; with a sweep of the hand I knocked the handle clear, so that it could not spin round like a catherine wheel and brain me, then eased the pressure on the brake and down came gaff and sail at the run.

I checked the descent when the gaff jaws were about head-high and put in the pawl again to hold it.

"Out parrel pin," drawled Jack, as he took a grip on the after end of the gaff.

I jumped on the hatches, unshipped the pin, and called back, "Pin out, heave away."

As Jack pulled the gaff towards him I swung the jaws clear on the port side of the mast then lowered away on the winch till the spar was safely resting on the mounds of black canvas, well out of the way of where the mast would come.

"Lower your mast," was the next order.

I leapt to the fall and surged away feverishly, fearing even now we should be too late to save it. It hung for a second, swayed slightly, then, in a graceful, majestic arc swung down through the darkness and settled comfortably over the hatches.

"Saved by the skin of our teeth," I muttered to myself when I saw the bunting of the vane flapping about on the cabin top, and wheeling round I expected to find us already under the bridge. But to my astonishment we were still the length of the wherry away! Jack was aiming her plumb through the centre of the arch and she answered the tiller as well as if the sail were up. I saw now how beautifully he had judged things and how ridiculous my own panic had been. But I would wager that anyone else in my position would have felt the same, until, like me, they had had the opportunity of seeing just how efficient a wherry's gear is and how quickly the sail and mast can be lowered.

Once clear of the bridge the mast was swung upright and the sail hoisted; this part of the operation took us four minutes and all told we were a little under ten minutes in negotiating the bridge. No one could expect greater efficiency than that from a sailing craft especially when it is remembered that at no time did the *Albion* ever lose steerage way.

We were now on the last mile or two to Beccles, the lighted clock-face in the church tower and the twinkling street lamps telling us our day's haul was nearly over.

There was still a drop left in the big, brown teapot and I filled up our mugs to help keep out the wind now blowing really coldly round the back of our heads. Jack rolled himself a cigarette and pushed the pastille tin over to me.

"Roll yourself one," he said with a grin, "and have a decent smoke!"

"All right," I answered, accepting what I knew was in the nature of a challenge, "if the mate can't have a bit of the skipper's baccy now and again I reckon it's a poor do," and I began rolling myself a 'tickler',

Albion loading reeds

Albion loading shingle in Norwich for Berney Arms

Albion discharging Russian timber in Norwich

Norfolk as it used to be, windmill and wherry. In a hard blow, the wherry has dowsed her peak to get round a sharp starboard turn. Even so, her wake shows how close she came to the bank

Neck-and-neck in Postwick Reach

almost with relish, for the bitter wind really demanded something drastic to warm the end of your nose.

Then, very casually, Jack remarked, "I didn't want to cut things too fine just now coming through the bridge seeing as how you hadn't ever shot a bridge before; wanted to leave plenty of time in case anything went wrong. Still," he chuckled, "you didn't do so bad, you'll learn!"

Half an hour later we moored up a few yards below Beccles bridge; the church clock was striking nine o'clock as we turned up our ropes. The quayside was deserted and the only sign of life was an occasional car going by on its way to Norwich or Lowestoft.

As I squared up the deck ready for unloading in the morning the dark clouds chasing in from the sea began fulfilling their promise of earlier in the day.

I went below into the welcome warmth and cheerfulness of the cabin; Jack had lit the two small, brass lamps over the mantelshelf and was washing his hands before having supper.

"Well," I said, "you'll be able to make those snowballs you were talking about at Buckenham if you've a mind to, it's just started coming down and the sky looks full of it."

"Thought it would," he answered, drying off his hands on a clean bit of deck cloth, "but I'd rather have a mug of tea and a bite to eat. What's in the locker?"

CHAPTER TWO

The Fleeing Dutchmen

The wherry's family tree—Viking hull—Dutch sail—elusive meaning of the word 'wherry'—express passenger carrier—slow entry into the cargo trade—wherries and keels in conflict—the wherry's victory and defeat.

IF the march of time had continued without interruption I could never have made the trip described in the last chapter. For trading wherries, like all other sailing craft in European waters, have had their day; and though we may regret their passing, because they were beautiful in themselves, and because they did the work of a bygone age to perfection, we should not try to put back the clock by attempting to revive them as a commercial proposition.

When we took over the *Albion* and got her sailing again, we artificially extended for a few years the working span of this particular type of vessel. It was fun doing it and her continued presence on the rivers of Norfolk and Suffolk gives pleasure to thousands of holidaymakers every summer. But there was no economic need for it; merchants did not require her services and what freights she gets are in the nature of charitable gifts.

But the mere fact of her survival demands that naval historians refer to the wherry in the present tense; they cannot yet dismiss her, like the clipper ship, the Lowestoft smack or the Yorkshire coble, as a thing of the past. She is still there for all to see, with her sleek, black hull and high-peaked sail, her gay paintwork, the lusty reek of tar, and her fathom-long streak of blood-red bunting fluttering aloft. In every line and every curve of her there is the mark of good breeding; whether you see her lying peacefully at an up-river staithe miles from anywhere, her big, black wing folded, swan-like, over her hatches, or threshing along over Breydon Water through a motley fleet of white-sailed pleasure craft, you are bound to wonder about her ancestry, to ask yourself how this perfect combination of shape and rig was evolved, and why there is no other craft like her anywhere in the world.

Her story begins, I think, more than a thousand years ago, when the Vikings sailed across the North Sea in their longships and landed on the shores of Norfolk and Suffolk. They found the district pleasant and fertile, many of them settled here, took to farming, and married native girls, thus bequeathing to us East Anglians the legacy of fair hair and blue, sailor's eyes. Many of our place names and a lot of our language we also owe to them.

They were not slow to realize the value of the many rivers and inlets, which then existed, as a means of transport. There were no roads worthy of the name and the smaller longships were well-suited to be cargo carriers. Instead of using their thirty or more oars they found less than half that number sufficient to get about in sheltered water, and the space vacated by the remaining rowers was used as stowage room.

Their size was just right for the job: length over all, 70 feet, beam, 17 feet, depth, 6 feet. Like all north European vessels of the period they were clinker built of oak. They were double-ended with a very pronounced sheer fore and aft rising to the familiar dragon-head at stem and stern. The planks were fastened with iron clinks while cow-hair and tar were used for caulking. They stepped one mast in a tabernacle for hoisting the famous square sail and so far as we know there were no shrouds or stays except one to the stem-head. They would sail with the wind a point before the beam, but the story book pictures of them crossing the seas with their shields ranged along the sides are, alas, just pleasant fancies. When passage making they were stowed in the boat and were only kept ready to hand like this when going into action.

Now, if we imagine a longship with her dragon-heads removed, we find a hull shape closely resembling a Norfolk wherry. And remove the dragon-heads in practice is just what the Vikings did. They found them an encumbrance working in confined waters, and the longer they lived here the more their own traditions decayed, so weakening their belief in the need for them. As their original craft grew old and rotten they set about building replacements, but not now for crossing the seas; they wanted vessels to carry cargo from one settlement to another, which they could also use for catching herring up and down the estuaries. It may well have been the herring shoals which kept the Vikings here; they are said to have come in search of them when this strange fish suddenly forsook the waters of the Baltic and deprived them of an essential source of food.

So the new ships they built were altered to suit these different requirements, and they were not above including some of the best points from the craft the English themselves were using. These were smaller, probably not more than 45 feet, almost flat-bottomed, and sprang from the Friesian and Saxon models which came over in the fifth century. They were called 'ceols', and the name must have been adopted for the new Viking craft, as it persists to this day all along the north-east and east coasts as 'keel'. The spirit of the old song, 'Weel may the keel row!' must, therefore, have echoed down at least a thousand years of English history.

With the arrival of the Normans, in 1066, active Danish influence came to an end, but being 'Northmen' themselves they used vessels directly descended from the longships, as the Bayeux tapestries show very clearly. They differed little from the English vessels, and it seems improbable that any great change took place in the trading craft of Norfolk and Suffolk until the latter half of the sixteenth century.

For more than five hundred years the square-sailed keel, helped now and again with oars, did the job of common carrier for the district. Passengers travelled in the keels, too, and for all the rough and ready conditions they preferred it to risking a journey by foot or on horse-back through the treacherous swamps and marshes which then lay between Norwich and the sea. But to travel from Yarmouth, say, to Norwich by river in the sixteenth century must have been a test of endurance. There was no accommodation as we know it, not even hatch covers, to go over the hold. You found what space you could among the piles of cargo, sweating or freezing to death according to the season, and endured as best you could the rigours of those thirty, cheerless miles.

Had I been forced to make such a passage I am pretty sure I should have waited for a good easterly wind; then, with a bit of luck, I might have reached Norwich in about eight hours. But in less favourable conditions we might have been at it for a couple of days if not longer. The only let-up for such travellers was when they came to one of the taverns placed, either by guess or by God, at strategic points along the route. The keel's huge, dark sail riding high over the marshland gave ample warning of her approach, and the innkeeper who knew his job would tend the fires, set a bunch of wildfowl turning on the spit, and see that ample pots of home-brew were mulled in time to greet his guests' arrival. We can imagine how thankfully they clambered ashore on a winter's night to thaw out stiff and frozen limbs before a welcoming hearth and put a dish of hot victuals into their famished stomachs.

Still, the fare was reasonable enough, threepence single between Norwich and Yarmouth. In Elizabethan times so many people travelled this way that the Norwich Corporation felt it necessary to make regulations for the conduct of the keelmen and the traffic in general. One quaint rule lays it down that those running the keels were forbidden to carry 'any suspect person, or common rogue, or harlot or suchlike'. Obviously a very high standard of tact and diplomacy was demanded of keel skippers in ascertaining the precise moral status of their intending passengers!

The real bar, of course, to fast and regular passage making was the square sail; it drove the keel along well enough with the wind astern and the tide fair, just as it drove the full rigged ship round the world until a few years ago. In fair weather there is nothing to equal the square sail for driving power. But on a twisting, turning river course it was never fair weather all the time. If one reach blew in their favour, like as not the next would muzzle them, then it was out quants and towlines to the next turn.

However leisurely life may have been then, with none of the mad rush and hustle we know today, there was still a growing demand for more efficient conveyance, for quicker and more reliable means of getting from place to place. And in Norfolk and Suffolk, because there were precious few roads in the eastern parts of the counties, that meant improved river transport.

The answer lay in the fore-and-aft rig, but the watermen of the Yare and Waveney knew nothing about it until well on in Elizabeth's reign. By then, their opposite numbers in the Low Countries had been using it for more than a century and a half; a sprit-sail, similar to that of the modern Thames barge, was illustrated in the year 1416. Looking back, it is hard to think how news of this revolutionary advance could have taken so long to travel over the North Sea. Perhaps sailors did bring tales of its invention, and how it enabled a vessel to sail against the wind as well as with it; perhaps, too, it was natural East Anglian obstinacy which made them do nothing about it, if they believed the tale at all. For any idea of being able to make a ship go against the wind was an unheard of thing; like trying to fly to the moon. There was something about it that smacked of witchcraft.

Yet, by 1550, the square sail had practically disappeared from the waterways of north-west Europe; England alone clung to it, in her usual insular way, and though her sea-dogs blazed new trails across the seven seas her small, workaday vessels were at least a century out of date.

We can see how much we were behind the times by looking at Braun and Hogenberg's *Atlas of the Cities of the World*, published in 1572. In the plate of London, which covers a stretch of the Thames from Lambeth Palace to the Tower, every craft is square-rigged, with one solitary exception, a tiny little thing, probably a peter-boat, which has a sprit-sail hoisted. This is the only fore-and-after to be seen in the English section.

But a glance at the plates of Nijmegen and Camperdown show all fore-and-aft craft, and no square-riggers; the same is true of Bruges, Antwerp, Amsterdam, Hamburg, Dunkirk, Groningen, Dordrecht and a host more.

We are, of course, considering only the craft that worked on rivers and canals, and about the harbours; they were not seagoing vessels and never traded to England, so our ship builders had no opportunity of running an eye over them, of weighing them up and copying them. However favourably our sailors may have reported on the new rig there was no response from the small yards that built the keels, no inclination to modify their centuries-old methods and give the new invention a try-out. Perhaps they had heard so many sailors' yarns before, which they did not believe, that they were in no mind to take this one any the more seriously. And who can really blame them when, as I have said, there was the smell of witchcraft about the very idea of being able to sail *against* the wind? Only by witnessing this black magic for themselves would they ever be convinced it was true.

Then, round about 1570, there occurred one of those curious accidents of history which was to provide them with just the evidence they needed, and make the trading vessels of Norfolk and Suffolk the most advanced in Britain. The accident in question was the revolt of 1568 which broke out in Holland against the oppression and religious persecutions of the Spaniards.

It may be true to say that the most fierce and terrible wars that have ever been fought, those that have seen the most bloodshed and the greatest refinements of torture, have been undertaken in the name of religion. The conduct of the 'Bloody' Duke of Alva in putting down the Dutch rebellion was certainly no exception; he gained his unsavoury title by acts of such unexampled cruelty, by such wanton and unprovoked massacres, that they set at nought the meek and pious principles of the faith he and his country professed.

We are not concerned here with the rights and wrongs of the conflict; what interests us is that it caused more than three thousand Dutchmen to flee their country and seek refuge in Norfolk and Suffolk. What interests us even more is how they got here, and what sort of craft they used to cross the North Sea.

As we saw during the Second World War, those who have to flee from an oppressor cannot pick and choose the craft for their escape; all manner of cockleshells reached our shores bearing Norwegians, Danes, Dutchmen, Belgians and Frenchmen, frail and flimsy craft, many of them, that would never have ventured on a sea crossing but for the desperate need to get away from the German invader.

Away back in 1570 people in the Low Countries had the same pressing need to escape the Spaniard; they seized whatever craft lay to hand, put all the provisions they could into them, and under cover of darkness slipped away from their native land and set course for Yarmouth. If salt water had not been in their blood they could never have bought their freedom by such desperate voyages; perhaps they would never have attempted them as it was if they had not had so much confidence in their fore-and-aft rigged vessels, small and unsuitable as they were. For it was those same little fore-and-afters, illustrated in the Braun and Hogenberg atlas, that brought the fleeing Dutchmen to East Anglia, and gave our shipbuilders the unexpected, but invaluable, opportunity of seeing them for themselves. There they were, any number of them, tied up along the Yarmouth quayside, and all they had to do was go and look at them.

The keelmen, too, had the chance of watching how they handled, and were not long in sizing up the new rig; here was something vastly superior to their own clumsy, square sail; if it worked in Holland, and could bring all these people safely across the North Sea, it would work in Norfolk waters, too. So, almost overnight, they were convinced that sailing against the wind was not black magic, but something anyone could do if they had the right sort of sail.

But there was no general stampede to get their keels converted to the new rig, because they could not be converted without a great deal of structural alteration. Their mast was stepped in a tabernacle amidships; the Dutchmen had theirs right forward. So it meant building new hulls to the Dutch pattern that would accommodate the mast in the new position; and it all took time, discussing what should be included, what should be left out, what could be improved and so on.

Above all there was the question of what size they should be; what trade would benefit most from speedier passages. Should they begin with small craft first, like the Dutchmen, and see how they answered; in short, should they build for cargo carrying or to take passengers?

They decided in the end to concentrate on fairly small craft, able to take twenty or so passengers, with a few small goods when required. There was more money in passengers than heavy cargoes and, of course, small craft were much cheaper to build.

So, within about a year of the first Dutch arrivals, the new craft began sliding down the ways. They were at once successful, proving not only superior to the local craft, but also to the Dutch vessels they were modelled on. This is not altogether surprising, for the Norfolk men stuck to the Viking hull shape, preferring it, quite understandably, to the less gainly Dutch construction. They were content to borrow from them only details of masting and rigging. That is why Norfolk craft never needed leeboards, a feature of Dutch waters right into the twentieth century.

It may also account for the rapid discarding of the sprit, though it is surprising that these hitherto conservative-minded old watermen should have taken the revolutionary step of hoisting their loose-footed sail on a gaff, the first ever stretched to a breeze in British waters. It was a remarkable, and quickly thought out, improvement, for it came into use within ten years of the Dutchmen's arrival.

Thanks to the foresight of Elizabeth, we can see what these craft looked like about the year 1580. With a nose for smelling out Spanish intentions she caused plans to be drawn of all the harbours on the east coast to help defend them in case of invasion. Yarmouth appears in great detail and a glance at the illustration reveals a spritsail rigged vessel sailing in the harbour between the crane and the bridge. She is clinker-built, with the mast right forward, and no stays of any description. She has a very pronounced sheer, fore and aft, and her crew of two are sailing her in workmanlike style up-river against the wind, but with a fair tide.

Close behind her comes an almost identical craft except for one striking difference; she is gaff-rigged. There is much less sheer to her, and if her sail were black, it would be easy to see in her the basic outline of the wherry as we know her now. The subtle marriage of longship hull and Dutch rig stands out clearly. Like her companion, she is making no bones about beating up the harbour, and I never look at this particular scene without wishing I could have been aboard one or other of the contestants; for contest I am sure it was, with the supporters of the gaff bent on showing a clean pair of heels to those who favoured the sprit, and vice versa!

The craft in the bottom right-hand corner is another wherry with a gaff, by all appearances quite a hefty spar, as four blocks are used to hoist it. The exaggerated sheer suggests one of the older hulls in which the gaff has been substituted for the original sprit, and her being at sea is quite in keeping with the times. Yarmouth was a difficult place to get into for ships of any size, and while waiting for water on the bar small craft would come off to them with food and stores, and land any passengers who wanted to go ashore. That seems to be the job this particular vessel is doing.

By the turn of the sixteenth century, therefore, two distinct types of craft were at work; the keel taking cargoes, but no longer passengers, who now went by wherry. The word 'wherry' was new to these parts and must have been borrowed from the Thames, where rowing-boats of special build, and bearing this name, plied for hire in the manner of aquatic taxis. It came to be a generic term for many kinds of passenger-carrying craft, and we find wherries plying between Ipswich and Harwich, at Spithead and Gravesend, on the Tyne and even as far away as Ireland. But apart from the name they had little in common, being quite different in build and rig.

Just why, and how, the word came to mean what it does remains a mystery. Some see it as a corruption of 'ferry', others as a derivation from 'wherret', to hurry, while another school of thought gives it a Scandinavian origin. This can hardly be so as there is no word in Icelandic, the tongue of the Vikings, Norwegian, Swedish, Danish, Dutch, Friesian or German from which it could possibly have come. And I feel sure it has no connection with a liquor, made in the West Country from crab apples, and called 'wherry', from the Welsh meaning 'bitter'!

In *The Sailor's Word Book* compiled by Admiral Smyth and published in 1867, a wherry is described as 'a sharp, light and shallow boat used in rivers and harbours for passengers'. Surprisingly enough, he makes no mention of Norfolk wherries, though he goes on to say the name was also applied to a decked vessel used in fishing in different parts of Great Britain, adding, 'numbers of them were notorious smugglers'. He suggests the name may be descended from the Roman *horia*, the *oare* of our early writers.

In several sixteenth-century voyages recorded by Hakluyt we find mention of 'whirries'. Raleigh had them on his expedition to Guiana in 1595. He says in a passage on the dangers of venturing up some fast-flowing rivers: 'Our vessels were no other than whirries, one little barge, a small cockboat, and a bad galiota.' Another time he carried a hundred men in 'one old galego which I caused to be furnished like a galley, and in one barge, two whirries and a shipboat.'

On Frobisher's second voyage in search of a north-west passage, in 1577, the native boats encountered are described in these terms: 'They have two sorts of boats made of leather, set out on the inner side with quarters of wood, artificially tied together with thongs of the same; the greater sort are not much unlike our wherries, wherein sixteen or twenty men may sit.'

The word wherry first appears locally in the *Norwich Rivers and Streets Book* (Chamberlain's Accounts), 1556–1618. An entry for the year 1604 records the payment of seven shillings for 'two wherries rowing down to Whitlingham'. It next occurs in a will in the Canterbury Court of Pleas by which James Smythe of Great Yarmouth bequeathed to John Cornellis a half-share in his wherry, the *Spred Eagle*. The date is 1610, and a point of interest is the name, the first we know belonging to a wherry.

If the *Albion* can trace her descent no further back than this she still spans three hundred and fifty years of history; but while she carries forty tons of cargo, her tiny ancestor probably took no more than five. But she had room for some twenty passengers, and their luggage, and could stow a few packs of light or perishable goods needed in a hurry. Like others of her kind, she also took mail between Norwich and Yarmouth, and in many ways did the same sort of work as the stage-coach. But her passengers travelled in much greater comfort and security than those who bumped and floundered over ill-made roads and primitive trackways, with the constant threat of armed robbery hanging over them from bands of wandering ne'er-do-wells. There were no such dangers lurking on the water, not in Norfolk anyway. The only case of river piracy I know of happened on the Thames, when some gentlemen being rowed to Chelsea were overtaken and relieved of their guineas and their gold watches.

An outbreak of the plague in 1635–6 brought swift action from Norwich Corporation, who wrote to Yarmouth seeking their help in limiting the spread of the dreaded disease. Their letter, and the reply, show how important wherry traffic had become by then, and how it was getting more and more trade in small goods.

Here is the letter Norwich sent to Yarmouth:

Our love remembered.
    The tymes doe give us occasion to desyre your best ayde and assistance, that by the help and goodness of Almighty God, theise two corporations of Norwich and Yarmouth, being yet free from the contagion of the plague, may, by God's blessing, be still so continued. And therefore we desire, if it may stand with your liking, that all wherrymen that take in any goods or passengers in your town for Norwich, may be compelled to take in at one and the self same place, and not elsewhere. And that none of them be permitted to take in any passengers that come from beyond the seas, from London, Newcastle, or other places infected, or feared to be infected, without a certificate from yr worpps. And that you would please to cause some officer to make known to all wherrymen that shall come from your town to this citty, that they land noe goods or passengers att any other place in this citty, than at the common stath of this citty, to the end that they may be there examined, and such enquiries made concerning them as shall be thought fitt; because we are

now giving to our wherrymen here, that they doe observe the same order in this place. And in this doing, we shall accompt ourselves much obliged to you, and will be ready to accomodate you in like performance, when vou shall have cause to require the same, and will rest

        Your very loveing friends,
         Thomas, Baker, Maior.
        Thos. Cory

Norwich, the first
of Septr, 1636.

Note that it was despatched on 1st September. It went to Yarmouth by wherry and was delivered so promptly that it was acted upon, and replied to, by the 3rd. Here is the answer Yarmouth sent to Norwich:

Right Worpll,
 Our kind respects remembred. Yor lre of the first in this instant recd. And accordingly have ourselves, in pson, strickly chardged our wherrymen in gen'rall that they neither take into, nor deliver out of, their wherrys any manner of goods or passengers, but at one certain known place in this towne, namely, the usual wherry key; and not any unknowne or suspected passengers, wthout or privity. And that they observe the like (according to the contents of yr lre) for your citty, namely at the common stath. We heartily thank you for yr good care taken herein, and recommended unto us: wherein we have hitherto been careful, and intend (God willing) for the future not to be wanting in conjoyning, or best help and endeavour for preventing thereof. Neither doe we knowe att present, thanks be given to the Lord, any in this towne infected, saving that this laste week one only pson died, who was suspected thereof, and as yet none els of the family sick. Wth or praiers to the Almighty God, that he will be pleased to stay his hand where it is, and grant a gen'rall pservation to the whole kingdome, if it be his blessed will, we rest,

        Yr very loving friends,
         Tho. Johnson } Bailiffs
         Robt Sayer }

Yarmouth, Saturday,
3 September, 1636.
    To or very loving friends
    the right worpll the Maior
    of the citty of Norwich
    and the Aldermen his brethren.

These two charming examples of civic courtesy and co-operation show very clearly how important wherries had become in the first sixty years of their existence. Reference to 'the common stath' and 'the usual wherry key' can only mean there was quite a sizeable fleet of them at work, and that together they had a monopoly of the passenger-carrying trade. I think that is why no mention is made of keels; had they still been taking passengers, then Norwich would certainly have sought the same supervision for them.

The fact that 'goods and passengers' are spoken of in the same breath suggests the inevitable was happening; the faster and more reliable craft were beginning to skim off the better paying items of cargo, leaving the keels with only the heavy hauls. Such was the general pattern of trade for the next two hundred years.

During this period the wherry remained small and speedy, the keel big and cumbersome. We get a good idea of what a keel could carry from the Norwich Chamberlain's Accounts for 1587–8. They record the cost of preparations for dealing with the threatened Spanish invasion. It may seem strange that these lumbering vessels were chartered as troop carriers, but that is just what happened. Norwich had to send three hundred soldiers to Yarmouth to help the coast defence forces there, and an item in the accounts shows that three keels were hired to take them. The holds were swept out and strewn with rushes, each craft embarking a hundred troops, and we can only hope a pleasant westerly breeze wafted them, without too many delays, to their destination, otherwise their passage must have been an unenviable one.

You need a fair bit of space to pack in a hundred men even if they only have to stand up. But if they must lie down and sleep, as these troops presumably did, then you need a lot more room. Because it was possible for so many men to be taken at once, I should put the lading of these keels at not much under 50 tons. At the period we are speaking of many coasting vessels were no bigger than this, so by any standards the Norfolk keel was a very substantial vessel for narrow, inland waters.

The tendency, as we shall see, was for them to get bigger still, whereas the wherry stayed much as she was for a century and a half. The first reasonably complete specification we have of one occurs in an advertisement, in the *Norwich Gazette*, for 23 December, 1727.

This is 140 years after the troop-carrying activities of the keels, yet the wherry has put on no weight at all, as the advertisement shows:

> For sale, 2 very good wherries, of about 8 Tuns Burden, late Mr. Summers's deceased; with all the Tackel, Masts, Sails, Ropes, Tilts, Hoops and Oars...

These examples were probably around 30 feet in length with a 7 foot beam. The gear that went with them makes it plain that oars and sails were both used, as conditions demanded, and mention of tilts and hoops gives a valuable clue to the wherries' success. Gone were the days when passengers took pot-luck in an open hold, with no protection whatever from the elements; wherries, it is obvious, provided a snug canvas wind-break, spread over semicircular frames, and this new standard of comfort made an instant appeal to would-be travellers.

Early the following year, on 6 April, 1728, another advertisement appeared, this time in the *Norwich Mercury*, which gives an interesting glimpse of how business was conducted on the rivers at this time:

> Norwich, 6 April, 1728.
>
> The Owners and Workers of the Day-Barges do hereby give Notice, That the Days of going from this Place to Yarmouth will be on Mondays, Tuesdays, Thursdays and Fridays exactly, between 8 and 9 of the Clock in the forenoon; and from Yarmouth Key the same Days and Time, with the utmost Care and Expedition, from the Green-Man Stath in Conisford; and that constant Attendance will be given at Mr. John Thompson's at the Sign of the Day-Barge and Flower de Luce in Conisford, Norwich, and at their Ware-house on the Key at Yarmouth. Their wherries for carrying of Merchants Packs and other Goods will go every Night in the Week from the Stath late Mr. Fell's; where they have a convenient Warehouse for the receiving and safe keeping of all such Goods as shall come to hand, and doubt not but to give a more intire satisfaction than has ever yet been done in this kind. To be performed (God willing) by
>
> | Edmund Jennis | John Sherwood |
> | Francis Sherwood | Thomas Fassacre |
> | Benjamin Pegg | William Brown |
> | Henry Robertson | Thomas Smyter |

I wonder how often these worthy fellows had to invoke the 'God willing' clause to excuse unpunctuality? It was, of course, a recognized provision of the times, and you meet it on most handbills, whether to do with the impending departure of ships or coaches. One proprietor was evidently a little irked by this, and advised all and sundry that his coach would depart on the Monday—'God willing,' if not, Tuesday—'whether or no!'

We can see from this advertisement how wherries were going in more and more for cargo carrying, with some being used solely for this purpose. It resulted from the merchants' need for a much speedier movement of goods between Norwich and Yarmouth and can be taken as a sign of the times.

For the whole country was reaping the benefit of an enormous increase in trade, thanks to a period of great colonial expansion, and in Norfolk this was reflected in an ever-growing demand for the woollen goods it manufactured. It is worth remembering that the worsted trousers and costumes we wear today, although now produced elsewhere, take their name from the little village of Worstead, in Norfolk, where this particular material was first made.

Norwich was not only an important producer of woollens itself, but the place to which goods from the country around were brought for export. They were forwarded down the Yare for transhipment into coasters at Yarmouth, whence they were taken to English or near-European ports, or to London, where they were put into larger ships to be carried overseas. The Norwich river was thus being called upon to carry a greater volume of traffic than it had ever done before, while the clamour on all hands was for goods to be taken more quickly, more regularly and, because they were valuable, with more protection, both from the weather and from petty pilfering. The advertisement shows how the watermen were responding to these demands, within the limits of the craft available.

The Turnpike Acts, being passed about this time, also helped to keep the wherry operators on their toes because, as roads came to be improved, they realized if they could not keep pace with the craving for speed, then goods would go by waggon instead of by wherry. It was a new and unheard-of threat to the river traffic; hitherto, carting goods overland had been slow, expensive and dangerous, where it had been possible at all, but now, with the better roads, waggons, drawn by teams of powerful horses, could lumber their way from Norwich to London in about three days.

Here was a challenge that had to be met; something drastic was needed to meet the new competition. But what could be done? In the backs of their minds the watermen had probably long known the answer, to build craft almost as big as keels and rig them as wherries. In this way they could combine the great carrying capacity of the one with the speed and handiness of the other. There were obvious difficulties, though none of them proved insuperable, and once the need was appreciated they set to with a will.

Growth was slow to begin with, capacity increasing from 8 to about 15 tons. Owners and builders felt their way carefully, because the bigger the craft, the more modifications were needed. They had good cause 'to hasten slowly', yet, within the comparatively short space of fifty years, they successfully sorted things out and brought the wherry to her final stage of development. By the end of the eighteenth century she was much as we know her today, and from then on only minor additions were made.

This big, new-style wherry, began at once competing with the keel, and over a period of about seventy-five years virtually sailed her off the rivers.

By 1798 there were no less than one hundred and twenty wherries on the register, as against only thirty-six keels. The average tonnage of those working on the Yare was 30; on the Waveney 27·7; and on the Bure 23·9, altogether a remarkable increase in size over so short a period.

Even so, it was only about half that of the keels, whose average tonnage on the Yare was 66·4; on the Waveney 58; and on the Bure 29·3. But because of their superior sailing qualities, wherries could take a freight to Norwich, unload, and be back in Yarmouth, before the keels had even got to the city. In the face of such competition the keels were bound to admit defeat and, as a result, only a handful were built after 1800. The rest dragged out their time as mud barges till at last they were shoved on the Breydon flats, and left to rot. You can sometimes see their bones now at low water, black, gaunt and forsaken, except for the gulls and cormorants which find them a comfortable resting place. Privileged birds, indeed, to perch on a thousand years of English history.

But before the keels finally gave up the struggle, they made a last

From a painting by M. E. Cotman, by courtesy Norwich Museums Committee

Wherries unloading coaster in Yarmouth Roads

From a painting by J. Moore in the author's collection

Wherries racing at sea off Yarmouth. The only picture known to exist showing them with foresails set

From James Stark's 'Scenery of the Rivers of Norfolk'

River at Norwich showing timber-laden keel and wherries, 1820s

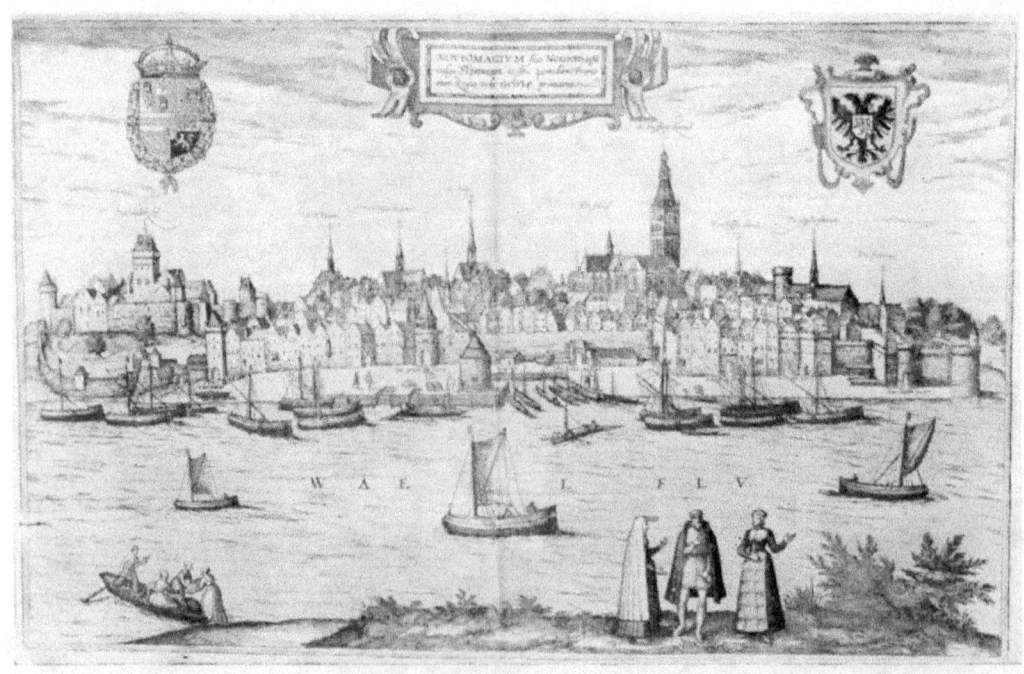

From Braun & Hogenberg's 'Atlas of the Cities of the World'

From Braun and Hogenberg's Atlas of the Cities of the World showing fore-and-aft rig at Nijmegen in the 1570s

ditch attempt to beat the wherry in the only way they could, by increasing their own considerable size, so that however swiftly the wherry sailed, she would find it impossible to bring up the same weight of goods, in the time the keel took, on her single, heavily-laden trip. To further this policy some really massive vessels were launched at Yarmouth round about 1770. First came a fleet of eight 70-tonners, the *Industry, Constitution, Conclusion, Union, Augustus, William, Flora* and *Royal Oak*, followed by a 75-tonner, the *William and Mary*. They met with a fair measure of success and were soon followed into the water by six 80-tonners, the *Marlborough, July Flower, Susanna, Polly, Beehive* and *Elizabeth and Ann*.

These were real heavyweights to be doing river work and must have been a rare handful in anything of a breeze; without a shoe-horn it seemed difficult to get anything bigger up to Norwich.

But a certain William Thomas, of Yarmouth, thought otherwise, and with great heart and abundant optimism, he launched an 85-tonner with *Recovery* bravely blazoned on her name board; then the *Edmund*, of 90 tons, went down the ways, followed by the even bigger *Supply*, of 95 tons. But at this point the keelmen were hoist with their own petard; such monsters could no longer be sailed with the normal crew of two, and it was found the *Edmund* and the *Supply* required no less than four men to get them to Norwich. So, whatever gains they had won were swallowed up by the extra mouths to feed. It had been a bonny fight while it lasted but they realized now it was one they could never hope to win. There was a final gesture of defiance when Anthony Cheeper, a Yarmouth merchant, launched the *Success*, 97 tons, and with him rests the distinction of having built the biggest keel and, indeed, the biggest sailing craft, ever to trade on Norfolk waters.

There is no doubt the wherries took this challenge very seriously while it lasted; for it was not only a battle between rival types of craft, but between the watermen of Yarmouth and Norwich. The former, hailing from the most important port on the east coast, had always earned their living off-loading the ships in their harbour, and carrying the goods, chiefly coal and timber, to places up-river. The Norwich men, on the other hand, had been mainly interested in passengers, and bringing down manufactured stuffs, for export. The real struggle began when the wherries, instead of sailing back light to Norwich, started looking round for freights of coal and timber; because of their speed they were soon in demand, and those that could load twenty tons or more never had to worry about going back empty.

Because of their geographical situation and the different jobs they had to do, Yarmouth was always the stronghold of the keel, Norwich that of the wherry. There were, of course, many Yarmouth wherries and Norwich keels, but that is broadly how the forces were disposed; there is not one Norwich owned keel among all the big fellows just mentioned.

This is not really surprising; Yarmouth were pinning their faith in the kind of craft which had served them so well in the past, while Norwich were content to rely on the one they were adapting, and with such obvious success, to their new requirements.

They went on increasing the size from 20 up to 40 tons, and when the last three big keels were launched at Yarmouth, replied with three wherries, the largest ever built up to then, the *Robert and Frances*, 43 tons; the *Robert and Mary*, 45 tons; and the *Mayflower*, 50 tons. Despite the size, two men could still work them, thanks to their easy rig and simple gear. It gave them final supremacy over their opponents, and by the early years of the nineteenth century their victory was complete. They became the accepted carriers of all goods on the waterways, and for fifty years they knew a period of real prosperity.

But from then on the sands of time began running out for all vessels driven by the wind. On the high seas, the last ounce of skill was going into the clipper ships to stave off the challenge of steam, a challenge felt just as much on inland waters. There were threats from other quarters too; railways began throwing out their tentacles in all directions, roads were being improved to take powerful steam tractors hauling strings of waggons, and then, slowly but surely, petrol engines started muscling in. There could be no hope, no reprieve, for the sailing ship, a gentle creation of wood and canvas, when Progress strode forward with such limbs of steel.

Thus, by the time the twentieth century dawned, this fine fleet of wherries had been decimated; their tough old bones were strewn by the waterside, up dykes, and along the Breydon flats, bearing sad and silent witness to the massacre. The lot of those that survived was, in a way, even more tragic, as they were forced to drag through a spell of poverty the like of which had never been seen.

Then came the First World War, and the chance of scraping together a shilling or two, but when it was over, only a handful had heart enough to continue the struggle.

The second war finished them off for good, with the sole exception of the *Albion*, and she had a very close call. What competition from road and railway had failed to accomplish, the arts of war nearly did. For one night in 1942 she was lying with the *Eudora*, alongside the quay at Norwich, when the enemy launched one of his infamous Baedeker raids on the city. An incendiary bomb crashed through the *Eudora's* hatches, set her on fire and completely destroyed her. The *Albion* was cut adrift in the nick of time and hauled to safety. There was something Phoenix-like about her escape, as if she was destined for a new lease of life, and to go on sailing into the age of atom bombs and moon rockets.

A time will doubtless come when all ships, and all sailors, will be as much museum pieces as bronze-age implements and the bones of mammoths; when nuclear-powered submarines, governed and directed by electronic devices, will move unseen and unmanned beneath the oceans; when men, women and children, fed on synthetic foods, will live all their lives in artificial light, deep down in the bowels of the earth, to escape the radioactive contamination of the air. When that time does come, people will never know sunlight nor the sparkle of waves upon the beach. For blind subservience to Progress, which never thinks to question whether, just because a thing can be done, it should be done, must surely, in the end, drive humanity to such straits.

But until that day arrives, the sight of the *Albion*, sailing about our rivers, may help to remind us that utility and beauty were not always incompatible; that invention and sanity can go together; and that, as George Borrow put it, 'there is still the wind on the heath'.

CHAPTER THREE

Made to Measure

Building a wherry—choosing the right timber—riverside 'yards'—fashioned by eye—the Gleaner—*hull and fittings—sail and rigging—names the wherrymen use—pitch-pine masts—vanes and 'Jenny Morgans'—the 'slipping keel'—chains for Yarmouth bridge—an anchor in name only.*

ONE fine summer's morning a few years ago I was sitting yarning with eighty-year-old Jacob Cox by the side of Barton Broad. We had a comfortable, shady berth on a wooden bench under some trees, and a couple of pint mugs stood within easy reach on a rustic table in front of us.

The unruffled water of the Broad lay sparkling in the bright sunshine. Every now and again we heard the gobble of a coot rummaging for his elevenses among the reeds. Overhead the darting redshanks sent their lonely, plaintive cry winging into the blue.

Two or three yachts were afloat but had no wind to work their sheets. They waited patiently while a group of lordly swans made better going, paddling to inspect some trifles thrown overboard from an anchored cruiser.

Breakfast chatter and the sizzle of frying bacon reached us from some late risers aboard a houseboat. A gentle plop told of a water rat swimming away to fresh feeding grounds.

Jacob grasped his mug, contemplated its contents with obvious pleasure, and then in the way so many countrymen have, poured the cooling draught into his mouth, instead of just drinking it. Passing the back of his free hand across his lips and accepting a cigarette from the packet I offered him, he lit it, and with the half-burned matchend, pointed to a grassy slope at the side of the staithe.

"That's where we built 'em, the little old *Ethnie* and the *Bertha*, though you'd never think it to look at the place now, would you?"

I asked him how long ago it was.

"How long? Let me see now, round about 1890 I should think, though it's a long time to remember exactly. We built them for Press Bros., the millers, not much over twenty tons they had to be, to get up the Dilham canal.

"And even all that time ago the right sort of wood to build them with was getting scarce. I used to go scouring all round the country in my pony and trap, whenever I knew a plantation was being felled, searching for all the bends I wanted, and the right sort of trees for sawing into strakes. And you had to get them a long while before you meant to use them because they had to season. A year for every inch we used to reckon, and as a wherry's planking is two inches thick, that meant the sawn wood had to lie out for at least two years."

"Was there any rule about this when the order was placed," I asked Jacob. "Did the prospective owner specify properly seasoned timber and so on?"

"No, there was never any need to. It soon got around what sort of a builder you were and what sort of materials you used. The good 'uns got all the work they could take, the others went out of business. Scamped work in my day didn't do you or anyone else any good, it got found out soon enough and you'd never get another job. Besides," he added, "what pride could any man worth his salt take in bad work?"

Nowadays, the art of wherry building has disappeared, along with the kindred crafts of millwrighting and the making of farm carts and waggons. It is a sign of the times that you can travel the length and breadth of Norfolk and Suffolk and not find a man to make you a six-foot cartwheel. Those who remember the accumulated skills that went into such things, the warm, homely atmosphere of the tiled and timbered workshops where they were fashioned, will regret the passing of these master craftsmen.

The life of the village often centred round their activities, yet for the most part they were men with little or no schooling; often they could neither read nor write. You will find no plans, no drawings of the things they made. With unerring instinct they knew what was right and what was wrong, and this instinct was a better guide to them than paper and pencil. An old shipwright once summed it up in a sentence—"If it's right it looks right, if it ain't it looks ugly."

They had much the same sort of instinct, or faculty, for calculating quantitites, which they could do almost down to the last square inch of material. I recall one old millwright, quite unlettered, who was called in to repair the cap of a Norfolk marsh pump. He began casting his eye over the job, quite casually, or so it appeared, though now and again he scratched curious marks with a rusty nail on a bit of wood. At last, after quickly scanning his hieroglyphics, he announced just what timber, and how much of it, he would need to do the work. It was ordered, delivered and in due course he finished the job. And when the floor was swept up, all that remained was a small pile of saw ends, hardly enough to light a fire with.

As if taking up my thoughts, Jacob went on to say how, when he was stocking up to build a wherry, he could reckon pretty well how many and what sort of trees he should buy to give him the necessary planks and bends. It was no good, he said, having three parts of seasoned wood and then having to finish off with new stuff. Everything had to be properly weathered, from stem to sternpost, and that meant getting in all you were likely to want with a bit to spare.

But Jacob never worried about anything he had over at the end of a job, spare lengths always came in useful for repair work.

"With all the wherries there were sailing about then," he went on, "there were always some that needed looking to. Old and tender they were, many of them, and you had to watch what you were about or they'd have come apart in your hands. I did hear say that some of them had been built round about the time of the Battle of Trafalgar, and if you'd have seen 'em you wouldn't have thought that was far out. After all, it was no unusual thing for a wooden ship, one that had been properly built that is, to stay afloat for eighty or ninety years, and that's how old some of 'em were in my young day."

The old-time wherry-building yard was really a 'yard' in name only. There were no cranes, gantries or equipment of any sort, no slipway even for launchings usually took place on rollers. Any fairly flat piece of ground sufficed, giving access to the water, and the best recommendation for any site was its closeness to the village inn. Building a wherry was thirsty work and demanded plenty of strong ale within easy reach.

"How long did it take you to build a wherry?" I asked Jacob.

"About a year, near as I recollect," he told me. "But, of course, you weren't at it all the time. Other jobs came along, repairs and such like, and you had to work them in as you went along, so to speak."

"Did you work entirely on your own?"

"No, I had one fellow helping me, a good chap, too. You couldn't manage just by yourself, you had to have someone else to give you a hand lifting, and so on."

"So the pair of you built a 20-ton wherry from the keel up in twelve months, with other odd jobs thrown in for good measure?"

"That's about it. But as you know there's a fair bit of ironwork in a wherry and all that was done by the blacksmith. Then there was the mast, gaff, blocks and sail, we had nothing to do with them either, they were made by the proper tradesmen in Yarmouth, same as the quants were. Twenty-two foot long they had to be, and you needed a nice, sweet bit of wood to be sure they wouldn't rive or snap when you put your weight on them. There was a knack, you know, in making all these bits and pieces," and he gave me a kind of confidential wink and nod of the head, "so your best plan was to get a tradesman to do 'em rather than meddle about yourself with something you didn't rightly understand.

"Anyhow, we had our hands full enough with the hull, that had to be complete so that when the mast went in, and the sail was bent, off she could go. To begin with, as I expect you know, the sail was its natural white colour. They let it stretch thoroughly for a month or two before they treated it and made it black. And black it was, real jet black, not some of those fancy colours you read about in books."

Here I heartily agreed with Jacob. It has always astonished me that any doubt could possibly exist about the colour of a wherry's sail. It is just simply black. And it is that colour because of the materials used to treat it. After being allowed to stretch, as Jacob said, it is unbent, laid on the ground, and brushed over with a mixture of seal oil and tar, and finally with a coat of herring oil. Very often, to get rid of some of the stickiness, black lead powder is added.

This 'dressing' is done at least once a year. A freshly dressed sail, seen against the blue summer sky and the rich green of the marshes, makes a truly magnificent picture. Only someone suffering from colour blindness could make any mistake about it. Yet most writers over the last hundred years must have suffered from this ailment, for you find such fanciful descriptions as, 'the dark tanned sail', 'the rich red of their sails', 'the huge brown-coloured sail', and, perhaps the choicest of all, 'the great *purple* sail' (my italics). It is hard to account for such fairy-tale descriptions because there the sails were in front of them, plain as pike-staffs, and all they had to do was put down on paper what they actually saw.

I can only think that black was too ordinary, too down-to-earth, too prosaic a colour to fit in with the flowery, highly charged, and extremely imaginative accounts these ladies and gentlemen wrote, after often no more than two or three weeks 'adventuring' on the Broads. But, for some reason, the district has always attracted this kind of visitor.

You will find on the shelves of local reference libraries great stacks of these 'travel books', each recounting the 'unique' experiences of its author as he (or she) 'voyaged' into 'the great unknown', 'exploring' the 'little frequented' and 'inaccessible' waters of the 'distant upper reaches', all of them liberally sprinkled with versions of everyday events calculated to chill the spine of credulous and unsuspecting readers. The pages fairly bristle with the most horrifying happenings; 'lee shores', 'gales', 'tempests', 'electric storms', even 'hurricanes'. And every chapter has its quota of pious nonsense; 'only the hand of providence saved us from this peril', or 'fortune must have smiled on us, indeed'. One feels that ascending the Amazon in a dug-out canoe would be child's play in comparison.

Fortunately, there were other writers, with more honesty of purpose, who described clearly and accurately what they saw. Their works will always be valuable as records of the past, but for the others, may the dust already thick upon them remain undisturbed until they pass at last into the limbo of things best forgotten.

Jacob nodded over his shoulder and our mugs were replenished. He always found talking thirsty work.

"Yes," he went on, "a wherry's sail was plain black, as black as your hat and no argument about it. Just the same as her topsides, black, too, as you'd expect seeing as how they were tarred. But one or two were a bit fancy under water, green and brown, which didn't look at all bad. Some of the pleasuring craft used to have a thin, white line to separate the green or brown from the black, and quite smart it was especially when they lay over in a breeze. For the most part, though, tar was reckoned the thing. I expect you've heard the saying, 'paint your windmill, tar your wherry every four years.' It's a good rule and if you don't let your own house go any longer then you'll never be worried about doors and windows falling to pieces."

The *Ethnie* and *Bertha* which Jacob Cox had built all those years ago, within a stone's throw of where we now sat, were typical 'north river' wherries. This expression was used to distinguish the small, shallow draught wherries, working on the rivers Bure and Ant, from their much larger sisters on the Yare and Waveney. But besides sailing the two north rivers, the *Ethnie* and *Bertha*, along with a couple of dozen others of similar size, were built with the express aim of negotiating the Dilham–Antingham canal.

This nine-mile-long navigation was sanctioned by Parliament in 1812 and completed in 1826. It was one of five canals built in Norfolk and Suffolk, the others being the Coltishall–Aylsham canal; the New Cut, part of the Lowestoft–Norwich navigation; the Blyth navigation linking Halesworth with the sea at Southwold; the Beccles–Bungay navigation.

Only the New Cut was a canal in the true sense of the word having been dug out of the solid earth as part of the plan to make Norwich a port. The rest were rivers made navigable by the installation of locks, though a lot of digging and banking had to be done to achieve this. All of them have now fallen into decay, with the exception of the New Cut between Reedham and Haddiscoe, and it is probably only a matter of time before British Railways are given leave of Parliament to fill this in. Its only purpose now is to provide a few more miles of sailing and motor-boating for holidaymakers.

It was originally intended to pass seagoing vessels from Lowestoft up to Norwich, and did so successfully for some years. But, as I mentioned in the opening chapter, it is now hard work to sail the *Albion* through fully laden. She is about the last commercial craft using the Cut.

The four other canals were built only to extend the wherry traffic, and the dimensions of the locks allowed nothing bigger to pass through. The maximum size for craft using the Dilham–Antigham canal was, length, 50 feet; beam, 12 feet 4 inches; draught, 3 feet 6 inches. The average width of the canal was 30 feet, with an original central depth of

4½ feet. The eight road bridges gave headroom in the centre of just over 8 feet. Near the various quays the canal was widened to 60 feet to provide turning bays.

Wherever locks occur on a navigable waterway vessels using it have to be tailor-made to fit. The *Ethnie* and *Bertha* were no exceptions, and Jacob Cox had to see they did not come out oversize yet still loaded 20 to 22 tons.

Building to strict measurements like this seldom affected the sailing qualities of a vessel, provided the builder knew what he was about. Sometimes it actually improved their performance, a good example being the Thames barge *Phoenician*. She was designed to go through Mutford lock at Oulton Broad and yet proved to be one of the fastest barges on the London river.

An occasion once offered for these little wherries to show what they were made of when a cargo of wheat arrived by sea at Yarmouth, for Walker's, of Ebridge mills, half-way up the Dilham canal. Six wherries were sent after it, the wind was fair for sailing both ways, and there was a full moon. By keeping going day and night they brought up 350 tons in a week, each making three round trips and covering some 200 miles.

Fleetness, handiness and the taking of heavy loads on a shallow draught, are the three outstanding qualities of a wherry. There are never more than two in the crew, often only one. This is possible because of her simple rig and the shape and function of the hull. And here, perhaps, we should take a look at her construction and the working of her gear.

The lines taken off the *Gleaner* some years ago may be regarded as typical. She was built by Allen's of Coltishall, and, as the *Orion*, belonged for many years to Woods, Sadd & Moore of Loddon. This firm of millers and coal merchants have their premises on the river Chet and employed wherries up to 1930 when the *Sirius*, the last of their fleet, was sold. Besides these two they owned the *Vega*, *Uranus*, *Ursa Minor*, *Lowestoft Trader* and *Benjamin*.

In 1922 they sold the *Orion* and she passed into the Gedge family, who changed her name to *Gleaner*. With a length of 57 feet and 14 feet beam, she loaded about 25 tons and was an average, handy-sized craft of the kind much favoured around the turn of the century.

MADE TO MEASURE

Wherries are among some of the biggest clinker-built craft, a method stemming, of course, from their Viking origins. They are built entirely of oak, with the exception of the garboard strake, which is sometimes Canadian rock elm. It is reckoned to withstand fresh water better than oak.

Her great carrying capacity, on a shallow draught, is achieved by her flat midship sections and the almost exaggerated flare of bow and stern. You can stand anywhere on a wherry's deck and not see her sides. The more she is loaded the more this flare gives her buoyancy, and it is quite normal to sail with the decks under water amidships.

The hull is divided into three sections, though the bulkheads are not watertight. From the stem to the mast is the forepeak, which allows swinging space for the foot of the mast and the counterpoise when it is raised and lowered. Shelves in the forepeak provide storage room for paint, tar, mops, shovels and so on.

The dominating feature here is the massive tabernacle supporting the mast, and just forward of this are the two winch stanchions. Supporting the tabernacle, on the after side, is the main beam, the biggest piece of timber in a wherry, and the bulkhead here forms the forward extremity of the hold.

This is lined throughout, or ceiled, with deal planking about an inch thick, and surrounding the hold are what would normally be called coamings. But wherrymen never use this term, calling them instead 'right-ups'. They are halved along their length, the top part being removable for convenience when loading or discharging. The lower, fixed part, is called the 'standing right-ups', and the removable part, the 'shifting right-ups'.

The wherry's name, the place where she comes from, and sometimes the owner's name, appear on two boards, either side of the mast, screwed into the right-ups at the fore end of the hold. In trading wherries they are usually painted, often in most spirited style, but pleasure wherries generally have natural wood boards, varnished, with gold-leafed, incised lettering. To my mind they never look right. We had them at first in the *Albion*, but soon replaced them with boards painted light blue, lettered and ornamented in cream. It made all the difference to her appearance.

The hold is covered by fifteen, sometimes sixteen, hatches, and one 'dead' hatch. This dead hatch is a fixture immediately aft of the tabernacle. The rest are portable and have a pronounced camber, both for shedding water easily and to give them strength. They have to be strong as they provide not only a covering for the hold, but working space when making or taking in sail, and when lowering and raising the mast. They must, therefore, be able to take the weight of two men over an area that may be as big as 35 feet by 14 feet, besides heavy mooring ropes and the gaff and sail when lowered.

Although the hatches vary in length, the camber is the same in each, so that they can be stacked on top of each other when the hold is opened up. Each one is numbered, from 1 to 15 or 16, with incised Roman numerals, to make sure they go in their correct places. This use of Roman numerals, incidentally, has long been an artful dodge of country carpenters, as they can use a flat chisel to cut from 1 to 99 without making a single curved stroke.

With one exception all the hatches overlap, and the purlins are grooved to shed any water that runs in between them. The exception is a 'taking off hatch', usually numbered 7 or 8, which can be removed independently of its neighbours. This arrangement enables the fore, or after, part of the hold to be worked without uncovering the whole of it, an advantage in bad weather.

When new a set of hatches should be completely waterproof, but even so they are generally covered by tarpaulins, or hatch cloths, when anything perishable, such as bulk wheat or bagged sugar, is being carried. They are battened down in the usual way with iron battens and wedges.

There is one other hatch, a small one called the 'carling board', which covers the space in the foredeck giving passage to the foot of the mast and the counterpoise. When a wherry is left unattended this carling board is secured to the deck with an iron strap and padlock.

The third section is the cabin, aft of the hold, and neatly following the lines of the right-ups and hatches. Entrance is by way of the sternsheets, through small double doors which are unshipped and stowed on the bunks when under way. This is done because, opening outwards, they would otherwise get in the way, especially closehauled, with the full scope of the mainsheet aboard. This is allowed to pay into the space between the bunks without cluttering up the sternsheets; a scheme greatly suiting the skipper, but of much discomfort to the mate, who finds himself tending the stove and brewing tea with his feet, and often the lower half of his body, coiled round with three-inch manila.

The stove is against the bulkhead facing the doors. It has a small oven and will roast meat or bake pies to perfection. On top it will fry steak, chops or bacon and boil vegetables. It burns coal, and is polished to such brilliance with black lead, that you can almost see to part your hair in it. Summer and winter the big, black kettle sings away, with the brown teapot close beside it.

The chimney leads out through the fore end of the cabin. A portable section, called the 'tall' chimney, is shipped when the wherry is alongside, but under way is removed to save fouling the sheet.

Above the stove is a small mantelshelf, housing a three-and-sixpenny alarm clock, and above that two small oil-lamps on gimbals. Between them hangs an aneroid barometer and a small mirror flanked, usually, by a few faded photographs of wives, sweethearts or old wherries.

By day the hair mattresses are rolled up and the blankets folded on top. This allows access to the lockers beneath the bunks where coal, kindling, potatoes and vegetables are stowed. Crockery, cutlery, tinned goods, lard, butter, sugar, tea and such like, are kept in two small cupboards either side of the doorway. Hand bowls, scrubbing brush, and cleaning materials find a place in small lockers round the sternsheets.

There is not much need for ventilation, but a little extra daylight is admitted through three unglazed openings, a skylight in the cabin top, and two sidelights. They can be opened and closed as required.

Going into a wherry's cabin for the first time you will notice at once the neatness and tidiness of everything, the polished lamps, the smart graining of all woodwork, and the clean, white deckhead. You will notice, too, there is no table; but this is not a hardship for wherrymen would find one an encumbrance.

You may think eating without a table a bit difficult but you soon get the hang of it. A meal in a wherry is certainly less elaborate than in some other places, where you have side plates, bread baskets, cruets, water jugs, glasses, and two or three sets of cutlery, with serviettes, ash-trays and flower vases thrown in for good measure. Here you need only the minimum of equipment, one dinner plate and a knife and fork. You sit on the bunk balancing the plate on your knees. Your mug of tea sits on the bunk beside you. A packet of salt passes, as required, from port to starboard. A hunk of bread rests on the side of the plate, and a good tip is to wedge it, in the early stages of the meal, between the two heaps of cabbage and potatoes. A sizeable piece of crumb is kept to mop up the last of the gravy, leaving a clean plate to receive duff and treacle. The last forkful of duff should absorb the final traces of treacle, so that a spotless plate can be put in the bowl for washing-up. Then some hot water is poured into the bowl, and while the plates and knives and forks are soaking, you stretch out full length, have a smoke, yarn for a while, and fall off for the inevitable forty winks.

Believe me, such a meal does you ten times more good than what you get in a city restaurant where, after lengthy queueing, you battle for a table, sink exhausted into a hard chair, gaze indefinitely at a stained, ash-strewn cloth, with oozing, dribbling sauce bottles for decoration, and then have thrown at you some ill-prepared, synthetic mess, so devoid of nourishment that half an hour afterwards you are crying out for a good, square meal. I will at any time exchange such refinements of so-called civilization for a chunk of honest roast beef, and a double helping of treacle duff, in a wherry's cabin, even if I do have to balance the plate on my knees.

Unlike most sailing ships a wherry's deck is almost completely free of gear. There are no bulwarks, no standing rigging, except from masthead to stemhead, and there is an unhindered walk throughout her whole length. These are by no means accidental characteristics but a combination of requirements evolved to fit her as perfectly as possible for the jobs she has to do.

The absence of bulwarks is explained by the need to use the decks as a source of motive power. They form unimpeded tracks for the wherrymen when quanting. With one end of the quant on the river bed, and the other against their shoulder, they lean forward, exerting all the weight they can, and walk slowly aft. As they do so the wherry moves forward, in confirmation of Newton's law, that every action has an equal, and opposite, reaction. I must confess, however, to having had serious doubts about this law when quanting against wind and tide in a particularly foul reach. The forward motion of the wherry has all too often seemed to bear but slight relation to my strenuous, back-aching toil.

If there were bulwarks, quanting would be difficult, if not impossible; and a wherry that could not be quanted would be almost useless. Shrouds and other standing rigging would also get in the way, and it is possible to do without them because of how the mast is stepped.

If a heavy spar, 40 feet high and 12 inches to 14 inches in diameter, is to be raised and lowered, with the minimum of effort and in the space available, then it can only be done with a counterbalance. This demands that it shall be pivoted and supported in a tabernacle of great strength. Wherry builders long ago solved the problem of combining the three factors (a) how much counterweight they could comfortably house, which was directly related to (b) where the point of balance must come, and (c) the minimum distance from the fulcrum to the extremity of the counterweight to give proper support for the mast in all conditions of weather.

The ease with which a wherry's mast can be lowered is something to marvel at. Anything up to 35 cwt. of lead, or iron, go into the balance weight, yet you can stand in the sternsheets and rock the mast gently up and down with one finger.

If you stand aft as far as you can get, your feet will be astride the 6 feet or 7 feet long tiller, extending to within a few inches of the cabin doors. It is slightly longer than the rudder, a massive thing to give effective control in restricted waters.

If you look down you will notice the deck you are standing on is planked in the usual way as far as the after end of the cabin. But alongside the hold, the deck consists of a single piece of wood only. Then comes the foredeck, planked again like the stern.

A prettily shaped covering board extends fore and aft, and through it come the mooring bitts, one on either side aft, two on either side forward. The wherryman's name for these bitts is 'timber heads', and he only speaks of the covering board from the stem to just aft of the forward timber heads, and from the stern to just forward of the after timber heads. The section between these two points narrows slightly and is called the 'plancea', a word probably derived from the French, *planche*, a plank.

The side deck, made as it is from a single piece of wood, is called the 'plankway'. It has to give a good foothold for quanting and is, therefore, usually treated with a mixture of tar and sawdust which dries up leaving a roughened surface. In winter, when everything is frozen and slippery, stove ashes are often sprinkled over the plankways.

One last deck fitting remains to be noticed; the winch. As already mentioned, it comes just before the mast, with its two stanchions securely anchored in the forepeak. It is worked with two handles, shipped at either end of the barrel, or on the counter-shaft, having a ratio of about four to one. A semicircular brake band about 2 inches wide engages on a drum, inboard of the main gear wheel, on the port side of the barrel.

To lower sail the mate ships a handle on the port side, makes a part turn sufficient to release the pawl, presses down hard with the brake lever, and removes the handle. The sail is now held aloft by the brake alone and when the skipper sings out, the pressure is eased slightly, and the sail allowed to come down at the run, till the end of the gaff has dipped and rests on the hatches. The mate applies the brake again while the skipper jumps from the sternsheets and lifts the gaff end off the hatches. The brake is then released once more and the whole spar, now horizontal, sinks on to the hatches.

The barrel and counter-shaft would be in the way of the mast when it was lowered if they were fixtures, so both are pivoted, or hinged, on the starboard stanchion and can be swung to one side.

One golden rule wherrymen have is never to leave a handle in the winch. It can be dangerous, if not deadly, to do so. Should the pawl fail to engage properly, or the brake not hold, a handle left in position would fly round at tremendous speed, come adrift and probably brain someone. But accidents of this kind are very few because it is instilled into wherrymen from boyhood always to unship a handle after use, and they do it by instinct and as a matter of course.

Because of the ingenious and quite unique arrangement of the single halliard, hoisting sail consists of no more than winding the winch. To see how this is possible let us take a look at the reeving of this halliard.

To distribute the weight fairly over the gaff there are two wire spans, called 'spens', linked on travellers by a chain martingale, which works in another traveller shackled to a single-sheaved block. This is called the 'spen' block.' Another, single-sheaved, block is shackled to an eye bolt just above the jaws of the gaff, and there is a third, double-sheaved, block at the masthead with a limited thwartship traverse allowed by the crane iron.

The end of the halliard is bent to the gaff a little above the throat block, leads up through the masthead block to the spen block, back again to the masthead block and down through the throat block. From there it passes up again and through a large sheave worked in the mast itself, and finally down to the winch.

When the sail is being hoisted the throat starts to go up first; when it is about half-way up a slight strain comes on the peak and it, too, begins to lift after having dragged a foot or two forward along the hatches. As we have just seen, the same thing happens in reverse when lowering, which is why the skipper has to hold the end up, coming aft all the time, while the jaws complete their descent. With the luff fully extended the gaff is in a roughly horizontal position, and the greatest strain comes on the halliard at the end of the hoist when, with the final peaking up, it has to support the whole weight of the sail. With this in mind the old-time rope-makers devised a halliard that was thin at the beginning, but gradually thickened, to coincide with the increasing strain. It was made in one piece in the rope-walk, but nowadays with everything machine-made, it is impossible to procure one. Sometimes, to get round the problem, a small and a larger rope are spliced together, but it is not quite the same thing.

The reason behind a tapered halliard was to allow sufficient accommodation on the winch barrel. Because the turns on the barrel increase its diameter, making hoisting that much harder, wherrymen have a special way of arranging them. The halliard is seized to the starboard end of the barrel and when hoisting, fleets across to port. When it is two-thirds the way across, it is hauled back on to the turns, and continues over to the starboard side again. Up to this point only the gaff is being raised so there is still not a great deal of weight to lift.

The flange throws it over to port once more, and by the time the real strain is reached the halliard has arrived at the end of the double layer of turns. From there it is allowed to slip down on to the unused part of the barrel, and the diminished diameter thus gained gives sufficient purchase for the peak to be set up without undue effort. Through long experience wherrymen can judge the whole thing so nicely that on the last pawl there are only about two inches of barrel left, which they use on passage for taking up any slack due to drying or stetching.

The forestay is of wire and has a soft eye in one end which slips over the top of the mast and comes to bear on the crane iron. The other end is shackled to a double-sheave block rove with a lower, single-sheaved one, secured to an eyebolt in the stemhead.

During the early part of the nineteenth century, by which time wherries had grown to about the size we know them today, their masts were made out of locally grown larch trees. In the latter half of the century Oregon and Scandinavian pine were tried but were not always found to be satisfactory owing to the strain of the very large sail. This was noticed by Martin Barber, master of the brig *Maid of the Yare*, then trading regularly to the Baltic. So when he came back from one trip he brought four pitch-pine logs with him which were shaped up and put into wherries belonging to Pope, of St. Margaret's wharf, Norwich. With their much greater strength they at once proved successful and thereafter anything but pitch-pine was rarely fitted in a wherry.

It was an Oregon mast we broke in the *Albion* when racing her on Breydon Water in 1952. At the time it was next to impossible to find a pitch-pine log big enough, so we had to fall back on Oregon. We had a good precedent for doing so as her first mast was made of it, out of a piece of timber brought by steamer from London specially for the job. Ellett, of Yarmouth, who, at the turn of the century was making nearly all the wherry masts, gaffs, quants and boathooks, had no log in stock big enough. Jack Powley of Bungay, who sailed the *Albion* for many years, and remembers her being launched, has told me Oregon was preferred to pitch-pine because of its lightness. They were afraid pitch-pine might put her down too much by the head.

When we had to replace the broken mast in 1952 we scoured the country for a piece of pitch-pine big enough, and after a desperate search heard of something that sounded suitable in Liverpool. After running the rule over it we found it was a foot short for height, but otherwise just what we wanted, 14 inches square, so we bought it and had it sent by rail to Great Yarmouth for shaping up. That piece of wood cost us the best part of £100, more than ten times the price of the *Albion*'s first mast in 1898, and I mention it to give some idea of the cost of ship preservation today. The £100 included rail charges, but we had another £30 to pay for making up. All told it was an expensive day's racing as the insurance company would only meet £50 of the cost.

But it turned out to be a very fine piece of timber, free of knots, which the previous one had not been, and with the rich, red colour pitch-pine should be. After seven year's service it is as good as when it first went in.

However, should it break again, then replacement may well prove impossible, because pitch-pine logs of this size are no longer imported. The forests where they once grew are now exhausted, particularly Mobile in America, so it would seem the only thing is to take a leaf from the book of a famous English admiral and start planting pine-cones!

When the new mast was stepped we found the extra weight did put her head down as her builder had feared it would fifty years earlier. But we corrected it by stowing several hundredweights of pig-iron round the sternsheets, though it decreased her carrying capacity by about a ton.

For telling accurately the direction of the wind the mast is surmounted by a 'vane', pronounced 'wane', which can be of two types, a high vane or a gate vane. The first is the more elaborate and comprises a figure, cut out of tin, on the windward side of the spindle, with a fixture above this to leeward for the bunting. A gate, or low, vane has no figure but a decorated plate to which the bunting is attached, and with this type everything is to leeward of the spindle.

Local artist-craftsmen found great scope for their talents in making these vanes and some very beautiful ones were to be seen in days gone by. A veritable portrait gallery of the famous, and not so famous, at one time graced the wherries' mastheads, one hand stretching triumphantly heaven-wards, the other, for constructional purposes, grasping the spindle. The wherry's name usually dictated what the figure should be; the *Red Rover*, for instance, displayed a villainous pirate brandishing a sword; the *Norfolk Hero* carried a very gallant Nelson; while the *Mermaid* had one such creature sitting, rather uncomfortably I always thought, on one haunch, with her tail stretched out beside her.

About the middle of last century there was a song which became very popular, and it told of a certain Welsh girl by the name of Jenny Morgan. Morgan's brewery, in Norwich, then owned several wherries and quickly adopted for their vanes the figure of this Welsh girl as a kind of trade-mark. She was depicted in a very long and full skirt, with rolls of wavy, fair hair surmounted by the characteristic inverted flower-pot hat, holding a bunch of leeks in her free hand. These vanes immediately became known as 'Jenny Morgans' and the name was loosely applied to vanes of all kinds. But strictly speaking only a Welsh girl vane should be so called.

Many of the gate vanes were equally imaginative, the plates being cut out like stencils to show all manner of decorative devices. A favourite was the 'circular saw', a circle with a serrated outer edge, and the initial letter of the wherry's name in the centre. Stars, too, were popular, with the initial letter in the centre. But where the plates were not cut to reveal designs in silhouette, they were painted to display some appropriate emblem, such as a rose.

During her sixty years the *Albion* has had three vanes; the first a gate vane with a gilded, twelve-pointed star; the second, also a gate vane, with the circular saw device surrounding her initial letter 'A'; and the third, a genuine 'Jenny Morgan', with flowing hair and bunch of leeks. This was presented to us by Barnard's, of Norwich, and was modelled on a very ancient Jenny Morgan which came to light in a Reedham barn. It still had some of the original paint on it so we were able to decorate our Welsh girl in her authentic colours.

The most striking and characteristic feature of a wherry is, of course, her great, black sail. There is no rig like it anywhere in the world, and it gives her the unique quality of being able to sail almost into the eye of the wind.

Wherrymen will tell you that the sail is more important than the craft; with a good sail they can get a bad wherry along, but with a bad sail they can get nowhere, however good the wherry. Sixty years ago Pike, of Yarmouth, made most of the sails including the first one for the *Albion*. The price was £12. In 1949 we had to pay £120.

The leach, head and luff are roped but the foot is not. A 'bonnet' can be laced to it in light airs and because it goes on the bottom is often called an 'Irishman's tops'l'. Robands secure it to the gaff and there are three sets of reef points. Another method of reducing sail in bad weather is to run 'goose-winged', or 'scandalized', that is to say with the peak dowsed, or lowered. The gaff line, leading from the peak to the deck, controls the gaff when gybing.

The luff is kept to the mast with hoops, once made of wood but now of iron, while for the jaws of the gaff there are 'trolleys' on a 'parrel lashing'.

The tack is shackled to an eye on the backboard of the tabernacle above the dead hatch. There are two mainsheet blocks, each with three sheaves, the lower one having a large hook with screw mousing which travels on a 'horsa' bolted to the cabin top. A cleat is incorporated in the iron strop of this block, but the sheet is normally turned up on two heavy-duty wooden cleats placed either side of the doors on the after end of the cabin. Below these, and slightly outboard of them, are two footrests. You have to use your whole body when steering, bringing the small of the back to bear on the tiller, and these footrests give a useful grip when you really want to throw your weight on to it.

A 2-inch thick rubbing strake extends round the hull, level with the covering boards and planceas, and is faced with half-round iron about $2\frac{1}{2}$-inch wide and $\frac{3}{8}$-inch thick. This is called the 'bin iron', and when a wherry is deeply laden she is always said to be 'down to her bins', Where this iron goes round the stem it is called the 'hairpin', because of its shape, while the overhangs of the covering boards, fore and aft, are termed the 'harpens', no doubt for the same reason. 'Harpen' is not far removed from the old Norfolk pronunciation of 'hairpin'.

One feature of a wherry seldom seen is the 'slipping keel'. But if you look on either side of the stem post you will notice two, curved iron straps, with an eye on the end of them. As the name implies, this keel can be attached or removed as required and the straps help to centre it up for fixing. Two lanyards with tell-tale knots ensure it is properly in position to take the two, sometimes three, self-centring bolts which hold it in position. When the keel is removed these bolt holes are made watertight with screw plugs.

The slipping keel was the last improvement made to the wherry and dates only from about 1880. Being made of wood it floats to the surface when released and very often, when approaching shoal water, it is unshipped and towed astern. You get the impression of a man tramping along the road with his boots slung over his shoulder. In the past, when a wherry was bound up to somewhere like Aylsham, she left it on the bank before entering the canal, and collected it on her return.

Crews became so adept at working it that you were reckoned a pretty poor hand if you shipped more than a bucketful of water when getting your bolt in. Although the *Albion* has a slipping keel she never uses it as her work is confined to those sections of the river where there is plenty of water. But it will slip if need be and does, of course, come off before she goes into dock.

One of the most important pieces of gear carried by a wherry is her 'dropping chain'. It helps in negotiating Yarmouth haven bridge, and works in much the same way as an anchor when it is dredged. I should explain that, except at slack water, there is a very fast run of tide through Yarmouth Bridge, which makes shooting in the ordinary way a very hazardous operation. Many a vessel has come to grief there, including the *Albion*, and it took three days to fish her up. But that was back in 1929 when she was the *Plane*.

With this chain a wherry can go through the bridge at any state of the tide, indeed, the faster it runs the more control there is. With sail and mast lowered the mate throws enough over the bows to swing her round, and she then drags stern-first towards the bridge. The slower she goes the better, as there is then more pressure on the rudder. The skipper sheers her to port or starboard as required till she is plumb in the centre of the arch, then, with the rudder amidships, lets her drop through.

Another important item is the 'swipe', an ingenious box pump made of elder wood. Apart from pop-guns, which used to give me great delight as a child, and which I made out of elder branches by removing the pith, I can think of no other use to which this wood is put. It is, however, almost impervious to water and can stand up to any amount of immersion, the reason it is chosen for these 'swipes'.

Pumping is invariably done in the forepeak because a loaded wherry is always slightly down by the head. A wooden lip, or spout, discharges on to the deck, the water running over the side. It is primed with a bucket of water and for all its simple construction is a most effective contrivance. As the bulkheads are not watertight the whole wherry can be pumped dry from this one position.

For loading and discharging cargo a wherry carries two 'long deals', two 'quarter deals', two barrows and two different sizes of 'right-up irons'. Long deals measure 22 feet by 11 feet by 3 inches and form a gangway from river bank or quayside. Quarter deals are 16 feet by 11 feet by 3 inches and are long enough to go right across the hold. They are also used in conjunction with the right-up irons which hook on the inside of the hold. The barrows are rather curious, being ordinary wheelbarrows without any legs, enabling them to stand on the width of a single plank.

Wherries engaged in the wood trade always have a pair or two of 'plankhooks' for hauling deals about the hold, and those doing much sugar beeting always have a couple of beet forks aboard. All carry a curious one-armed device known as a 'rond anchor'. It is nothing like an anchor in the ordinary sense but is driven into the ground to provide a mooring when there is no convenient tree or post.

The rest of the equipment is very much what you would expect to find in a vessel of this sort; a boathook, two or three cork fenders, a light towline 100 feet in length, mooring ropes, a stone water jar, a rag mop and a 'killer'. This last is not as bad as it sounds but a wooden bowl for washing the hands, peeling potatoes and dishing up crocks. It derives from the Anglo-Saxon, *kylle*.

I have tried to describe a typical Norfolk wherry, her construction, rig, fittings and the way she is worked. But you can only go so far in general terms because there are exceptions to every rule. A number of wherries differed in certain details from the normal pattern, while others were temporarily modified for special duties or occasions. I will explain these differences, and the reasons for them, in the next chapter.

CHAPTER FOUR

Shrouds, Topsails and Spinnakers

Launching overland—Albion Brighton's last wherry—famous Reedham craft—a wherry's earnings—Edward Fitzgerald prophesies—builders in town and country—the Wonder—*shipbuilding in Norwich—a 'horse packet'—'steam' wherries—strange sails—'white nosings' and distinctive colours.*

WHEN the Norfolk Wherry Trust bought the *Albion* for preservation in 1949 a number of well-meaning people criticized our choice on the grounds that she was carvel built and, therefore, not a typical wherry. It was a perfectly valid criticism because she does differ in construction from any other trading wherry ever built. I may say here that while we should have liked a clinker-built craft, we really had no choice in the matter, there being no other hull available in good enough condition to merit preservation.

But we have never regretted our action for Billy Brighton, of Oulton salt-water broad, who built her, certainly intended her to last. It was he, in fact, who suggested her carvel build and as he was responsible for many fine wherries, besides smacks and yachts, I think we may regard the *Albion* as an authentic specimen.

When W. D. & A. E. Walker, the Bungay millers, first decided on a new craft they had in mind an iron wherry thinking it would stand up better to all the lock work on the navigation between Beccles and Bungay. Brighton was against this and suggested instead a wooden wherry, but of carvel construction. She was the last Brighton built and undoubtedly his finest. To see her stretching away up Breydon at the present time it is hard to realize she already has more than three-score years behind her. Besides her unusual build several other points are worth mentioning. For instance, not only did Brighton make her garboard strakes of Canadian rock elm, but the next two as well, and they are still in her. The only planking we had to replace was between wind and water, and that was due more to rubbing and chafing than to decay. Then again, she must have been the only wherry ever launched without a single brushful of tar on her; she entered the water with a green bottom, and red oxide above the waterline, while her seams were filled with marine glue. She was also the first craft to have internal iron-bound blocks.

Before moving to Oulton Broad, Brighton carried on business at Bungay where he built his first wherry, the *Waveney*, when only seventeen. She was afterwards bought by Di Thain of Somerton and re-named the *Eva Rosa*.

The story goes that as a lad he kept plaguing his father to buy wood and when at last he had collected enough he turned to and started on the *Waveney*. He succeeded in making such a good job of her that Welton, of Somerleyton, ordered the *Blanche* from him, and after that he never looked back. He went on to build some of the prettiest yachts on Norfolk and Suffolk waters and became a well-known figure at local regattas.

Brighton was not a man to let difficulties stand in his way. When he built the *Waveney*, the only suitable bit of land he could find was a quarter of a mile from the river, and when it came to launching she had to be hauled over the marshes on rollers. This operation, however, proved most popular with the lads of the village, roped in to lend a hand, for their exertions were liberally rewarded with beer from a cask lashed on deck.

The *Blanche*, too, also quenched a lot of thirsts at her launch. He built her on the Honey Pot meadow at Bungay, later the town bowling green, and she had to be taken on a trolley through the streets to the Staithe and launched into a dyke sideways.

Whether young Brighton found this free beer was eating up his profits I cannot say, but he did no more building at Bungay and began looking round for a yard of his own. At that time, when men counted more than machines, the age of the journeyman craftsman was not over, and it was quite common for wherry builders to go from place to place and build craft wherever a prospective owner might have a supply of timber. We find Ben Benns, the famous Yarmouth builder, moving to Barton Turf to lay down the *Little Georgie*, and to Somerton to build the *Lord Roberts*. Brighton did much the same and built craft at Coldham Hall and Yarmouth before settling down with his own yard at Oulton.

Once there, he found his reputation had preceded him and was soon given the chance to enlarge his experience and try his hand at smacks and yachts as well. Looking back it seems fitting that his active career should have ended with the building of the *Albion*. He always held she was the best of his wherries and must have looked on her as his swan-song, for he actually sold his yard while she was still on the ways.

It may be that she is the last of his works afloat today. If so, then she is surely a worthy memorial to a type of man we shall, alas, see no more; the master-builder, in every sense of the word.

It is impossible to give anything like a complete list now of all those who, at one time or another, plied the trade of wherry building. Very few records or accounts were kept and official registrations are mostly silent about when and where they were built. But from the evidence available, and the remarkable memories of many old wherrymen, it is possible to learn where most of the yards were seventy or eighty years ago.

Pride of place certainly goes to Reedham, where Hall's built such fleet and famous craft as the *Bell, Maud, Dora, Our Boys, British Queen* and the incomparable *Fawn*. This little 25-tonner was the most perfect thing ever to hoist a black sail, and with her crack skipper, Ophir Powley, at the tiller, there was nothing that could look at her. Just what sort of magic went into her building we shall never know, but her praises will be sung to the full in the chapter 'Clippers of the Tideway'.

There were really two yards at Reedham, one belonging to Charles Hall, the other to his brother James. Charles was the senior member and had with him his son Dan and cousin Tom.

Three famous pleasure wherries also came from their yard, the *Solace, Hathor* and *Ecila*, as well as the passenger steamer *Jenny Lind* which wafted many thousands of happy holidaymakers up and down the Norwich river.

Hall's price for building a trading wherry was in the region of £10 a ton, which means the *Fawn* cost about £250. That was for the hull alone and did not include mast, sail, quants and one or two other small items. But all told the cost was well under £300.

In those days a wherry could prove a pretty sound investment. Looking at several old notebooks kept by skippers it is clear one could pay for herself within five or six years. The crew received no wages but worked on a share basis; a third went to the owner, called the 'wherry's share', and the remainder was divided between skipper and mate. This was done by mutual agreement but usually on a fifty-fifty basis.

The following list shows the *Bell*'s earnings for her owner over a period of nearly five years. The total is not far short of the £350 he paid for her.

		£	s.	d.
1895	November to December	11	17	4
1896	January to December	64	18	1
1897	,, ,, ,,	70	15	3
1898	,, ,, ,,	63	3	7
1899	,, ,, ,,	68	17	1
1900	,, ,, August	41	12	5
		£321	3	9

These amounts are the 'wherry's share' only, or a third of her gross earnings. Assuming the balance to have been equally divided by her crew, then skipper and mate each received the same sum. In the best year, 1897, it works out at a weekly wage of about 28 shillings. This was well above the prevailing rate for agricultural labourers and North Sea fishermen, but a wherryman, of course, had two homes to keep going. He had to feed himself on board and provide for his wife and family, a more expensive business than if they had all been living together. Such wages seem a poor reward for the responsibility of taking cargoes, often worth hundreds of pounds, yet many an old-timer has told me they were much more happy and content then than youngsters today.

I well remember one teak-skinned old skipper, close on the heels of eighty, taking my arm in a still vice-like grip and saying, "Why, blast, old partner, when yew cud draw along into a pub, lay down a tanner, order a pint, a packet o' fags and a box of matches, and get change out of it, wot was the use of more money?"

Hall's, of Reedham, built more wherries than anyone else but they were closely followed by Allen's, of Coltishall. Because of their position on the River Bure, just above Wroxham, they went in for a slightly smaller type of wherry. The *Hilda* and *Cornucopia* were good examples of the Allen build, both 20 tons or a little over. This yard claims the distinction, though a rather melancholy one, of having built the last wherry ever launched, the *Ella*. That was in 1912, and curiously enough, the last Norfolk wind pump to be erected was put up in the same year.

Wright, of Beccles, produced a range of strong, handy craft of varying sizes. The smallest was the *Matilda*, 26 tons, followed by the *Olive*, 28 tons; the *Courier*, 30 tons; and the *Cygnet*, 40 tons. Most of these were either owned or employed by Crisp the local maltster. Wright built the *Emerald*, 35 tons, specially for him round about 1880 and she may well have been the last wherry launched at Beccles.

Edward FitzGerald used to sail from Lowestoft up to Beccles in his yacht the *Scandal* and occasionally got Wright to do odd jobs for him. Writing to his friend Frederick Spalding in February 1862, he said: "Wright has laid down the keel of a new wherry, on speculation, but I am afraid that the railway which is now approaching Beccles will injure his business." That is just what happened, though Wright was not the only victim. The railway, aided in due course by the motor lorry, put every wherryman and every wherry builder out of business. Steel tracks and macadam highways became the thing, even though they were expensive to maintain, while the surface of the river cost nothing. But mark the irony of this thing called Progress. Having creamed the best of the trade for a hundred years, the railway gets a fit of the sulks and closes down. Greater and greater burdens are thrown on the roads, which, in these parts, have not been materially improved for fifty years; slower and slower move the ever more powerful juggernauts; and more and more victims get crushed to death beneath their wheels.

FitzGerald goes on to tell his friend how he took Wright to task over an unsatisfactory job: "I showed him two of the guilty screws which had almost let my leaden keel part from the wooden one; he says he had desired the smith not to make *too* large heads, and the smith accordingly made them too small; and some apprentice had, he supposes, fixed them in without further inspection. There is such honesty and cheerfulness in Wright's Saxon eyes and countenance when he faces such a charge as disarms all one's wrath."

Joe Teasdel, of Stalham, built at least three wherries, one, the *Dorothy*, a tiny little thing of only 14 tons, intended to go to Skinner Taylor's farm up his dyke by Dilham Cut. The *Ceres*, slightly bigger, was designed to do the same. Teasdel's largest venture, the *Unexpected*, 30 tons, was built for Riches, of Catfield. But she proved altogether too big for the narrow cut and was sold away to Yarmouth.

Besides Billy Brighton's, only two wherries were built in the Lowestoft district, the *Chieftain* of 34 tons, by Kemp of Oulton Broad, and the *Number One*, 45 tons, by Charles Reynolds of Lowestoft, and that was as long ago as 1850.

Yarmouth, on the other hand, had four or five first-class builders, the best known being Ben Benns. I have already mentioned him as a journeyman builder in connection with the *Little Georgie* and the *Lord Roberts*, when he went to work at Barton and Somerton. He also worked on Hall's yard at Reedham, and at Coldham Hall, but back at Yarmouth he produced the *Louisa* and the *Zephyr*, 30 tons. The wherry for which he will always be remembered, however, was the *Wonder*, most appropriately named as she was a giant of no less than 90 tons, far and away the biggest ever built.

There was originally some idea of using her as a coaster and for taking cargo out of vessels in Yarmouth Roads. She did go to sea on one occasion, but never again. She proved very hard to handle and in an effort to make things easier was given an experimental foresail. It helped a little but she always remained a trial to everyone who had her, only the strongest men venturing to take her tiller.

'Skeweye' Tyrrell had her for a while and called her 'a great old cow'. He told me that many a time he arrived in Yarmouth after a scant wind all the way down from Norwich, and had hardly a shred of skin left on his backside when he got there. Nobody shed any tears when Hobrough, of Norwich, bought her for conversion into a dredger.

The only other craft approaching her for size was the *Wanderer*, of about 70 tons. Little is known of her as she first went into the water more than a hundred years ago. Unlike the *Wonder*, however, she is reckoned to have been fast and handy.

Valentine Gibbs, of Yarmouth, built a very small wherry, the *Faith*, of only 13 tons, which he sailed himself for some time. From Bessey & Palmer came the *Dauntless*, 26 tons, and the *Fir*, ex *Crowhurst*, 40 tons, which Jack Cates was skipper of between the wars.

Barber's produced the swift little *Lady Violet*, the *Lowestoft Trader*, *Earl of Beaconsfield*, 30 tons, and the *Forget-Me-Not*. From Cossey's came the *Rambler*, intended mainly as a pleasure wherry, though she was stripped out during the winter and used for trading.

Richard Wooden had a small yard opposite Flint House, Southgates Road, Yarmouth, where he lived, and from there launched the *Ena May* in 1895. She was the last wherry to be built on the east, or Yarmouth side of the harbour. To Bessey & Palmer's *Crowhurst*, mentioned above, belongs the distinction of being the last wherry built anywhere in Yarmouth.

Winter, of Bungay, was responsible for the fine-looking and powerful *Eudora*, belonging to the same owners as the *Albion*, W. D. & A. E. Walker, the Bungay millers. Anyone visiting the Wherry Inn at Geldeston, between Beccles and Bungay, will see a vigorously painted sign of the *Eudora* under sail among the willow trees of the Waveney. It was done from a photograph taken about 1900.

Norwich was very poorly served for wherry builders during the latter half of last century. Only a handful of craft were launched in that time, which is surprising because of the considerable activity going on immediately before.

The earliest records of shipbuilding in Norwich date from 1372 when Edward III ordered the city to build him a balinger. This type of vessel was around a hundred tons, very long and low in shape, and propelled by oars as well as sails.

The king would certainly not have given this order to Norwich had he not been advised that facilities existed for carrying it out. But the first reaction of the city fathers was to try and farm the job out to Yarmouth. They sent a deputation to negotiate terms with the local shipwrights but it was not received with much enthusiasm. So they decided to build the king's ship in Norwich after all, but to look elsewhere for a master shipwright. They found one, John Pondere, at

Ipswich, and came to an agreement that he and his companions should journey to Norwich and work on her as 'the Bailiffs and Community shall wish'. A cart was sent to Ipswich 'for carrying their necessaries hither' which suggests the city was anxious to get started as soon as possible to keep in the king's good books. They had already made an agreement 'to buy timber, and to do all other matters'.

In later centuries Norwich had several small yards where keels and wherries were built, and by 1800 these were big enough to launch coasting brigs. In 1801, a builder by the name of Houghton, launched one of 120 tons burden, an event providing quite a spectacle for the local residents. He built another two years later and this time there was no restraining the onlookers, as the following newspaper report shows: 'She went off the stocks with all her rigging up and drove into the water with perfect safety, when the people on board began to rock her, and a number impudently ascending the rigging, which, not having any ballast on board, and the people going over to the starboard side, overswayed her and all on board were plunged into the river. Only one was drowned.'

The construction of this kind of ship was greatly encouraged by the passing of the Lowestoft–Norwich Navigation Act of 1827. Within two years the *Spring* had come from Batley's yard, near Carrow Bridge, and the year after J. Watts launched from his slip in St. Faith's Lane, a fine steamship of 20 h.p. measuring 80 feet in length. She was called the *Emperor* and was built to augment the steam packet service between Norwich and Yarmouth, started in 1813 by the *Royal Soveriegn*. Watts is described as a manufacturer of steam engines as well as a shipbuilder, and if he was actually responsible for her machinery then he can be credited with having made the first steam engine in Norfolk.

In June the following year, 1831, Thomas Batley had another vessel ready for the Lowestoft, Beccles and Norwich Shipping Company and she was duly launched 'amid the plaudits and acclamations of the spectators'.

The extent to which Norwich was ship-conscious in those days may be seen from this eye-witness account of the arrival of the *Squire* and the *City of Norwich* on the opening of the Navigation from Lowestoft in September 1833: 'The shores were lined with tens of thousands of the population to witness the vessels passing through Carrow Bridge, which they did without once having touched the ground on their voyage from Lowestoft, amid loud cheering and firing of guns. The Union Flag was hoisted on St. Peter Mancroft steeple, the bells rang rejoicing peals and colours were displayed on the banks and other places.' The ringing of St. Peter's bells was an appropriate touch as they had earlier been brought to Norwich by river.

Much was expected from this new waterway. Optimism ran high that Norwich would, in fact, become a port, and in keeping with the spirit of the times a public house was confidently named the Clarence Harbour. But the high hopes entertained were never realized and within a few years the navigation fell into disuse. No more seagoing ships were built in the city and one after another the small yards closed down.

Only a few plots of land remained by the riverside where a little boat building and repair work was carried on and, very occasionally, a wherry was built.

William Patch had one of these plots near the boom tower in Pockthorpe, and he built at least two wherries, the *Hand of Providence*, 28 tons, and the *Jenny Morgan*. Harry Gallant had a piece of land opposite Colman's factory, possibly Thomas Batley's old yard, and he built the *Tiger*, of 38 tons.

Stephen Field and William Hobrough both had small establishments at Thorpe, a short way down the river from Norwich. Hobrough is reputed to have built an occasional wherry but he mostly contented himself with buying up old craft, taking out their gear and running them as motor barges. When they reached the end of their days he sank them in his notorious graveyard on Rockland Broad. Just how many he put to rest there will never be known but any list would include the following: *Albert*, *Myth*, *Leveret*, *Empress*, *Tiger*, *Madge*, *Cambria*, *Providence*, *Chieftain*, *Diligent*, *Unexpected*, *Gleaner* and *Star of Hope*.

The bones of these veterans make a sorry sight rotting among the reeds. Even so, in death they paid their tribute to the living, for when we were needing lead to make the counterpoise for the *Albion*'s mast, I rowed round these hulks at low tide with Edward Ellis to see what we could find. He lives by neighbouring Wheatfen Broad and know-

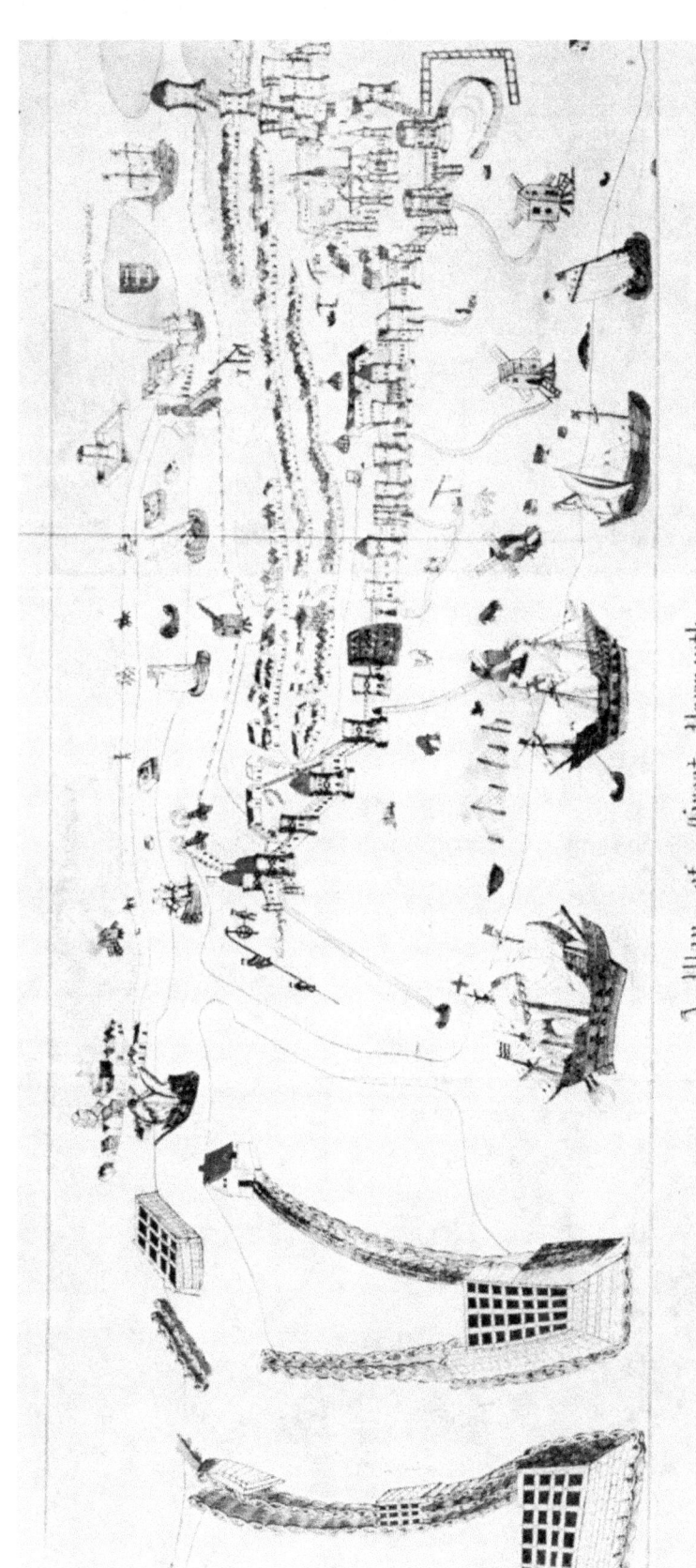

Plan of Yarmouth Harbour, temp. Elizabeth I, from the Cottonian Collection in the British Museum

With the arrival of Dutch refugees, the fore-and-aft rig comes to Norfolk

From James Stark's 'Scenery of the Rivers of Norfolk'

Burgh castle water frolic, 1830s

From James Stark's 'Scenery of the Rivers of Norfolk'

Entrance to Yarmouth Harbour, 1830

ing these wrecks well, thought we might find some useful salvage in the form of lead tingles, pipes and so on. Our visit was well rewarded. We collected altogether about three hundredweights, our prize piece being a massive lead pump installed by some enterprising old skipper long years ago. Whoever he was, I am sure he would have been content to know we were using it to help the *Albion* sail again.

The *Empress*, fourth in the above list, had rather a unique beginning. She was the only wherry built by Stephen Field, though he never intended her for a sailing craft. She was laid down as a 'steam' wherry for the Beccles–Lowestoft run but after her launch it was decided not to install machinery. She was eventually quanted down to Reedham where Halls were called in to finish her off as a sailing wherry. She was a big vessel of 48 tons and was engaged for many years bringing coal from the brigs at Lowestoft to the gas works in Norwich.

Steam, as already mentioned, had been used for the Norwich–Yarmouth packet service since 1813, when the *Royal Sovereign* began running. But it had a nasty setback soon after when the boiler of one craft blew up at Norwich and scared intending passengers off these 'infernal' engines. It was after that some enterprising gentleman stepped in with a remarkable invention he called The Horse Packet. To eliminate both the dangers of the steam engine and the uncertainties of sailing, he hit on the idea of using horses, walking round in a circle, to drive small paddle wheels.

When Robert Stevenson made the last of his three tours of the English lighthouses in 1818, he visited Yarmouth and was so taken with this vessel that he set down this description of her: 'The Horse Packet is about 60 feet in length and 18 feet beam. It has a principal cabin and ladies' room in forward end and a common cabin aft. It is worked by 4 horses in a file which walk in a circus of 18 feet diameter by which they are too much confined and so do only half work. The driving-shaft has two bevelled wheels, one at each end, by which the motion is communicated from the horses to the axle of the paddle wheels of 7 feet diameter. The boat goes at the rate of about 6 miles an hour. The proprietors find this as cheap a plan as the steam engine. The horses and driver are not covered from the weather—the driver sometimes rides, but is always in the circus with his horses. The crew consists of 4 men.'

From the dimensions Stevenson gives it seems likely that a medium-sized keel had been converted. It was certainly a very ingenious affair, though how long it retained the confidence of the public I cannot say. With no further explosions on the steamers it seems probable they soon regained their popularity, if for no other reason than the regularity of the service they were able to maintain.

Without passengers it is doubtful if these steamers could have been made to pay and the idea of a 'steam' wherry, to be used solely for cargo carrying, was not seriously considered till almost the end of the century. Even then second thoughts prevailed, as we have seen in the case of the *Empress*. In any case it was rather absurd to think of putting a steam engine into a wherry hull and expecting it to perform satisfactorily.

Fortunately, John Crisp & Sons, the Beccles maltsters, realized that when they decided to add steam vessels to their fleet of wherries. Round about 1895 they placed an order for the *Opal* which, although always known as a steam wherry, bore little or no resemblance to one. She was not built in Norfolk but at Gainsborough, by Watson's, and was launched in 1896. She was of steel construction and measured 74 feet in length, 14 feet 4 inches in beam with a depth of hold of 5 feet 3 inches. Her gross tonnage was 46 and she had a small compound steam engine of 10 nominal horse-power.

After completion she was towed round by sea to Crisp's wharf at Lowestoft and went straight into service carrying barley, malt and general cargo between Beccles, Lowestoft, Yarmouth and Norwich.

This little craft still survives, in the service of the Great Yarmouth Shipping Company, and must be the oldest steamboat working on the East Coast. To give an idea how she has spanned the years, in 1912, during the Norwich floods, she helped to carry sandbags for damming the water, and again in 1953, after the sea broke through, she went into action taking materials to fill the breaches in Breydon sea wall.

She is a pretty little vessel with her machinery aft leaving a clear hold forward. The deck line rises in a graceful sheer to a schooner-shaped bow and the effect is completed with a nice counter stern. Like the London tugs, her mast and funnel are lowered to pass under bridges.

She can carry 65 tons of general cargo and nowadays usually has one or two steel lighters in tow, each carrying 80 or 90 tons, so she is still a very useful proposition.

She was not the only 'steam wherry', Crisp's having also the twin-screwed *Topaz*, and Steward & Patteson, the *Annie*. She was very like the *Opal* and was launched at Yarmouth in 1898. Both have long since been broken up.

About this time there was a move to build wherries of iron instead of wood. It will be remembered that this was Walkers' idea when they first discussed building the *Albion* with Brighton, and they must have had in mind the three iron craft Fellows', of Yarmouth, built for Woods, Sadd & Moore in 1895 and 1896, the *Uranus*, *Vega* and *Sirius*.

They loaded about 30 tons but were pretty ungainly things to look at. They lacked the fine shape of an authentic wherry, were too low at their ends, and would not sail for toffee. The *Uranus* soon got the name 'wild horse', because nobody could do anything with her. The tale goes that one skipper used to get so angry that he would go forward with a coal-hammer and thump her on the stemhead once or twice 'to knock some sense into her' as he put it.

They were also most uncomfortable to live in. In summer the cabins got as hot as ovens, while in winter they were bitterly cold, with condensation everywhere. This 'sweating', above all else, made them unpopular with wherrymen. They felt that after a hard day on deck they were entitled to a little warmth and comfort in their cabins. The experiment of building 'iron pots' was never repeated, and what few wherries were subsequently built, were all of wood.

A number of craft could be distinguished from their companions because they were doing special jobs. One of these was timber lugging, the carrying of heavy oak logs of the kind used in shipbuilding. A wherry tackles these big logs by using her mast as a derrick. To allow plenty of room, gaff and sail are landed and the main sheet used to reeve a single purchase, stropped to the crane iron and brought to the winch, previously cleared of the halliard. A chain sling to go round the trunks and stout mooring ropes complete the gear.

The *Albion* has dragged three-quarter ton butts up over the sea wall with only two hands on the winch and two more easing away with spikes, and although some of them lay twenty yards off it seldom took more than ten minutes to get one aboard. As the strain comes on the winch the wherry heels over gradually to about ten degrees. The spike is then used to give the log a start and it slides forward two or three yards as she rights herself; then round with the winch again, over comes the wherry, a heave with the spike, and the log takes another spring forward. Branches laid down to act as rollers make the going easier and by stages like this the trunk is soon worked alongside. By easing the forestay the mast is raked to allow the log to swing into its required position in the hold.

Both mast and tabernacle are subjected to a lot of strain and wherries regularly engaged in this trade used to rig temporary shrouds. They were shackled to small chain plates, specially fitted for the purpose, but were unrigged before getting under way. Going on board a wherry and seeing these chain plates you knew at once what sort of work she did.

In the early part of last century the winch and single halliard were by no means general. Contemporary prints of Yarmouth harbour show wherries hoisting sail with throat and peak halliards, but no winch. Towards the middle of the century, winches made of wrought-iron and bolted to the cheek boards of the tabernacle, came into use, though it is hard to see what advantage they had over the more usual type. Older craft may have fitted them as an addition, requiring no structural alterations, to take advantage of the single hoist system.

At least four wherries had double halliards, worked in conjunction with a winch, the *Firefly*, *Lucy*, *Kathleen* and the giant *Wonder*. The *Kathleen* was exceptional in another way having a centre beam with pillar underneath to support her hatches. Several of the larger wherries, such as the *Norfolk Hero*, *Tiger*, *William*, *Lucy*, *Florence* and the *Wonder*, had fore-and-aft beams and cross beams to take half-hatches.

Few of the big wherries had sternsheets, steering being done from the deck, which was carried right up to the cabin. Steps led down into the cabin, headroom being provided by a small sliding hatch in the cabin top, known as the 'cabin slip'. To accommodate this slip the horsa was placed further forward and in wherries of this type the tiller had a pronounced upward sweep so that the haunches could still be brought to bear on it. Curiously enough, although they had no actual sternsheets, these craft were always called 'high sternsheet' wherries.

None of the points so far mentioned in this chapter affected the wherries' appearance, but when we come to sails it is a different story. I have already mentioned the *Wonder*'s foresail, but she was by no means the only one to have such an addition. In the Yarmouth and Lowestoft Sea Regattas wherries set foresails, and in some cases, topsails. In the only picture known to exist of wherries racing at sea every competitor has a foresail up, but these additional sails were never part of their normal equipment. They were borrowed from any craft in harbour willing to lend them.

I should have liked to include a photograph of wherries with these two additional sails, but one has never come my way. It nearly did once when an old wherry-builder assured me his sister had one of the Yarmouth Regatta showing three or four wherries with topsails set. Alas! when I saw him again he told me she had put it on the copper fire only a couple of weeks before.

When racing, the *Volunteer, Beaconsfield, Lowestoft Trader* and *Fawn* used to carry big spinnakers, and the *Swift* often set one on ordinary trading trips. They were boomed out on a boathook and sheeted to a timber head.

Clarke & Reeve, the Norwich carriers, had a small fleet of very unusual wherries so far as rig went. With one exception, the *Hannah*, 18 tons, they all had yards instead of gaffs, and were, in fact, luggers, This is what they were always called. Altogether, there were seven of them rigged in this curious way, the *Accommodation*, 30 tons: *Norwich Trader*, 32 tons; *Maria*, 32 tons; *Gratitude*, 32 tons; *James*, 50 tons; *Tiger*, 38 tons; and *William*, 30 tons. The whole fleet was broken up many years ago and I have never heard how they handled.

Like farm waggons, wherries are painted with the countryman's love of bright, cheerful colours, and to see one fresh from her annual refit, every inch shining and sparkling, is a real delight.

The hull, of course, is tarred and therefore black, though underwater you find occasionally green or red. The plankways are black, too, but the covering boards and planceas are invariably white.

The standing right-ups are blue, the shifting right-ups white, and and over them comes the dazzling glory of the hatches which, without exception, are vermilion. It is hard to describe in words the effect of this mass of rich, red colour against the black hull and the blues and whites of the right-ups, but anyone who has seen it will agree it is unique among British sailing vessels.

The cabin top is also vermilion and the sides continue the colours of the right-ups. The after end and the doors are handsomely decorated in blues, yellows, whites and reds, with all ironwork black.

The head of the rudder post is white, picked out with touches of red and blue, and the tiller is white to within a foot or eighteen inches of the end where it terminates with a red or blue band and a crown knot. A similar knot is found on either side of the horsa to absorb the shock of the mainsheet when gybing.

Timber heads and winch stanchions are white, with all ironwork black, but the carling board is vermilion like the other hatches. The shells of all blocks are vermilion, too, with black strops, while gaff, spen wires and martingale are white.

The mast is scraped and oiled with linseed, treatment that brings out all the rich colours of the wood. On top of the mast comes the vane, or Jenny Morgan, to crown everything with a splash of gay colour, its fathom of red bunting streaming out against the sky and acting as a foil to the vermilion of the hatches.

The last four or five feet of mast are painted according to the distinctive colours of the owners. The pattern is to have three or four feet of plain colour from the top of the mast terminating below with a series of different coloured bands three or four inches wide. As an example, the *Albion*, when she belonged to Walker's of Bungay, had a bright green masthead with yellow and blue bands and these colours were carried by all their other wherries, the *Iolanthe, Mayflower, Hope, Eudora, Maria* and *Enfield*. The Loddon wherries of Woods, Sadd & Moore, were blue with four red and white bands, while Wright, of Beccles, favoured black with a single white band.

Many wherries were skipper-owned but they still went in for distinguishing colours up aloft. Leonard Welton, of Somerleyton, who had the *Blanche*, spurned ordinary painted bands and fitted solid brass ones beneath his strip of bright blue paint. Whenever he lowered for a bridge he rubbed them over with a rag and polish, kept handy in the cabin, 'so they shouldn't lose their shine', as he used to say. A list of owners with their distinguishing colours will be found in Appendix Four.

I have left till last a feature which many regard as the most characteristic of a wherry's decoration, the white quadrants on either bow. They are called 'nosings' and have caused a lot of argument about their purpose and origin. Some thirty years ago I remember reading in a local newspaper that they probably had a significance at one time which had now been forgotten. That like the eyes painted on Maltese boats, and which are also found on the carvings of those of ancient Egypt, they may have originated as a symbol of something or have been a mascot to bring good luck.

They are, in fact, very utilitarian in origin, serving only to warn other craft of their approach at night; wherrymen would never have a light of any sort on deck as it prevented them seeing where they were going. This will be appreciated by anyone who has sailed any sort of vessel over a twisting river course on a pitch black night; you must be able to see the banks and be able to steer by them. Even striking a match to light a cigarette can blind you and send you up on the mud, as I know only too well.

Of course, by law, wherries should have carried lights, but they never did, and so far as I can discover nothing was ever done to make them. And when, as sometimes happened, there was a collision, no claim was ever made on the grounds that one or other was not carrying lights.

The white nosings can, therefore, be regarded as a good East Anglian compromise between what was the law, and what was practicable, often enough two very different things in this part of the world.

They were adopted by all commercial craft on the Norwich river and the big steel lighters of today still retain them. And, somehow, the little *Opal* would never look quite right without those two white quadrants to grace her schooner bow.

CHAPTER FIVE

Marl, Mud and Merchandise

Berney Arms—cement factories on the Yare and Waveney—the old Britannia —a fleet of mudders—Horstead marl—the Little Spark—smelt fishing and winter frosts—low tides and floods—Daniel Defoe and Yarmouth Quay— the trade of Norwich—many cargoes—a sad tale about port wine—timber rafts—2,000 miles a year.

ONE morning, in January 1950, the telephone rang and a voice at the other end asked if the *Albion* could take a load of sand, shingle and cement from Norwich to Berney Arms. I said yes, quoted a price, which was agreed to, and for the next two days lorries from Thorpe gravel pits tipped their loads into her. It was surprising how many it took to load 30 tons. Then came the cement, stowed against the after bulkhead, and on the third day the *Albion* quanted through the city, raised her mast, and made sail for Berney Arms.

It was the first freight to be taken out of Norwich by sailing wherry for more than twenty-seven years and created quite a stir. But there was no other way of getting these materials to such an isolated spot as Berney Arms. It takes its name from an inn which once stood on the north bank of the River Yare where it enters Breydon Water. The nearest road is three miles away and the rough, marsh track leading to it is a quagmire in winter. The railway passes close by but there is no siding, so heavy goods must go by water.

The hamlet of Berney Arms consists of two farmhouses, a row of four small cottages, the remains of the old inn, and the tallest windmill in Norfolk. When January gales lash in over Breydon from the sea, when the marshes are spread deep with snow and the dykes are frozen hard, I know of no more bleak and desolate spot on the face of the earth. Yet there is a wonderful majesty about it, for civilization, with all its attendant squalor, has passed it by. You look out over an immense, unspoiled sweep of country, stretching round all four points of the compass, with little else for company but the call of curlew and a glimpse of spoonbills feeding on the flats.

You may wonder if an innkeeper ever made ends meet in such a place, and why, indeed, an inn was ever built here. The answer is to be found in the fine, towering windmill, whose tarred brickwork and white-painted sails rise impressively out of the flat marshland, dominating the whole scene around. It drained the marshes until a decade ago, when an electric pump took over, yet, strangely enough, it was not built as a drainage mill but to drive the crusher in a cement factory. Up to fifty or sixty years ago this was an area given over to the manufacture of large quantities of cement on account of the presence, within easy reach, of the two essential materials, chalk and mud.

Thousands of tons of both were brought to the factory here at Berney Arms every year, the chalk from Norwich and the mud from Oulton fresh-water broad. All of it came by wherry.

There was another factory directly opposite at Burgh Castle which got its mud and chalk from the same sources and, of course, by wherry. The Burgh Castle Cement Company had its own fleet; Berney Arms relied on chartered craft.

The inn, therefore, was built to slake the thirsts of workers and wherrymen engaged in this dusty business, and sixty years ago it did a thriving trade. There were always wherries hanging on waiting to load or discharge, and their crews were joined in the Berney Arms bar by a motley gang of smelt-fishers and wildfowlers from Breydon.

Nowadays, there is little to remind one of all that hard work and hard drinking. The fabric of the inn still stands, though filling the prosaic role of private residence, and the foundations of the factory may still be traced. But otherwise, only the mill remains as it was, though, alas, its sails will turn no more.

Over at Burgh Castle there is even less to be seen. The site of the factory is buried in thick scrub, and the quay heading has completely crumbled away. Anyone not acquainted with the history of the place would find it hard to believe that within living memory a fleet of wherries used to trade here. They were the *Britannia, Fanny, Frank, Morton, Emma, Herbert, Mary* and *Mermaid*.

The real veteran of this group was the *Britannia*, which saw more than a hundred years of service before being broken up, in 1929. It was, of course, fairly common for seagoing ships, carrying dry cargoes, to last a hundred years, but freshwater craft seldom reached that age. The *Britannia* loaded about 22 tons, had a small transom stern, and the slightly raking stem met with in the early eighteen-hundreds. She packed plenty of adventures into her long life, but none quite like that of 30 January, 1877, which was very nearly her last.

She was lying at Barrack Quay, Yarmouth, loaded with coal, when one of Fellows' boats cut her adrift. Driven by a strong wind and flood tide, she crashed into the Haven bridge, fetching out her mast; slowly she was forced through, getting badly damaged as she went, and, sweeping on upstream, finally struck the mud and sank near the Knowle.

She could easily have been a total loss, but next day her fleet sister, the *Mary*, came to her aid, and with the help of Tiger Smith's keel she was got up. Hall's, of Reedham, took her in hand and had her sailing again after a couple of weeks. About this time she was sailed by W. H. Thaxter.

The *Fanny* carried 30 tons and belonged originally to H. Barber, of Yarmouth. The *Morton*, a 24-tonner, was first owned by Sam Nightingale of Lacons, when she was sailed by Len Smith. Coming into the cement trade, 'Guinea' Poole, and later George Knights, had her. She spent part of her career icing for the Lowestoft smacks, a trade giving work to many wherries, in winter time, before the coming of manufactured ice.

They went out on to the broads and rivers and ladled up the broken pieces with a wire-netting scoop on the end of a pole. There was a noise like breaking glass as each scoopful pitched into the hold. When full up they took it to the ice-houses for storage till required by the smacks. It kept for a long time and the smacks often put to sea in the height of summer with ice collected from Oulton Broad in December or January. In mild winters, when the broads and rivers failed to freeze, ice was sometimes imported by the shipload from Scandinavia.

The *Emma* was probably as much a veteran as the *Britannia*. She was launched as the *Intrepid*, carried something under 30 tons, and was sailed for a time, like the *Morton*, by George Knights. His brother

James also had her for a spell and on 19 February, 1876, he took 26 tons of mud from Oulton to Burgh for the sum of 12s. 6d., or 6d. the ton. In 1888 Harry Russell was drowned out of her.

The *Herbert* was known up and down the rivers as 'The Monk', but why nobody knows. She was sailed for a while by George Thaxter and was a real old-timer, lugsail rigged like Clarke & Reeve's fleet.

The *Mary*, as mentioned, helped to raise the *Britannia*, and the last one on the list, the *Mermaid*, before going to Burgh belonged to Mrs. Warnes, mistress of the Foundry Bridge Tavern, Norwich. In the great May gale of 1860 her mast was sprung so badly you could get your fist in the split. The *Mermaid* had many skippers in her time including Edmund Royall, Rodney Holmes and 'Piper' Hawes.

She boasted an impressive mermaid vane and the story goes that it was painted for Piper in Yarmouth market-place by a kerbside artist called Miller. As a very small boy I remember seeing Miller painting in the Norwich streets and always quite a crowd gathered to watch him, for the good reason that he was armless and did everything with his toes. The *Mermaid*'s vane may well have been his only 'commission', though from what I recall he painted extremely well.

George Knights, who sailed the *Morton* and *Emma* for the Burgh Castle company, was in his youth a freight checker at Berney Arms. He kept a notebook of those days and some of the entries for February and March 1876 give a good idea of the rates prevailing then. All the chalk in the following list came from Norwich or Whitlingham:

> The *Gem*, 30 tons chalk, £1 10s. 6d. Sailed by Robert Brady. His X mark.
> The *Edward*, 20 tons chalk, £1 1s. 6d. James Harvey.
> The *Fairy Queen*, 24 tons chalk, £1 6s. od. Wm. Tooley.
> The *James and Jessie*, 33 tons chalk, £1 15s. 9d. S. Gibbs. His X mark.
> The *Pearl*, chalk, £1 6s. od. S. Holmes. His X mark.
> The *Charles and Henry*, 30 tons chalk from Whitlingham, £1 12s. 6d. John Saul. His X mark.
> The *Adam and Eve*, 24 tons chalk, £1 4s. od. John Watts.

All these were chartered craft and the *Adam and Eve* belonged to Mrs. Howes of Norwich. She kept the Adam and Eve public house in Palace Street and named her wherry after it.

The cement factories got most of their chalk from the Norwich area. Marl Pit Lane proclaims where the workings were in Norwich, though supporters of the City Football Club, in the old days, may not have realized that 'The Nest', where the 'Canaries' played, was actually built on the site of these workings.

The chalk was brought down in trucks to the quay, just below Bishop's bridge, and tipped straight into the wherries. In later years, when the contents of Norwich dustbins were disposed of by wherry, this same quay became a corporation tip. Craft engaged in this refuse trade had one thing in common with the 'rough stuff' barges of the Thames—you could smell them a mile away. Wherrymen, literally, turned up their noses at it, except when there was nothing better to be had.

In Marshall's *Rural Economy of Norfolk*, published in 1787, we can see how valuable marl also was for agriculture, and how cheaply it could be obtained by water. He writes: 'Before the use of marl (which has not been brought by water, I apprehend, above ten or fifteen years) the farmers could grow no turneps; the land letting for ten or twelve shillings an acre: now, the turneps upon it are remarkably fine; and the land lets at full twenty shillings an acre: a rent the occupiers could not pay, were it not for marl.

'The distance between Wood-Bastwick and the marl pits at Thorpe next Norwich, is not, by land, more than six or seven miles; yet the farmers find it cheaper to fetch their marl fifty miles by water, and then carry it, perhaps, half a mile from the staith to the ground, than fetch it the six or seven miles by land.'

There were other quarries round at Coltishall, where very small wherries, of about 12 tons, lightered chalk out of Horstead Marl Hole, for the bigger craft to take downstream. Millican has a note about these workings in his *History of Horstead and Stanninghall*, and writes: 'For many centuries the chalk beds provided material for the local lime-kilns, now in disuse, but perhaps even more important, from a commercial point of view, were the huge deposits of chalk-marl for which Horstead was noted in the eighteenth and nineteenth centuries. This marl was used for agricultural purposes, not only in the immediate neighbourhood, but also in more distant localities to which it was transported in wherries along a system of canals leading to the River Bure. The diggings, still to be seen in the south-eastern portion of the parish, bear witness to the extent of this industry. Deep valleys and canals were cut which are now covered with luxuriant vegetation ... The thirsty diggers and wherrymen were provided with refreshment at the Grove's End public house, built on the bank of the Bure when this industry was at its height.'

One of these Horstead marl wherries, the *Little Spark*, achieved considerable fame after being converted for pleasuring by Dr. Emerson, and re-christened the *Maid of the Mist*. Emerson wrote four very readable books on broadland life, but I like best *On English Lagoons*, wherein he describes a year's cruising in the *Maid of the Mist*, from September 1890 to August 1891. He was no fair-weather sailor and deliberately chose to sample the rigours of a winter afloat.

His affectionate description of the *Maid* is worth quoting: 'The history of my boat may serve as an example of the innate virtue that lurks in the heart of such craft, for the *Maid of the Mist* is one of a numerous class.

'Built in the year when the Prince of Wales took unto himself a bride, the *Little Spark*, as she was named, began life as a common labourer—she carried marl between the pits and the big river wherries —not even her beautiful lines, for she is one of the prettiest models afloat, saving her from such base uses.

'After marling, she fell into the hands of the extinct Columbia fishing fleet, and was employed upon the baser toil of icing—that was terribly rough on her skin and did much to spoil her complexion and age her.

'When that ill-considered venture collapsed she fell into the possession of one, Gaby Thomas. I know not to what base uses she was put by him—she even carried ash-pit siftings—was once sunk and fished up again, and finally Gaby died, but the *Spark* flew onwards, passing through many hands, until she fell into the clutches of old Tommy, the one-eyed winkle-seller.

'He, too, used her for icing, and it was at such work that I saw my beauty and determined to possess her.'

One can tell he was proud of his little vessel and, needless to say, lavished a great deal of care on her conversion. She well repaid his trouble, providing a swift and dependable conveyance to every out-of-the-way corner of the district accessible by water.

There was, inevitably, some haggling before the purchase was complete, but at last he got her: 'The one-eyed winkle merchant hummed and hah-ed, and sold her for a small sum, his single eye glittering greedily as he signed the receipt and pocketed the money. I quickly gave her over to the dressmakers and she was in five weeks converted.'

Emerson gives glimpses of life on the water which few, now, can remember. One day, for instance, the *Maid of the Mist* brought up on Breydon and the crew were able to watch some of the locals at their work. 'Nearby,' he writes, 'a fisherman was tanning his smelt nets (for shrimping was over and smelting had begun) with kutch. The fishermen hereabouts use oak bark or kutch. The old man filled his cauldron with water, breaking several pounds of kutch into it.

'When the mixture was boiling, he packed in the light flaxen-coloured nets, cooking them for an hour, smoking his pipe stolidly meanwhile. After they were tanned, he and his boy spread them upon the marsh.

'At eight o'clock they rowed past in their coble under the young moon, the newly-browned nets piled high on the stern seat, on their way to smelt on the Breydon flats.'

It is many a long day since the last catch of smelts was made on Breydon. The great place was on the mud flats near Burgh Castle, and a drag net was used, similar to those still worked on the Norfolk and Suffolk coasts for catching salmon trout. Before the season started, long chains were dragged over the mud, to smooth it out and remove anything that might rend the nets. When these waters were free from the detergents, sewage and crude excrement from pleasure craft, which have now virtually turned the broads into a huge, open cesspool, immense shoals of smelts visited Breydon every autumn.

They often swam on to the plankways of deeply laden wherries where they became stranded, like flying-fish in the southern oceans. There was no need to see them to know they were aboard for there was always that fragrant smell of cucumbers to tell you.

Now and again smelts still turn up on the fishmonger's slab and they are well worth buying. Smeared with fresh butter and lightly grilled, they are delicious, with a delicate flavour all their own.

By sailing in winter, Emerson could see for himself what wherrying was like, for the men whose daily bread it was, when the sun was low in the sky, and the long nights brought snow-laden gales and intense cold. It was a very different picture from the one those other 'adventurers' saw, the glib scribes who lounged comfortably in warm sunshine, under blue skies, drifting idly on gentle summer breezes, and penning their monotonous superficialities about 'the beauty of it all'.

The winter of 1890–91 was a hard one. Everything froze solid and only brute force and long toil could force a passage. Emerson describes what he saw at Geldeston:

'The wherrymen got into a rough coble and began to break the ice below the lock. This floe was about an inch thick. Standing in the stern, they pushed the forefoot of the boat on to the edge of the ice as far as it was possible, then walked forward, crushing it with their weight, for the ice was too thick to break by rocking the boat from side to side.

'After they had broken a narrow passage up to the lock, the sleepers were raised and the water allowed to run down, the sail filled, and five men took a towline, and by means of these three powers, man, wind and water, the two great 30 ton craft, loaded with bricks, were forced through the channel.'

The *Maid of the Mist* followed in the wake of the big traders, though Emerson was far from happy about the conditions: 'It was unpleasant to hear the sharp, jagged blocks grinding against her ribs, and we did not bless the icers who were busy all round us gathering the cold harvest into old ships'-boats, broken down wherries and dismasted smacks, scooping up the broken pieces, and tossing them into their holds with the sound of broken china.'

Christmas 1890 was a white one in every way, and though it may have been seasonable, it meant sparse fare for many people whose supplies came by river. The *Maid of the Mist* spent the festive season at Oulton Broad and her owner describes the following incident: 'In the harbour we moored against a wherry laden with Christmas supplies —plums, raisins, soap; but her cargo never reached home. The next day she was frozen up; she could not continue her voyage till after Christmas. And when at length navigation was reopened, though she was one of the first to cross the broad, at the far end she struck a block of ice and sank, plum-pudding ingredients, soap and all.'

Wherries were never at the mercy of the elements in quite the same way as seagoing vessels, but they had their own particular problems to contend with, and when winters were more severe than they are now, freeze-ups like this were a constant hazard. Even as late as 1929, three wherries, the *Eudora*, *Goodwill* and *Secunda* were held fast for a month on Oulton Broad, while the *Meteor* lay helpless at Haddiscoe. They broke the ice on the broad and found it was $7\frac{1}{2}$ inches thick; next day a football match was played on it.

The exceptionally low tides which occur from time to time on the River Yare could also make things difficult especially when craft were caught at the top of a shallow cut or dyke. For some reason the river fails to respond to the tidal ebb and flow at Yarmouth and for several days remains at a very low level. On one occasion it continued to ebb throughout the twenty-four hours leaving nearly every craft high and dry.

No less than thirteen wherries once got stranded at Loddon when the River Chet dried completely out. It was two weeks before they floated again.

Sometimes it worked the other way round, and a long spell of high water would make it impossible to get under bridges. The little 14-ton *Ceres*, after being converted for pleasuring, and re-named the *Dorothy*, was caught like this in 1912. It was the year of the Norwich floods and at the time she was taking a party of London gentlemen for a holiday cruise on the north river. They left Wroxham and got safely above Ludham bridge, when the water began to rise. They soon found they could neither get through Wayford bridge nor return through Ludham, and had to spend their holiday idly sailing up and down the short stretch of water between. Eventually their patience was exhausted, and Cecil Bunn, the skipper, decided on a desperate remedy; he landed all the cushions, bedding and other perishable gear, pulled out the plugs, half filled her with water, and dragged her through Ludham bridge to freedom.

The floods of 1912 occurred in summer and were due to heavy and continuous rain. An even worse calamity occurred in January 1809, when a rapid thaw, following a long period of frost and snow, deluged the lower parts of Norwich and put many houses six and seven feet deep in water. The flooded meadows and marshes outside the city looked like a sea, and the damage done amounted to more than a million pounds.

From a water colour by Austin in the author's collection

Norwich about 1900, looking up river to Bishop's Bridge—

From a water colour by Marshall in the possession of Q. E. Gurney, Esq.

—and down river from Bishop's Bridge

Albion's Jenny Morgan

Albion at sea on passage from Yarmouth to Lowestoft, 8th August, 1951

Strange to say, with all this water about, wherries were unable to get to Yarmouth. They tried, but were forced to return because they could not find the channel. To the east lay one great sheet of water and it was impossible to tell where the river went. Many spent an anxious time sailing about in farmyards, and over the gardens of deserted cottages, because river banks and all the familiar landmarks had disappeared. They put back thankfully to the comparative safety of the city, even though mooring was difficult, and often dangerous, with quay headings a fathom or more below the surface.

I came across an interesting note on the river traffic of Norwich in Crosby's *Complete Pocket Gazetteer of England and Wales*, published in 1815. 'Norwich,' the author says, 'adds greatly to the trade of Yarmouth, by the transportation of about 40,000 chaldrons of coals yearly, wine, fish, oil, Irish yarn and all heavy goods, which come from thence by the River Yare; and in peace-time by the exportation of its manufactures to Russia, Germany, Holland, Denmark, Norway, Spain, Portugal, Italy, etc.'

The author had obviously been at some pains to inform himself about the craft engaged in this trade, for he goes on: 'The keels and wherries which navigate between Norwich and Yarmouth are acknowledged to be superior to any other small craft in England for carrying a larger burthen, and being worked at a smaller expense. Their burthen is from 15 to 50 tons; they have but one mast, which lets down, and carry only one, large sail. They are covered close by hatches and have a cabin superior to many coasting vessels in which, oftentimes, the keelman (or wherryman, and his family live; they require only two persons to navigate them, and sometimes perform their passage (thirty-two miles) in five hours.'

Some ninety years earlier, Daniel Defoe, in his *Tour Through the Eastern Counties*, had made his now famous remark that Yarmouth quay was the finest in England, if not in Europe. His view that it was not inferior even to Marseilles was, perhaps, a little exaggerated, but he gives an impressive picture of Yarmouth harbour leaving us in no doubt about the amount of trade it handled: 'The ships ride here so close and as it were keeping up one another, with their head-fasts on shore, that for half a mile together they go across the stream with their bowsprits over the land, their bows, or heads, touching the very wharf, so that one may walk from ship to ship as on a floating bridge, all along by the shore side, the quay reaching from the drawbridge almost to the South gate is so spacious and wide that in some places it is near one hundred yards from the houses to the wharf. In this pleasant and agreeable range of houses are some very magnificent buildings, and among the rest, the Custom House and Town Hall, and some merchants' houses which look like little palaces, rather than the dwelling-houses of private men.'

He describes the autumn herring fishing, when the land was covered with people, and the river with barques and boats, and how he counted, in one tide, no less than one hundred and ten barques and fishing vessels coming up the river laden with herrings caught the night before.

Yet this was only a branch of the great trade carried on at Yarmouth: 'Another part of this commerce is in the exporting these herrings after they are cured, and for this their merchants have a great trade to Genoa, Leghorn, Naples, Messina and Venice, as also to Spain and Portugal, also exporting with their herring very great quantities of worstead stuffs, and stuffs made of silk and worsted, camblets, etc., the manufactures of the neighbouring city of Norwich and of the places adjacent.

'Besides this, they carry on a very considerable trade with Holland, whose opposite neighbours they are, and a vast quantity of woollen manufactures they export to the Dutch every year.

'They have also a considerable trade to Norway and to the Baltic from whence they bring back deals and fir timber, oaken plank, baulks, spars, oars, pitch, tar, hemp, flax, spruce canvas and sail cloth; with all manner of naval stores which they generally have a consumption for in their own port where they build a very great number of ships every year, besides refitting and repairing the old.

'Add to this the coal trade between Newcastle and the river Thames, in which they are so improved of late years, that they have now a greater share of it than any other town in England, and have quite worked the Ipswich men out of it who had formerly the chief share of the colliery in their hands.

'For the carrying on all these trades, they must have a very great number of ships, either of their own, or employed by them, and it may in some measure be judged of by this, that in the year 1697, I had an account from the town register, that there was then 1,123 sail of ships using the sea, and belonged to the town, besides such ships as the merchants of Yarmouth might be concerned in and be part owners of, belonging to any other ports.'

Defoe visited the Eastern Counties during a period of rising prosperity, when the weaving industries of Norwich and the surrounding districts were flourishing, to such an extent that there was reckoned to be no man, woman or child unemployed. Children, of four or five years, could earn enough to keep themselves.

The annual value of manufactured woollen goods at this time amounted to a million and a quarter pounds. Travellers from Norwich went the length and breadth of Europe after orders and their pattern cards were displayed in every town and city as far east as Moscow. They introduced Norwich goods to France, Spain, Portugal, Germany, Poland and Russia.

The great Fairs of Frankfurt, Leipsig and Salerno saw Norwich fabrics to the fore. More and more bay-yarn had to be imported from Ireland and Norwich was working up as much of this as the rest of the whole country. The East India Company placed an order every year for 20,000 to 25,000 pieces of fine camlets.

Fine camlets, worsted damask and flowered satins were then the staple articles, and it was with these that Norwich reached the peak of its prosperity, from about 1750 up to the outbreak of the French wars. After that, it steadily declined, as foreign markets became closed and the power looms of Yorkshire took an ever greater share of the trade. The West Riding became a formidable rival in worsted fabrics, and the growing adoption of cottons for wear in England left Norwich largely dependent on foreign trade. That was ruined, partly, by the American War, and completely, by the French Revolution.

Crosby was, therefore, quite correct in remarking how much the industries of the city increased the trade of Yarmouth. Defoe, too, was quick to observe that the ships leaving Yarmouth for Spain, Portugal and the Mediterranean with pickled herrings, were just as heavily laden with Norwich silks and worsteds. Indeed, apart from fish, Yarmouth had little to export on its own account.

Of course, trade in coal and consumer goods kept a sizeable fleet working in and out of the port, but here again the town used only a fraction of what came in. The rest was sent up to Norwich, Beccles, Bungay and all the other places along the rivers.

It is quite interesting to look at the rates charged two hundred years ago to bring goods by sea, and shows us the sort of things then in demand. Rates from foreign ports worked out at about 15s. a ton, but we can break this down into more detail for the coasting trade.

General groceries, for instance, came from London to Yarmouth for 8s. to 10s. a ton. Cheese, on the other hand, which was exported from Yarmouth to London in large quantities, cost 15s. Hops, grown extensively in the Blofield district, went for 5s. a bag.

The prices of other items from London to Yarmouth were: spirits, 5s. a pipe; rum, 4s. a puncheon; porter, 1s. 6d. a barrel; wood, 8s. a ton; oranges and lemons, 1s. a chest; nuts, 1s. a sack; bales and butts of leather, 1s. a cwt.; sugar, 4s. a hogshead; shot, 2s. a firkin; clover seed, 2s. a sack.

Had you gone shopping you would have found prices like the following: French olives, 9s. a gallon; fine cheshire cheese, 3d. a lb.; quart glass bottles, 2d. each; printed cottons and linens, 1s. 6d. a yard; cotton hose for girls, 1s. to 1s. 6d. a pair; butter, 6d. a lb.; rum, warranted neat and full proof, 7s. 3d. a puncheon; cod, 3d. a lb.; skate, 2d. a lb.; cider, 10d. a gallon; oranges, 38s. a chest. Had you been a builder wanting burnt lime it would have cost 11s. a chaldron. A Yarmouth chaldron, by the way, consisted of 20 sacks, each weighing 137 lbs., or 2,740 lbs. It was 500 lbs., or roughly $4\frac{1}{2}$ cwts. more than a ton.

General cargoes from abroad accounted for a wide variety of goods and among the more important were: iron for blacksmiths from Sweden; white rags and pipe staves from Hamburg; pipe and sheet lead from Naples; pipe staves from Danzig; iron, hemp and canvas from St. Petersburg; wine and salt from Lisbon; wines from Guernsey; wines and oils from Malaga; hemp and timber from Riga; oranges, lemons and figs from Seville; pantiles from Holland; tar from Stockholm; yarn from Ireland. From other places came deals, battens, palings, all sorts of wainscot, hogshead and barrel staves, glass bottles, mahogany and so on.

In the home trade, potatoes came from Boston; pipe clay from Poole;

coal from Newcastle, Scotland and Milford; stones from Portland; allum from Whitby; salt from Liverpool; pantiles from Hull.

These details may help to explain why Defoe found more than a thousand ships on the Yarmouth register in 1697. While the number is impressive, it must be remembered that most of them were quite small, with a capacity of 100 tons or under; a great many were, therefore, needed to handle the trade of the port.

The majority of the smallest ships were employed in the coasting and collier runs. During the peak of prosperity in Norwich, a fleet of brigs and brigantines maintained the service between London and Yarmouth, those most frequently mentioned being the *Sarah, Happy Return, Providence, Fair Trader, Success, Dove, Robert, Ellen and Mary, Endeavour, Hopewell* and *Thomas and Mary*.

In the foreign trade, certain ships concentrated on one port, some on another, and there were eight main groups of places to which they went: Genoa and Leghorn; Seville, Cadiz and Malaga; Hamburg and Altona; Danzig and Koningsberg; Rotterdam; Ostend and Bruges; St. Petersburg; and Naples.

There were many other ports, of course, to which Yarmouth ships went as occasion demanded, the most generally frequented being Copenhagen and Elsinore, Memel, Bilboa, Oporto, St. Lucar and Lisbon.

With business booming everywhere, keelmen and wherrymen had all the work they could cope with. Not a chaldron of coal nor a bale of goods passed between Norwich and Yarmouth but what they took it, and fortune smiled as it had never done before. Just what this prosperity meant we can see from a vivid description of the city given by Lord Macaulay. It relates to the close of the seventeenth century.

'Norwich was the capital of a large and fruitful province. It was the residence of a bishop and of a Chapter. It was the chief seat of the manufacture of the realm. Some even distinguished by learning and science had recently dwelt there; and no place in the kingdom, except the capital and the universities, had more attractions for the curious.

'The library, the museum, the aviary, and the botanical gardens of Sir Thomas Browne, were thought by the Fellows of the Royal Society, well worthy of a long pilgrimage.

'Norwich had also a court in miniature. In the heart of the city stood an old palace of the Duke of Norfolk, said to be the largest town house in the kingdom out of London. In this mansion, to which were annexed a tennis court, a bowling green, and a wilderness stretching along the banks of the Wensum, the noble family of Howard frequently resided.

'Drink was served to guests in goblets of pure gold. The very tongs and shovels were of silver. Pictures of Italian masters adorned the walls. The cabinets were filled with a fine collection of gems purchased by the Earl of Arundel, whose marbles are now among the ornaments of Oxford.

'Here, in the year 1671, Charles and his court were sumptuously entertained. Here, too, all comers were annually welcomed from Christmas to Twelfth-night. Ale flowed in oceans for the populace. Three coaches, one of which had been built at a cost of £500, to contain 14 persons, were sent every afternoon round the city to bring ladies to the festivities; and the dances were always followed by a luxurious banquet.

'When the Duke of Norfolk came to Norwich he was greeted like a king returning to his capital. The bells of St. Peter Mancroft were rung; the guns of the Castle were fired; and the Mayor and Aldermen waited on their illustrious fellow-citizen with complimentary addresses.

'In the year 1693, the population of Norwich was found, by actual enumeration, to be between 28,000 and 29,000 souls.'

After Waterloo, with most of its foreign markets gone, and with growing competition from north-country mills, the fortunes of Norwich were in decline. Unemployment became rife, with wages for hand-loom weavers lucky enough to have work, a mere pittance of about 7s. 2d. a week. Inevitably, discontent and unrest grew, leading to strikes and riots. The position was aggravated by the return of great numbers of sailors and soldiers from the war. Few of them had been given their proper pay on discharge, and even less had any prospect of finding work. It was a post-war slump of the kind we have since become very familiar with, and recovery was slow.

The keelmen and wherrymen were naturally affected like everyone else, but they managed to keep going with work provided by the many small industries situated alongside the rivers. Of these, brick-making was probably the most important, and at one time there were more than a dozen fields, all close to the river, and all relying on wherries for transport. The best known were at Somerleyton, Reedham and Surlingham, though Whitlingham was reckoned to have excellent brick earths, and the finest tile earths in Norfolk.

Almost the whole of Yarmouth is built with bricks brought by wherry, and fifty years back you could always see stacks of them on Stone Cutters' Quay, near the Haven bridge. Wherrymen did their own unloading for which they received 6d. a thousand. An average wherry load was 12,000 to 14,000 bricks, and the rate 2s. 6d. a thousand.

Sawn Scandinavian timber provided plenty of work up to Norwich. It was brought over by the onker barques and stacked, much as it is today, along the Southtown quays. To load a wherry with this sort of timber calls for a lot of skill.

When her hold is full she only has about two-thirds her lading, owing to the lightness of wood, which means taking the rest above hatches. This is called 'waling', and is done by building stacks along both plankways till they are level, and inter-locked with, the timber in the hold. The whole width of the craft is now used to build one solid stack two or three feet above the right-ups. The skill comes in making the stack firm and rigid; if it were not, a trail of four-by-twos would be left all the way to Norwich.

Coal has always been the wherrymen's bread-and-butter trade. As the population of the country increased more houses had to be built, towns and villages expanded, and the demand for it grew apace. When gas works came into operation the demand increased still further, and the one at Norwich continued to get coal by wherry till long after the First World War.

By the side of many country staithes you can, to this day, see red brick buildings, rather like small barns; they were, in fact, used as store houses for the coal wherries brought up from Yarmouth. They belonged to local merchants, who generally dealt in corn as well as coal, and more often than not part of the store house served as a granary as well. This enabled wherries to have a return load instead of going away light.

Wheat and barley always kept a great many craft at work with mills and malthouses to supply at Beccles, Bungay, Norwich, Coltishall, Oulton Broad, Ranworth, and many other places. Large quantities of malt were taken down to Yarmouth for export to London and across to Holland and Ireland.

Until the coming of the railway, all the fish consumed in Norwich arrived by wherry. As Defoe mentions, loads of herrings used to be carried inland from Yarmouth on every tide. They were discharged and sold at Fye-bridge Staithe, and in 1821 could be bought at twelve a penny because of a glut at Yarmouth. Other fish could be had in season, including salt cod, from the Faroes and Iceland. Fresh-water fish from the rivers were then part of the ordinary diet and could be bought in the usual way. Wherries on passage often put a small trawl net over the stern and generally caught enough to earn an extra shilling or two. In later years they towed two scythe-blades over the bottom, arranged in the shape of a T, to help clear the navigation of weeds.

So pure was the River Yare in 1771 that an 80 lb. sturgeon was caught at Buckenham ferry. Salmon, too, were landed, while occasionally a seal, and even a porpoise, came exploring the Norwich river.

Herring roes seem an unlikely sort of wherry cargo, especially in bulk, but one merchant at least had the bright idea of fetching home a large purchase in this way. Unfortunately, there was quite a breeze going over Breydon, and the continual motion soon reduced them to a thick, milky mess. They had to be sold for manure, and it took a month or more to get rid of the sickly smell of stale herring oil. So far as I know the experiment was never repeated.

Oak sawdust, or 'shruff', for smoking kippers, and billet wood for bloaters, was once burnt by the ton in Yarmouth and gave several wherries regular employment. One, the *Bessie*, sailed by Billy Bygrave, brought shruff down from the Norwich sawmills, and returned with sand. It was long before the days of linoleum, when the floors of many public, and private houses were laid with stone pamments. Sand was the best thing for scouring them and keeping them fresh, and it was stocked by most riverside dealers and publicans. Children were sent out by their mothers on Saturday mornings to buy it, a ha'porth or farthing's worth being the usual week's supply.

The Norwich and Yarmouth breweries provided a fair bit of work when they used wherries to supply their riverside houses. The *Bell* was employed from 7–13 August, 1897, taking 'Pop and beer up and down' for Pattesons, of Norwich. 'Pop', presumably, was ginger-beer.

It was not her regular work, and it seems the brewery called her in to augment the holidaymakers' supplies during an exceptionally hot spell.

London stout, or porter, was once a favourite drink in Norwich, and was brought by sea to Yarmouth in the s.s. *Capulet*, belonging to the General Steam Navigation Company. It was there transferred into wherries and completed its journey to Norwich under sail.

Port wine, today, reverses the sequence; it begins its journey down the River Douro in sailing barges, and finishes it by steamer. Not so very long ago it also finished its journey to Norwich under sail, in the holds of wherries, and there is the story of one rascally skipper who thought he would make a bit for himself out of one such cargo.

He had four pipes on board, about 420 gallons, and on his way to Norwich stopped at a certain riverside inn. With the publican's help he drove back the hoops, drilled spile-holes where they had been, and drew off about three gallons from each pipe. He then poured water in to make up the measure and after plugging the holes, replaced the hoops. The deed might well have gone undetected, but unfortunately for the thieves, the added water turned the wine sour, and some inquiries followed. As a result, skipper and publican were charged, found guilty, and sentenced to fourteen years transportation.

That happened in 1830, a time when you flouted the law at your peril. There was no incentive for crime when punishments were harsh and ruthless, which may be why so little was committed on the rivers. Two cases that did occur will suffice to show the severity of the law.

In 1773, Cornelius Jekyll, a keelman of Norwich, was accused of stealing a pig and five chickens from Jeremiah Alburrow, of Reedham. His keel was searched, and he was found hiding in the cabin, along with the pig and the chickens. He was ordered to be transported for seven years.

At Ely, a waterman was charged with stealing three bushels of rye from a lighter, and after being found guilty, was ordered to be burned on the hand.

About this time a rather different kind of offence came before the magistrates when a keelman, by the name of Drake, was charged with 'wilfully running his keel foul upon a pleasure boat to the great endangering of their lives'. He was fined the very considerable sum, for those days, of five guineas.

Anything likely to injure or impede the navigation was, understandably, frowned upon. Those who have sailed over Breydon Water will recall the posts marking the fairway; they were there as long ago as 1765 and seem to have been uprooted then just as often as they are today. Keelmen were accused of running into them, and the Town Clerk of Yarmouth offered a reward of five guineas to anyone giving information leading to a successful prosecution.

Nowadays, as we sit back and watch the broads and rivers being choked to death and overgrown with weeds, it is instructive to discover how the problem was dealt with in days gone by. An official notice, issued in November 1741, helps us to do this:

> Ordered that the Constables of the several Towns and Parishes between Norwich and Hardley Cross, do attend on Monday, the 23rd inst., near the River side within their respective Jurisdictions or Boundaries, to inform the Inspector of the names of such Owners of Lands adjoining to the River aforesaid, as have not cut their Banks and drawn their Hoves and Weeds, and removed all other Impediments in the said Rivers and Creeks, for which they were lately presented by a Jury of Sewers, on pain of being sued for their Neglect.

Until well on into the second half of last century there was enough traffic to keep open many cuts and dykes which have now totally disappeared. William Thain, in 1946, set down his memories of wherrying, from the time when he first went with his father, Dionysius Thain, in the eighteen-sixties. Old Dionysius was the 'Di' Thain who bought Brighton's first wherry, the *Waveney*, and re-christened her *Eva Rosa*. The interesting thing about this account is the number of places they traded to regularly which are now completely inaccessible.

William was born at Stracey Arms in 1855, making him ninety-one when he recounted his experiences. He begins by saying how, when he was very young, he used to go with his father in his wherry, the *Pharos*, a small craft of 15 or 16 tons. They went in her through the North Walsham and Dilham Canal to North Walsham Staithe, and on occasion, up as far as Antingham.

When he was fourteen he took charge of one of his father's wherries called the *Onward*, bigger than the *Pharos*, being 36 feet long and able to carry 22 tons. He sailed this wherry entirely by himself.

He often loaded corn at Somerton Staithe from farms at Martham, Ashby, Thurne and Winterton, which he took to Yarmouth for the maltsters and millers there. He went from Somerton across Martham Broad, into the Dungeon Dyke, thence into Heigham River, and on down the Bure.

He made trips from Somerton, with corn, to the Parish Staithe at Hickling, behind the Pleasure Boat inn, and to get there went through Kendal Dyke, over Heigham Sounds, across Whiteslea, and over Hickling Broad.

Sometimes he had a cargo of timber for Stalham Staithe, which meant crossing Sutton Broad, and going on up Stalham Dyke. On other occasions he sailed up light to Horstead to load marl from the Horstead Marl Holes. Most of this went down to Martham or Potter Heigham for use on the land. At other times he went through the lock at Coltishall and sailed up as far as Aylsham.

He often discharged manure at Black Horse Staithe, in Hoveton Little Broad, and he went with cargoes of barley to the malthouses at Ranworth. Sometimes he sailed through the Fleet Dyke, across South Walsham Broad, then up through another wide dyke, into Malthouse Broad.

There were two staithes on South Walsham Broad, one, the public staithe, on the north side, the other, known as Debbage's staithe, on the west. He used both of them to bring up coal and coke, and to take away corn.

Nowadays, you would need a wherry on wheels to reach most of the out-of-the-way places visited regularly by William Thain eighty or ninety years ago, striking evidence of how waterborne traffic has declined.

But we all know how grass springs up on roads that are never used, and much the same sort of thing has happened to the small cuts and dykes that were once so valuable to farmers and country tradesmen. The moment they ceased to need wherries for bringing up raw materials and taking away produce, the reed beds began their advance on the waters. After only a few years it was hard to tell where these once navigable channels had been, so choked and overgrown were they; a year or two more and they were solid earth, a token of how swiftly nature on the march can change the face of familiar things.

A wide assortment of country trades were established on the riverside solely to make use of wherries for transport. Tanneries, for instance, like those at Beccles and Barton, were built where they were so that plentiful supplies of oak bark could reach them by water. The Horning turf marshes could be worked only because the river ran close by and the cut peat could be delivered by wherry.

Thatched roofs were popular in east Norfolk largely because reeds cost so little to cut and bring from the river banks. Hay, too, wherever possible, was carted by wherry, and sometimes enormous loads were carried. It was piled up in the hold, overflowed on to the plankways, and rose up another five or six feet, after the manner of a Thames 'stackie' barge. They looked for all the world like floating haystacks drifting quietly down the river.

When a load is carried like this above the level of the right-ups, a wherry is said to be 'boked'. This curious word is also applied to the body portion of a cart or barrow, having sides or to which sides can be temporarily fitted, to increase its load. In the country, a 'boke load' is any large, top-heavy, bulky load.

The old notebooks kept by skippers long years ago, which I have already referred to, give a good picture of the work they got through in a year, with all the variety of things they were called upon to carry. In 1899, for example, the *Bell* loaded, carried and discharged no less than 60 freights. Besides this she did three spells of lightering, one with copper ore at Yarmouth, one taking granite to Caister Denes, and another with deals and firewood at Yarmouth. More than half the total, 32, were freights of deals up to Norwich, and the remaining 28 were made up as follows: 5, general goods; 3, stones; 3, rubbish; 3, coal; 2, grain; 2, granite; 1 each, cattle cake, flour, tiles, chalk, cinder ashes, firewood, boards, wheat, cinders and mustard seed.

On two trips to Norwich she earned an extra 25s. towing rafts. They were arranged in a long string, as wide, or a bit wider, than the wherry herself, and slowed down progress so much that, even with a fair wind, it took three days to reach Norwich.

The *Norfolk Hero* once sailed into the city with a raft 100 yards long and 20 feet wide. The crew could not get it round some of the sharp bends and had to take it to pieces and sail it round in sections.

Timber-lugging wherries were seldom satisfied with what they could get in their holds, and for good measure lashed a 2 or 3 ton butt on each side of them. It speaks volumes for the wherrymen's skill that they could still get about with such encumbrances.

Taking a final look at the *Bell*'s doings in 1899, we find that her year's work amounted to about 2,500 tons, excluding the rafts, and that the distance she sailed, roughly 2,000 miles, would have taken her to Gibraltar or Newfoundland.

In recent times all this trade has disappeared. There is not now a freight to be had from the Norwich rubbish tips, and only sugar-beet offers a little seasonal work between October and January. It has earned a few pounds for the *Albion*, and several motor-hulks still scratch a living out of it.

But on the rare occasions when work is to be had in Yarmouth, wherrymen are debarred from loading their own craft. It has been their job since as long as anyone can remember, but in the new order of things they must stand around kicking their heels while nominees of the Dock Labour Board do it for them. The cost just about doubles the freight charges to Norwich so, wherever possible, goods now go by road or rail.

The last nail has been driven in the wherry's coffin, and with all her trade taken away she has become useless and obsolete; the *Albion*, for all her good looks and proud bearing, is as much a relic of the past as the Tower of London.

All the same, it would be a pity if either were allowed to crumble away and disappear—there is so much of English history in both.

CHAPTER SIX

Southwold Harbour and the Blyth Navigation

Yarmouth's seven harbours—keels and wherries in the Roads—by sea to Southwold—cargoes for Halesworth—wherries in new waters—the hindrance of a bad harbour—making matters worse—greed of the landlords—Patrick Stead battles for justice—facts and figures—two monuments—a struggle to survive—pioneering the iron wherry—decay and ruin—Fred Lambert's last gamble.

THE people of Yarmouth have had many headaches over their harbour. It took seven attempts before they could make one to stay open, and the struggle to do it lasted from the middle of the fourteenth century to the middle of the sixteenth. Even then it was a continual source of anxiety because the entrance periodically silted up, making it difficult, if not impossible, for fully-laden ships to get in or out.

The formation of bars, caused by tidal action and the deposits of slow-running rivers, was always a problem on the East Coast, nor was it ever really solved, because once the railways came interest in harbours declined, and most of them were left to fall into decay, like Wells and Blakeney.

The same fate now seems in store for Yarmouth, where piers and other works, like old London Bridge, are falling down, causing lengthy disputes about where the money is to come from to put matters right.

But there is hardly the same need, now, for a satisfactory harbour at Yarmouth as there was two hundred years ago when it provided the link between the industries of Norfolk and Suffolk and their vital foreign markets.

The town was then fully alive to the need for keeping its harbour open and in good trim, though it still took a lot of money to do it. Before duties were levied on goods entering the port, several startling means were adopted for raising funds, one being to appropriate the plate, bells, ornaments and money belonging to the parish church of St. Nicholas. That was in 1548, and a hundred years later they went one better and petitioned Parliament for all the lead on the roof of Norwich Cathedral, a request that was not granted.

We gain a very clear impression of what the harbour entrance was like in 1830 from a plate in James Stark's *Scenery of the Rivers of Norfolk*. It shows a coasting keel from the Humber working out round the south pier in a north-easterly breeze. She has warped herself over the shoals across the mouth, and a beach boat can be seen recovering her anchor. Just inside, to the right, wherries are loading sand, and a fleet of colliers opposite wait for a change of wind before setting off for Newcastle. It is plain enough what a job they will have to cross the bar when the wind does come fair.

The sand built up so much at times there was insufficient water for the smallest coasting vessels to enter or leave. This state of affairs naturally played havoc with the business interests of the district, the more so because, even at the best of times, large vessels could rarely get in except at the top of spring tides. They could only do it then after discharging part of their cargo in the Roads.

The keelmen and wherrymen were not very anxious to see the harbour improved because theirs was the job of lightening vessels at sea. It meant additional work, and extra pay, and as they only went off in fine weather there was little danger to it.

Ships had just the same trouble leaving, of course, as they did getting in. That meant loading as much as they could get over the bar with, bringing up, and taking the rest from keels and wherries.

During the autumn of 1755, when the newly-harvested grain was being sent away from Yarmouth, a rare case occurred of a keel being lost. She was taking wheat to a ship in the Roads when it suddenly came on to blow. Keels were ungainly things at any time to handle, and in trying to fetch back into harbour she missed the entrance and drove ashore. A wherry would doubtless have made it without much trouble. However, the wind must have kindled up into a proper gale for the next night another keel, bound up-river to Bungay with coal and deals, sank just above the Haven bridge.

After the keels had disappeared all work in the Roads was carried on by wherries, and they continued doing it right down to the First World War. Instead of sailing, they were sometimes towed to sea, like the *Dora*, *Princess* and *Wanderer*, who went out behind the tug *United* in August 1898. They lay alongside while the ship's derricks loaded them, then sailed back to harbour and on up to Carrow works, Norwich.

The *Uranus* was about the last to load at sea, sometime between 1914 and 1918. She took linseed and cotton seed cake out of a steamer, and should have been accompanied by the *Sirius*. But 'Times' Holt, her skipper, did not care for the idea and refused to go, even though it was a flat calm.

Whether Norfolk keels were ever engaged in the coasting trade is very hard to say. Their rig was not really suitable, and about the only place they might have gone to was Southwold, until Lowestoft became a port, in 1833. The only piece of evidence I can find having any bearing on the subject is an advertisement of 1766. It reads: 'A small keel, almost as good as new, with mast, sail and all other proper rigging. She carries seven lasts of barley, or ten chaldrons of coals, and draws very little more than two feet and a half of water. She is very strong built, and seem well calculated for Halesworth new river, or any shoal water. For further particulars, inquire of Mr. John Whiteside, shipbuilder of Yarmouth.'

The 'Halesworth new river', or River Blyth Navigation, had been opened five years, since 1761. It was not connected by water with the broads district, so anyone in Halesworth wishing to buy John Whiteside's keel would have had to bring her round by sea, through Southwold harbour. When Whiteside mentioned Halesworth he probably knew that craft about this size had already gone there to work on the new navigation.

This is suggested by a report of its opening which describes the arrival in Halesworth of the first craft from Southwold, carrying 9 chaldrons of coal, and drawing about 3 feet of water. She was roughly the same size as the one up for sale.

Eleven years later, in 1772, when the effects of the Free British Herring Fishery Society were dispersed at Southwold, we find 'two small keels' among the items for sale.

It seems clear that keels were not averse to having a taste of salt water now and again, though it would be wrong to assume they went on regular coasting passages. They may have done, but there is no evidence to prove it.

A point to remember about their presence in Southwold is that they could have been built there. The yards were there to do it, but it would have meant local shipwrights going to Yarmouth after measurements and rigging plans, a rather unlikely procedure when merchants could go along and buy keels 'off the peg'. I feel pretty sure that is what they did, and that the first keels used on the River Blyth sailed round from Norfolk.

It was the farthest south they ever worked though they found conditions much the same as at Yarmouth. Southwold had an equally poor harbour and there was plenty of lightering to be done at sea before ships could enter.

In past centuries Southwold and Dunwich were important centres for the North Sea fisheries and, like Yarmouth, sent a fleet of whalers to the Arctic every year. To supply this industry, both places imported large quantities of raw materials such as salt from Lisbon and pipe-staves and deals from Norway.

Large supplies of timber also came in for the different shipbuilders who were in a flourishing state up to the middle of the eighteenth century. In October 1764, a 100-ton brig was launched named the *Farmers' Liberty*, and three days later a sloop called the *Southwold* went down the ways.

It was about this time the people of Halesworth began wondering whether their river, which emptied into the sea at Southwold, could not be used to carry goods between the two places. Halesworth was then a flourishing market town, with large malthouses, an iron foundry, an agricultural implement factory, and a corn exchange. As the centre of a large and prosperous farming district it would obviously benefit if craft could reach the town with coal, coke, timber, and suchlike, direct from the ships at Southwold.

Thomas Knights, a local brewer, started things moving, and after a public meeting in the Angel Inn, an act of Parliament was applied for to make the Blyth navigable. Work started in 1757 and four years later, on 23 July, 1761, the first craft sailed into the town. The event was reported in the most glowing terms:

> This day we had the pleasure of receiving into our bason a keel from Southwold laden with coals and drawing upwards of 3 feet of water. We can assure the publick that the works for facilitating the navigation of our river are constructed and finished with the greatest art, and as they afford the most pleasing probability of a particular benefit to this town, so do they no less promise to the country round a more extensive influence.
>
> The barge was attended from the Town lock up to the great bason by a numerous concourse of people, assembled not more to satisfy their curiosity at the novelty of the sight than to join in the general joy and triumph on the occasion.

For the next thirty years or so the navigation more than lived up to the high hopes entertained for it. Keels were employed exclusively in the early stages, but gradually their place was taken by wherries; their superior sailing qualities made them much more suitable for the extremely narrow waters of the Blyth.

The trip from Halesworth to Southwold and back took two days, with four locks to negotiate, at Bulcamp, Blyford, Mells and Halesworth. There was a quay at Blyford as well as Halesworth, and in Southwold loading was done from the ships whose regular berth was at Blackshore, three-quarters of a mile inside the harbour on the north bank.

The launching of the wherry *Halesworth*, in 1772, reflects the enthusiasm of those days; she was built in the town and, therefore, very appropriately named. She loaded 34 tons and had a crew of three, with William Forman as skipper. An extra hand was carried because of the narrowness of the Blyth over most of its length, which often meant long spells of trekking in a head-wind.

She was, I believe, the only craft ever built in Halesworth, and whoever was responsible made a good job of her as she lasted until 1818. During her lifetime she sailed in company with another locally built wherry, the 32-ton *Halesworth Trader*. She was launched in 1799 and was the first wherry to be built at Southwold. Skippered by William Blanden, she also had a crew of three. We shall meet the name Blanden again later on in this chapter.

By about 1850 there were at least a dozen craft in service, three of them wherries belonging to Robert Burleigh, a maltster in Halesworth. These were the *Hankey*, *Hope* and *Fanny*, and all of them came originally from Yarmouth. Burleigh also got Billy Brighton to build him a wherry-yacht, named the *Helen*, after one of his daughters. He used her on the broads during the summer, but at the end of the season she was brought round to Southwold and up the Blyth, to her home port of Halesworth. Her berth was in a cut just above the drawbridge. She eventually passed to Bullen, of Oulton Broad, where she became a houseboat with the name *Vera*, and was afloat well into the nineteen-twenties.

Burleigh had as well the ketch-barge *Mayland*, 120 tons, which took malt and corn up to London, and came back with stout and chalk. On his death, in 1883, she and the three wherries were sold by auction at the Swan Inn, Southwold, and all, except the *Fanny*, left the port. She was broken up at Halesworth quay.

Of the other owners, Thompson George, of the Old Brewery, had three craft, though whether keels or wherries I cannot say; Tippell, the printer, had two, and a further two belonged to George Butcher, of Wenhaston. One of these later belonged to Turner, of Wenhaston, and lay at Blyford bridge long after the navigation had closed, in 1884. She at last sank at her moorings and was broken up. Mrs. Chapman, mistress of the Fishing Buss Inn, Blackshore, also had one.

A large wherry for these waters, the 40-ton *Iron Duke*, was owned by Harvey, of Harvey's Academy, Halesworth. As her name suggests, she was built of iron, and is reputed to have come from a Southwold yard, but I have always thought it strange that a place like this, experienced only in building wooden ships, should have pioneered a craft of this kind. She must have appeared at least twenty years before the *Uranus*, the first of the iron wherries launched by Fellows' at Yarmouth.

I have mentioned Blackshore as the place where seagoing ships unloaded, but quite a few came as far up as Blythburgh bridge. The last to do so was the *Woodland Lass*, sometime in the eighteen-seventies, when she brought timber for Bicker's, of Wangford.

The success, or otherwise, of the Blyth Navigation was always dependent on there being an efficient harbour at Southwold. Unfortunately, this was not always the case; the entrance was frequently blocked, and trade came to a standstill. There was a very bad period in 1839 when it became so choked up that carriages could pass over to

Walberswick. This state of affairs persisted for several days, and all the time a fleet of vessels lay trapped inside, while others beat about in the Roads waiting to enter. One of them, the *British Queen*, was cast ashore and lost.

Things were not always as bad as this, but even at the best of times it was a job to get a fully-laden ship in without first lightening her. It was such a normal procedure that the masters and principal owners ordered a special lighter from Yarmouth. She was called the *Good Intent*, and was really a wherry of about 40 tons, big enough to make quite a hole in an average coaster's cargo. She was launched in 1790, and cost £200. She proved a good investment and went on earning money for her sponsors for twenty-five years. Even then her useful career was not over, as they sold her to the Harbour Commissioners for £50 to be turned into a dredger.

As with all East Coast harbours, the trouble at Southwold was lack of scour. Not enough water was collected on the flood to carry away the sand and other detritus on the ebb. Instead of being taken out to sea, it was deposited at the entrance, creating at times an impenetrable bar. What scour there was came, almost entirely, from the water flowing over Blythburgh flats, an extensive basin of saltings some way inland. This basin was to the harbour what a cistern is to a lavatory pan; the means of flushing it out regularly and keeping it clear of obstructions. Every right-thinking person in the district knew the importance of these flats, that they must be retained as they were at all costs, and never encroached upon.

But there were others, the landowning gentry of the neighbourhood, who looked at things very differently, who were stirred only by motives of self-interest, and cared not a fig for the common merchants, shipowners and mariners who earned their bread-and-butter out of the harbour. For a long time they had been casting covetous eyes on these very saltings around Blythburgh.

By the beginning of the eighteenth century they could restrain themselves no longer; they began throwing up embankments to keep out the tides, and adding the reclaimed land to their estates. They pushed ahead to such purpose, and sealed off such vast areas, that in the course of fifty years the harbour was paralysed. Stranded ships, ruined trade, and the general distress gave no pause to their activities; rather, they seemed to act as an incentive, for every possible opportunity was taken to raise more and more embankments, and add more acres to their property. Southwold Corporation was as bad as the worst of them, taking all it could lay its hands on, without a thought for the harbour.

Figures tell the story better than words: prior to 1770, 700 acres were enclosed; in 1780, 100 acres; in 1804, 100 acres; in 1807, 100 acres; in 1818, 43 acres; a total of 1,043 acres. Between 1818 and 1845 the work went forward at an even greater rate, till it reached the astonishing figure of 2,704 acres, or $4\frac{1}{4}$ square miles.

Assuming these saltings were flooded to a depth of only one foot at high tide, then the harbour had been robbed of the scouring effect of 800,000,000 gallons of water passing out to sea, twice a day.

Half-hearted efforts were made to keep it free by artificial means: it was dug out, by hand, in 1776, 1784 and 1792, and no less than thirteen times between 1805 and 1818. But there was generally so little depth that vessels could only be got in with the help of powerful capstans, dragging them over the bar.

It seems unbelievable that a handful of men could bring such disaster to a district, but the dice were heavily loaded in the landowners' favour. They possessed great political power and never hesitated to use it, in promoting their own personal affairs. The Act of Parliament of 1746, 'to open, cleanse, scour, widen, depthen, repair and improve the haven at Southwold' provides a good example of how they went about things.

Under this Act, Commissioners were to be appointed to see the necessary works were carried out, and it represented a very grave threat to the interests of the landowners. For any competent engineer would demand at the outset that a stop be put to any further embanking, that those already built should be taken down, and the tides allowed to flow freely again over the saltings. It was the only way of putting things right but, or course, it would not suit the landowners' book at all. Such a possibility had to be nipped in the bud at once.

We can picture them, gathering in great anxiety round ancestral hearths; the putting together of noble heads over rummers of hot toddy; the broadening smiles as they saw the light; then the nods and winks to influential guests, down in the country for a few weeks after the toils of Westminster; the understandings; the promises; the gentlemen's agreements.

In the fullness of time an announcement gave the names of those appointed to be Commissioners for the Harbour of Southwold; they were all landowners. By dint of a little wire-pulling, and a word or two in the right places, they had got the harbour at their mercy. They could push forward with their land-grabbing free from any shadow of interference. Only the Harbour Commissioners had power to question their actions—and they were the Harbour Commissioners. The whole thing was masterly in its simplicity.

What matter if the harbour was destroyed? It was no concern of theirs and could go to the devil. Their estates would benefit and that was all that counted.

It would be easy enough to fob off those troublesome merchants foolish enough to want to get their ships in and out. A few labourers could be put to digging out the channel, if that would keep them quiet. But these tradesmen must learn to fend for themselves and not expect to be wet-nursed by the gentry.

The same simple, but infallible, methods were used in all future Acts, those of 1756, 1789, 1809 and 1830. Commissioners under the 1789 Act comprised the High Steward and Bailiffs of Southwold, fourteen knights of the shire, baronets and squires, five parsons, and four others whose status is not given. In the 1809 Act, all those still alive were reappointed, with the addition of three more landowners.

The Act of 1830 was vigorously resisted by traders in both Southwold and Halesworth. The merchant class felt very strongly they should have a voice in running the harbour, such as it was, as they paid all the dues that went to its upkeep. They organized a petition against it which was only withdrawn on the assurance of Lord Stradbroke, the chairman, that five Commissioners would be appointed from among the merchants of Halesworth. But he never kept his promise, and the chief users of the port were prevented from having any say in its management.

Even when we allow for the corruption and intrigue that was rife in those days, the record of Southwold seems quite unparalleled. In other places, such as Dundee, Leith, Glasgow and Liverpool, Comissioners were periodically elected from among the shipowners, merchants, ratepayers and inhabitants. The interests of all classes were taken into proper account. But at Southwold, the only people with a say were the riparian owners, who had not the slightest concern for the harbour. It could go to the dogs for all they cared. All that can be said in their favour is that, as Commissioners, they never intended to promote its welfare; they sought these positions only to make quite sure that no one could tell them to return the lands they had stolen. It was the best, and simplest way of managing the affair, and they had no scruples about doing it.

But their path was not always one of roses. They often had to contend with outbursts of public indignation and were forced, from time to time, to make a pretence of carrying out their duties. They brought it to quite a fine art. When it was obvious a gesture was necessary, they adopted the simple expedient of calling in some well-known engineer, asking him to carry out a survey, and submit his proposals.

After about a year the report was received. Then it was discussed at great length, the various proposals taken note of, and selected pieces printed in the newspapers, after which, when the public was felt to be suitably placated, the whole thing was put away on the shelf, and forgotten.

They were, of course, only too pleased to carry out some of the minor, and comparatively unimportant, proposals, such as dredging (that is why they bought the *Good Intent*), building and extending piers, repairing quay-headings, but they availed nothing so long as the embankments remained.

Yet every engineer called in stated, in the most unmistakable terms, that they, and they alone, were the root cause of all the trouble. The famous John Rennie was invited to carry out a survey in 1820, and in his report he said:

> There is little doubt that the harbour of Southwold has, at former periods, been of a much greater depth than it now is; and that for many years past, it has been getting gradually more shallow, owing to the embankment of the salt marshes, over which the tide used to flow, and the stopping of the creeks which communicated with the channel of the River Blyth ... Thus, not only shingle and sand, brought in by the tide, but also alluvial matter, brought down by the freshes of the Blyth, subsided and gradually lessened the depth of the channel ...

He then went on to tell the Commissioners, in the clearest language possible that: 'Unless those embankments are destroyed, but little that I can advise will be of much use.'

Nine years later, William Cubitt, then engaged on building Lowestoft harbour, reported in much the same terms. Again, in 1841, James Walker, the distinguished harbour engineer, after making a thorough survey as far up as Bulcamp lock, stated that the injury to the haven was due, almost entirely, to the vast areas which had been cut off from tidal flooding.

The way these reports were received may be seen from a letter, written by one of the Commissioners, the Rev. Clissold, of Wrentham, to his chairman in 1840. Setting at nought the conclusions of these eminent and experienced engineers, he not only defended the embankments, but proposed that Buss Creek should be stopped up, and the money derived from the land reclaimed, applied to the improvement of the harbour. Suggestions of this kind were mostly inspired, and were all part of the game; they could be given plenty of publicity and helped to distract the public from the real issues.

The last expert opinion we need take note of is that of Captain E. K. Calver, R.N., given at the Tidal Harbours Inquiry in 1845. As Admiralty Surveyor he put forward plans for improving Southwold, and in them he remarked that were the embankments removed, and the marshes at their original level, the amount of tidal water would be quadrupled; and that although the River Blyth might have benefited in some small measure by embankments, the bar, and the entrance to the river, had suffered out of all proportion.

But his words, like all the others, might have been addressed to a brick wall. For more than a hundred years a succession of Commissioners pursued their policy of putting private gain before the common interest. As I have said, it did occasionally lead to agitation and demands for a thorough investigation into the running of the harbour, but they were always clever enough to ride such waves of public disapproval, and to leave the impression that their only concern was with its welfare and of all who used it.

Towards the end, however, they nearly met their match in the person of Patrick Stead. He was an energetic and progressive-minded Scotsman who migrated, by way of Great Yarmouth, to Halesworth, where he took over the maltings in Quay Street, round about 1824. He soon became one of the chief users of the Navigation, and was elected a River Commissioner in 1826. Largely through his efforts, the Blyth experienced its greatest period of prosperity, and would have known even more but for the deplorable state of Southwold harbour.

He was not long at Halesworth before discovering how matters stood there. The constant interruptions to his trade he found intolerable, and lost no time in seeking out the cause. Having found it, he started a campaign against the Harbour Commissioners which lasted for twenty-five years. He sought to put a curb, once and for all, on their activities, and to give Southwold a harbour worthy of the name. He might well have succeeded had not the odds against him been so great.

What he did succeed in doing was to lay bare the whole sordid story, and to provide facts and figures to make the Commissioners squirm. They stood utterly condemned on his evidence, and though he failed to loosen their grip on the stolen lands, or throw down their embankments, the moral victory was his.

Matters came to a head with the great blocking-up of 1839 when, it will be remembered, a number of ships were trapped inside the harbour. All of them were carrying his goods. He was bound to suffer great loss and inconvenience, and promptly brought up the matter at the next meeting of the River Commissioners. He wanted to know why the Harbour Commissioners had done nothing about the Rennie proposals; he claimed the river-users were the victims of the Act of 1830 which, he stated, had been got through Parliament by influence. If that were not the case, how could sixteen landowners and fourteen parsons have named themselves Commissioners?; he questioned the integrity of Lord Stradbroke, and referred to his broken promise; he demanded an immediate public inquiry to be held in Southwold.

This was a body-blow for the landlords; try as they would, they could not wriggle out of it, and reluctantly arranged for evidence to be heard in Southwold Town Hall on 1 August, 1839. No doubt anticipating the nature of the evidence that would be brought, they instructed their surveyor, Lieutenant Ellis, R.N., to make a hasty report on the harbour. When ready, it was found to attribute all the troubles to nature, which, under the circumstances, was what might have been expected.

But Patrick Stead and his fellow River Commissioners brought some well-known Southwold sea captains to give evidence of a different kind. They included Rowland Twaddle of the *Sarah Ann*; John Magub, senior, of the *Perseverance*; Marshall Twaddle of the *Sophia*; John Magub, junior, of the *Vigilant*; Meshac Lilly of the *Liberty*; Henry Smith of the *Three Friends*; John Palmer of the *Suffolk*; and John Chittleburgh of the *Mary Ann*.

Every one of them declared it was the embankments which had ruined the harbour and brought it to its present derelict state.

Several of the pilots were called, who spoke in much the same terms, and then it was the turn of William Blanden. Blanden, it will be recalled, was skipper of the *Halesworth Trader*, and at the time of the inquiry was quite an old man. Nevertheless, he spoke in clear and simple words, and here is a transcript of what he said:

> William Blanden, of Halesworth, states that he is 70 years of age, has been a wherryman between Halesworth and Southwold 59 years; that about 50 years ago ships traded at Southwold of similar size as now trade there. That he never remembers ships being detained there for want of water or upon the bar until after the marshes were taken in, and that we (the wherrymen) amongst ourselves, then said and considered, that at the time of the embankments being made they would ruin the harbour, which up till then had been good. That no better harbour ever wanted to be than it had been there up to the date of the embankments.
>
> That the tides over 40 or 50 years ago ran a wonderful deal stronger than now, when we always required to bring up our wherries with an anchor, but that now we find a quant is quite sufficient, unless during a strong wind running with the tide.
>
> That there was no shingle lay within the harbour and the water flowed and ebbed the whole breadth between the piers.
>
> That at Blythburgh bridge the tides used to flow all over the marshes (Bulcamp side), above bridge, on ordinary tides. Great creeks there used to get full of water like sluices, and the tide used before that to run far stronger than it does now and we used to stop the wherries with an anchor above bridge in order to pass under the bridge.
>
> About 40 or 50 years ago I used to go pinpatching* all over the marshes,

---

* Winkle gathering.

called the salts and flats, and they always were under water, neap tides and spring tides.

There was a large creek with a great deal of water in it where I have been up several times with my craft, where I laid her in.

Pinpatching I never was questioned about or refused, and all the public went as a matter of right and asked nobody at all. We took our own leave and nobody said anything to us.

No one fed cattle and none could be fed, being always under water, and I have sunk in the mud above the knees to the crotch, and I used to have a hod to assist me out and to hold the pinpatches.

Those marshes were at the Long Reach, and right up to the New Cut, and were all taken in 30 or 40 years ago, say 2 to 300 acres at least, all that certainly. Since that time the harbour has been getting worse and worse, and there has not been back water enough to keep the harbour scoured out. The floods not being nearly so strong now as then (40 or 50 years ago), I could now run my wherry down against the flood with a fair wind double the distance what I could have done with a similar then.

We never had to go to the Roads or Bay in old times to lighten the ships as they got in then without lightening, and I have seen ships drawing nine or ten feet of water come in at half flood, and come and lie alongside the piers afloat. The ships used to come in as soon as it was flood upon the bar and would get over it in an hour or two. Larger ships came in then than now (the *British Laurel* and the old *Providence*).

The only thing that can be done now is to get more back water and to run out the north pier 40 or 50 yards.

This evidence of William Blanden's, together with that of the captains, pilots and others, told only of physical deterioration; Patrick Stead showed what it all added up to in terms of pounds, shillings and pence. No one had been hit harder than himself by the intrigues and double-dealing of the Harbour Commissioners, and we can see him, that August day, bristling with anger and bursting to get to grips with them. This was his testimony:

You are a merchant and maltster at Halesworth?—Yes.
How long have you traded at Southwold?—Upwards of twenty years.
How much corn and malt do you export?—From 15,000 to 20,000 quarters annually.
How many coals, &c. do you import?—About 2,000 or 3,000 tons of coals, 500 tons of chalk, besides other kinds of merchandise.

What proportion of the Southwold dues do you consider you pay?—Nearly one half of the revenue of the port.

Do you consider that the grower of the corn and the consumer of the coals, &c. pay these dues, or who pays them?—I consider that the merchant pays them. When the merchant freights a ship, the captain adds the dues to the freight, and so charges the merchant with them. It is at the option of the merchant at what port the farmer delivers his corn; and, therefore, the farmer living at nearly the same distance from any port, would always deliver at the cheaper port, if required so to do by the buyer. At Snape, Aldborough, Ipswich and Woodbridge, no dues are paid; at Lowestoft, Yarmouth and Lynn, the dues are 1d. per quarter; at Southwold, 2d. per quarter; at Halesworth (add the River Blyth dues, 1d.) 3d. per quarter.

The merchant, therefore, trading at Southwold has to pay these dues, besides being liable to an additional expense for the damage, inconvenience and detention which shipowners constantly experience at Southwold.

For example, last winter, freights were much higher, and more difficult to be obtained, at Southwold than at Yarmouth. Whilst the current freight at Yarmouth to Newcastle was 1s. per quarter, ships could not be had at Southwold under 2s. 6d. per quarter for Newcastle, and so on.

Independently of this, the merchant is exposed to loss of market, damage on the bar, detention, additional premium of insurance, and other serious contingent risks and loss, entailing a cancer upon, and rendering the trade of Southwold comparatively insignificant.

With regard to coals, I may say that farmers will generally take their coals in their return empty wagons from the cheaper place; if the farmer deliver his corn at Snape, he can procure coals there free of all dues; or if at Beccles, by paying only 6d. per ton. Whereas at Southwold there is to pay:

	s.	d.	
Harbour dues	1	2	per ton
River dues to Halesworth	0	9	,, ,,
	1	11	
Additional freight for bad harbour, 1s. to 2s. per ton	1	6	
Showing an excess of cost of	3	5	,, ,,

which the Halesworth merchant has to pay, if he compete with those other ports and sell at the same price, or he must lose his trade in coals.

From these causes, a large proportion of the grain grown in the rich and fertile landed district, to which the port of Southwold ought to be the main outlet, is now conveyed through Bungay, the ports of Beccles, Yarmouth and Lowestoft, on the north; and Snape, Aldborough, Ipswich and Woodbridge, on the south. And thus the exports and imports of Southwold do not amount to one-third of what its situation entitles it to command.

Have you experienced much inconvenience in shipping from Southwold?—I have experienced incalculable loss and inconvenience from repeated cases of damage and detention to ships upon and by the bar. I have lately had cargoes inward-bound beating about for a long time in the bay and nearest roadsteads, at great hazard. In fact, they have been so many, that the Yarmouth shipowners (particularly since the publication of your surveyor's report) will not allow their vessels to go to Southwold with, or for, any cargoes; nor can I charter ships now at any port for Southwold, from the bad character which the harbour has obtained. Insurances cannot be effected under an extravagant rate.

The freight of coal ships is generally 1s. 6d. per ton higher at Southwold than at Yarmouth. They could not be freighted at all last winter for Southwold at any price at Newcastle, and the consequence was, I could not at Southwold get culm or coals for my cinder ovens, or cinders for my malt houses. I was compelled to cart those, as well as a very large quantity of lime, at great loss, from Beccles and Bungay.

Have you met with more or less inconvenience of late than formerly?— Very much more of late by the repeated detention of ships for days and weeks together, causing ruinous loss of market, damage and disputes. After ships are loaded up in the harbour, they have frequently to unload their cargoes every spring tide, in the attempt to get over the bar; when they have reached the bay, they must then wait suitable weather to reload their cargoes; at times to ride in great peril, with boat and captain on shore, attending to their lighters.

I could instance many dangerous cases, attended with great expense. The *Perseverance*, in May last, discharged 80 tons of coals in the bay before she could get over the bar; and in loading her subsequently, five wherry loads with 500 quarters of malt, at the risk of the ship and owners, had to be put on board in the open sea.

I loaded two cargoes of barley in December last at Southwold, one by the *William*, bound to Newcastle, and another by a beautiful new schooner, the *Hawk*, of and for Perth, both of which were totally lost, and with the latter, every soul perished. The parties to whom these shipments were made ascribe the loss of property and life to the wretched state of Southwold harbour, and to the detention which occasioned those ships to be at sea in the dreadful gale in January 1839; and I have orders from them never again to ship any corn for their account from Southwold.

I have received similar orders from many other correspondents, and to such an extent that I have all but resolved to give up shipping grain from Southwold, the personal risk being so great, independent of what one's friends suffer.

[Here Stead gave some technical evidence, with suggestions for improving the port.]

As the revenue of Southwold is small, how is the expense of improvement to be borne?—If the harbour were improved, the extension of its trade would most assuredly follow, and hence the means would be found in the increase of the revenue; for much of its legitimate commerce (probably two-thirds) is now carried on through other channels.

Do you think a larger revenue would be obtained by an advance of dues?—I think not. I submit that increased commerce should be encouraged by facilities to trade, as at Yarmouth, where the dues are not one half; and I refer to the corn shipments annually at the respective ports upon this coast, in proof of the comparative smallness in quantity shipped from Southwold:

At	Corn and Malt	At	Corn and Malt
Maldon	121,493 qrs.	Yarmouth	327,188 qrs.
Colchester	101,539 ,,	Cley and Wells	102,693 ,,
Ipswich	170,025 ,,	Lynn	242,892 ,,
Harwich	101,842 ,,	Wisbech	107,261 ,,
Woodbridge	69,209 ,,	Boston	251,832 ,,
Aldborough	55,690 ,,	Southwold	29,658 ,,

Coals shipped at Yarmouth, 170,000 tons—at Southwold, 9,843 tons, being one-seventeenth part as compared with Yarmouth.

What, in your opinion, would most effectually promote the trade of Southwold?—A better harbour, and a new Bill. It is impossible, in my opinion, to carry on trade at Southwold in the same manner it has been of late. Unless a new Act of Parliament be obtained, so as not to exclude from the Commission practical and nautical men, I submit that the confidence of the public and parties interested cannot be supported.

Patrick Stead concluded his evidence by referring to improvements made to other harbours, and repeated, most vehemently, that 'it was the banking in of the marshes which has occasioned the interruption and misfortunes of the harbour.'

The Commissioners' cupboard door was flung open with a vengeance, revealing a pretty nasty skeleton within. Stead had torn off their masks and exposed them for what they were, men without scruple or a shred of public conscience.

But they still strove to put a bold face on things and arranged for another survey to be made. This, as already stated, was carried out by James Walker, and he submitted his report in 1841. It only served to confirm Patrick Stead's charges, and it was plain that the Commissioners would be driven, at last, to do something.

And they did. They played what they hoped was their trump card. They applied for a new Act of Parliament, which Stead had demanded, to unite the River and Harbour Commissions into one body, responsible for the whole navigation up to Halesworth. But that was only part of its aim; the sting was in the clauses making their embankments legal, and giving them the title to all the lands enclosed.

It was a cunning and desperate move; cunning, because it would have obtained official blessing for their depredations; desperate, because it was now the only way of silencing the public clamour that these lands be returned to the community.

Had the Bill been passed, riots might well have broken out; perhaps the landowners knew this. As they gathered round the ancestral hearths, drinking hot toddy from the same rummers their grandfathers had used, this new generation of intriguers may have sensed the bottom falling out of their world, and concluded, regretfully, that England was not the place it was.

But they need have had no qualms. When the General Enclosure Act became law in 1845 it gave them everything they wanted; a title to all their stolen land and security of tenure. It was a gift out of the blue, and the rummers were called upon to work overtime. They dropped their new Bill like a hot brick. There was no longer need to put a face on things, no call for further fine words; the harbour could be damned. And it was, slowly decaying into the pitiful object we know today.

Patrick Stead had put up a gallant fight and performed a valuable public service in exposing what went on in high places. He was a David in a land of Goliaths, but for all the odds he battled fiercely for what he held to be common justice and the rights of the ordinary people.

I often pass by Blythburgh Water and the surrounding marshes, but I never do so without feeling the spirit of Patrick Stead is close beside me, pointing to the different embankments and all those acres cut off from the tides; and in my imagination I hear him say: 'Look you there, man, that's what caused us all our misery, what broke the trade of Halesworth, and ruined Southwold. Those banks you see yonder were all put up by greedy, soulless men, who cared not a jot for what happened to the rest of us. Look well at them and remember, they stand as a monument to all those who turned Southwold into the port that was murdered.'

In the early fifties Stead sold out at Halesworth and returned to Scotland, where he died in 1869. But he never forgot Halesworth. If you drive there now from Bungay you will see, on the left-hand side as you enter the town, the Patrick Stead Hospital. It was built with one of the many large gifts he made to charity. And if you go in the church you will see a window placed there in his memory. May they long remain to tell us of his courageous stand against the corrupt use of political power—none the less admirable because it was unsuccessful.

There is little left to tell of the River Blyth or the harbour. The latter fell into such a state that by 1882 G. Christopher Davies was constrained to write: 'The piers are tumbling to pieces and the great worn capstans, which are used for hauling vessels *through the shingle*, looked almost past use. . . . All round are speaking evidences of its decadence as a port, rotting barges, disused smacks, and desolute wharves.'

The days of vigorous, bustling activity were past; the creeping paralysis of neglect lay its cold fingers over quays and slipways. The pride of Southwold and its haven passed away amid a desolation of crumbling timber and forsaken berths; nothing remained but the eternal calling of the sea and the song of the beach winds. They alone, told of all that had been before.

Yet even in such ruin, traditions and ways of life die hard. There were still families with yards, and slips leading down to the little water that was left, and they strove gamely to carry on. They pioneered iron wherries with the building of the *Iron Duke*, and launched another with the defiant name *Walberswick*. Both eventually found their way to Norfolk waters.

Wherry Inn, Gelderston

Wherry Inn, Halesworth

Keel & Wherry Inn, Norwich

The New Cut, Haddiscoe. A photograph taken more than fifty years ago showing the arctic conditions often met with

Jack Cates tending the *Albion*'s sheet

Roy Clark

Sam Gibbs became skipper of the *Iron Duke* when she arrived at Yarmouth and was bought by Prentice Bros., of Runham Vauxhall. They worked her for a long time, taking artificial manures from their factory at Haddiscoe, and re-named her the *James and Jessie*. Her activities in the chemical trade gained for her the engaging nickname 'Acid Drop'. She was broken up at Teasdell's yard, Yarmouth, prior to the First World War.

The *Walberswick* was a little smaller than the *Iron Duke*, and was bought new by Joe Jay. She later belonged to Tom Barber and Ben Ingram, of Yarmouth, who used her for icing in the early eighties, and from them she passed to Colman's, of Norwich.

Both of them reached Norfolk via Lowestoft, but the way they did so is worthy of record. Neither had mast nor sail, so they waited for a fine day, pushed out of Southwold harbour at the top of the tide, and quanted down to Lowestoft on the ebb. They had to keep close inshore all the way so the quants could reach the bottom, and were finally run up the beach at Lowestoft and sold as they lay.

Only one more wherry ever passed between the Southwold pierheads, and that was the *Star*, of Oulton Broad. She was bought by Fred G. Lambert, a Halesworth man connected with the Blanden family, who believed, even in the early years of this century, that a wherry could still be made to pay on the Blyth. He always had a soft spot for the Navigation and hated to see it growing more and more derelict. So he bought the *Star* from Everitt, of Oulton Broad, and started trading with coal from the odd vessel putting into Southwold.

He worked up as far as Blythburgh, then set to repairing Bulcamp lock, and took the *Star* through Blyford bridge right up to Wenhaston. He estimated a thousand pounds would have got the whole navigation working again, but no one was interested in putting up the money.

But Lambert busied himself in the stretches that were navigable till, in 1911, he saw it was hopeless. One morning, with the mists swirling in from the sea, he quanted the little *Star* up to the hard at Walberswick; there he left her to be broken up.

The black sail had been lowered for the last time and trade on the Blyth was over.

CHAPTER SEVEN

Blue Water Wherries and Far-away Havens

Coasting wherries—the cunning of 'Rattler' Kemp—colliers, grain ships and timber barques—a bold venture—taking precautions—the North of Europe Steam Navigation Company and the City of Norwich—*salt water for four—down Channel—arrival at Portsmouth—work in strange places—safe return.*

There was never the same concern years ago about what constituted a seagoing ship as there is today. Our distant ancestors rowed skin-covered boats across the Channel and never thought for one moment they were unseaworthy. If half a coconut shell can drift safely across the Atlantic, then the smallest craft need take no harm, even in bad weather, unless it be through lack of sea-room. Slocum, in the *Spray*, showed what a small ship can survive.

Many of the old North Sea coasters were under a hundred tons burden, and vessels of fifty, forty or thirty tons were quite common. Nowadays, apart from being uneconomical, it is doubtful if they would ever be allowed to put to sea. The one concession these small ships made to bad weather was to lay up for the winter. There used to be tier upon tier of them at Yarmouth, with watchmen living aboard all the time to guard against fire.

By the beginning of last century, quite a few wherries were as big, if not bigger, than the ships they had to unload. But they would never have been considered fit to go to sea except for the need to lighten ships in the Roads. Had it not been for this work, wherries would never have been seen beyond the pier-heads.

As it was, their crews gained first-hand experience of open water, and from this grew the confidence to undertake coasting passages. Not every wherry went to sea, of course, but quite a few had a taste for salt water, and among their more stay-at-home companions rated as 'sea-timers' or 'blue-watermen'.

Many beautiful sea pieces were done by the Norwich School of painters and among them is one by Miles Edmund Cotman which shows wherries discharging a coaster in Yarmouth Roads. It is a lively scene packed with interest and we can see one wherry already alongside and another about to lower sail and join her. In the distance, on the right, a third can be made out just leaving harbour. This picture now hangs in the Norwich Castle Museum.

For a long time wherries could only go coasting to Southwold, but after the opening of Lowestoft harbour they often sailed there from Yarmouth. It was much quicker than going over Breydon, up the Waveney, along Oulton Dyke and across the broad. If freights were offering in Lowestoft, and wherries at Yarmouth were looking for jobs, they lost no time in putting to sea after them. They could do it in an hour and a half as against the best part of a day going inland.

The chief trade to Southwold was coke for the Halesworth malthouses, and bricks, which came mostly from Somerleyton. Sand and shingle often made up a return freight. These materials were always in demand for building, and for scouring floors, and when a wherry could get a load nowhere else, she sometimes went on the beach and shovelled a ton or two aboard between tides.

Billy Godison in the *Emerald*, and Charlie Clarke in the *Ruby*, did a lot of coke-carrying to Southwold, and 'Rattler' Kemp in the *Go Forward* was a regular visitor with bricks. The *Amelia*, sailed by John Mann, also went there with Somerleyton bricks and many a time made the passage to Lowestoft, by sea, from Yarmouth, for Lucas Bros., the building contractors.

On one occasion, Guinea Poole in the *Morton*, and Jimmy Shepherd in the *Volunteer*, earned themselves an extra pound or two running ice by sea from Yarmouth to Lowestoft. Oulton fresh-water broad was frozen solid and the smacks could get no supplies from the ice-house, so the *Morton* and *Volunteer* loaded up on Breydon and took round 60 tons. They did not sail, however, but were towed, no doubt because of the weather.

The *Lowestoft Trader*, although built at Yarmouth, was appropriately named, as she put in a lot of sea time trading there. The *Nil Desperandum* met with misfortune early in life and as a result made a forced passage to Southwold. Soon after launching she collided with a schooner in Oulton Dyke, and because her owner could not meet the claim that followed, the *Nil Desperandum* was sailed to Southwold and held for debt. In due course she was put up for sale and bought by Bull, the lime-burner of Oulton Broad. She then returned to her home waters.

However accustomed wherrymen got to being at sea there was always an element of adventure about their trips, and an experience that befell 'Rattler' Kemp and Billy Thaxter, in the *Go Forward*, shows the sort of thing that was always liable to happen.

The *Go Forward* was bound to Southwold with her usual cargo of bricks from Somerleyton, and it was beginning to get dark by the time they reached Gun Hill. Suddenly a hail came to them out of the gloom.

"Where are you for?" inquired a voice from a small boat Rattler could see dimly, coming off to them from the shore.

"Into the harbour," he shouted back.

"Then you'll have to take me aboard, I'm the pilot," answered the voice.

At this Rattler blew up. He had taken his wherry into Southwold enough times without needing anyone to show him the way, and he was damned if he was going to line the pockets of any good-for-nothing scoundrel out of his hard-earned freight money.

The argument became heated. Many matters fell under discussion and frequently embraced the ancestry of the disputants; and while the one persisted in contending his services were required by law, the other, with equal determination, swore that the *Go Forward* would be the exception to any such tommy-rot rule.

I cannot say with what choice epithets this verbal contest ended. All I know is that with ill-concealed disgust Rattler put the wherry about, and stood back to Lowestoft.

By now it was quite dark, and there was nothing the would-be pilot could do but pull back to the beach, consoling himself on the way, perhaps, with the thought, that if he had been dished of a job, the wherry had been done out of a useful freight. If they were his thoughts, then he was greatly underestimating his opponent.

For at first light in the morning, Rattler and Billy were gaily unloading their bricks on to Southwold quay, without a care in the world.

They say it's no good getting old if you don't get crafty, and Rattler certainly had not made that mistake. As soon as they had given the pilot the slip, he came about once more, edged along the coast, and quietly felt his way into harbour. It was all done in the dark, of course, and lesser mortals might well have hesitated to get in with a rowing-boat. But his favourite saying was: "If there's water, I reckon she'll go." And she did, as a very chastened pilot discovered when he came on the quay later that morning.

Rattler was skipper of the *Go Forward* for close on twenty years, and always kept her looking smart and trim. She was built at Yarmouth and launched on 12 July, 1898, with a feature which distinguished her from all other craft on the river, a beautifully fitted cabin in the finest mahogany. She carried about 27 tons, and is still afloat, though stripped of her gear, and working as a mud hulk.

In those days, the seas about our coasts were not so bare and desolate, so devoid of shipping, as they are today. When wherries poked their noses out of harbour they sailed in company with a throng of vessels, brigs, brigantines, schooners, barques; whole fleets weaving their way through the treacherous shoals, up to London and down to Newcastle; colliers, grain ships and timber barques passed by in their hundreds; out from Yarmouth and Lowestoft came the brown-sailed smacks and the swift, three-masted yawls; cheeky little shrimp boats added to the scene, sporting topsails, bowsprits and foresails, and from every beach, between Aldeburgh and Sheringham, punts, skiffs and doblers were off shooting long-lines, or dragging heavy beam-trawls, over the sole grounds close inshore.

At that time, when craft like these, of every shape, size and rig, were at sea doing a useful job of work, there was nothing remarkable in the idea of sending Norfolk wherries to Portsmouth. When Lucas Bros. decided they would be useful in helping to build Gosport Barracks, they obviously saw no particular difficulty in getting them there.

But what the wherrymen thought about such a long trip, with the prospect of working in strange, tidal waters, I do not know. Perhaps the extra pay was an incentive, but most likely they looked forward to the whole thing as a bit of an adventure and a welcome change from the ordinary routine.

Lucas Bros. were an enterprising firm. They put up hundreds of houses in the modern parts of Lowestoft, built York railway station, part of Liverpool Street station, and fulfilled a number of important contracts abroad. Having got the job at Gosport they wanted to lose no time making a start, though their great problem was getting materials to the site. They had to be fetched from as far away as Langston, Southampton and the Isle of Wight, and that is what they wanted wherries for.

The interesting thing is that wherries were already at Portsmouth, though of quite different build and rig to the Norfolk variety. They were used mostly for taking provisions to the anchored warships at Spithead. They were steered with yoke and rudder-lines, were undecked, clinker-built, double-ended, and carried two spritsails and a foresail.

There were also the cargo-carriers proper, Cowes ketches, or Solent barges as they were called, double-ended, but carvel-built. They had almost flat floors, rather resembling Humber keels, though smaller, and without being quite so bluff, either fore or aft. They were decked for about two-thirds their length, and ketched-rigged.

It is a little hard to understand why Lucas Bros. did not use them as they were all ready to hand. It may have been they were too expensive, or else drew too much water, though I think they much preferred having their own fleet they could do what they liked with. It made them independent of the local watermen who, apart from anything else, may well have resented an important contract like this going to a firm from away.

For the most part, I feel sure, the wherrymen took this trip in their stride, though one or two precautions were obviously necessary. First and foremost, they almost certainly rigged temporary shrouds. A great fear of all wherrymen at sea is that the mast may jump the tabernacle and go through the bottom. It is only resting on a pin, and should it come adrift in short, choppy seas, there is nothing to stop it. Shrouds, therefore, kept really taut, were the best guarantee against such an accident.

They also needed an anchor, probably shackled to the dropping chains, a compass, some extra fenders, and a place for port and starboard lights. But that was about all, apart from an extra keg of water and a few additions to the food locker.

Eight craft were selected, to sail in two groups of four. The first group, comprising the *Mahala*, 24 tons; the *Carrow*, 35 tons; the *Accommodation*, 36 tons; and the *Number One*, 45 tons, was assembled at Lowestoft, in March 1857. Decked out in fresh paint, with newly-dressed sails and well-oiled masts, these adventurers stood by waiting for a favourable wind.

I doubt if they aroused very much interest for all their trim appearance. At the time, Lowestoft was alive with ships of every kind, and had only lately become the terminus of a fleet of paddle-steamers starting a regular service between England and Denmark. Its aim was to foster trade in live cattle between the two countries and began running in 1851. By 1857, the year we are considering, it was in full swing and operating specially constructed cattle steamers.

The instigator of this ambitious project was Samuel Morton Peto, partner in the firm which built the Houses of Parliament, Clerkenwell Prison, Hungerford Market and the Lyceum Theatre. Peto, by acting as guarantor for a sum of £50,000, made possible the Great Exhibition of 1851, and the building of the Crystal Palace. Four years later, during the Crimean War, one of his ships, the *Leipsig*, took out locomotives, waggons, drivers, smiths and materials for building a railway from Balaclava to the front. For this service he was made a baronet, and he also represented Norwich in Parliament.

Lowestoft harbour was in the doldrums until Peto bought it, in 1844. He immediately launched a company, with a capital of £200,000, and in a few years put it on its feet. In 1857 it was used by 780 vessels, with a gross registered tonnage of 53,980, while another 584 entered, either for refuge or repair.

Having got the harbour going, Peto set about attracting some of the continental trade to Lowestoft. He did this with his North of Europe Steam Navigation Company. It took over the Hanseatic Company together with two of its vessels, the *Hamburg* and *Leipsig*, trading between Grimsby and Hamburg. Three other vessels, the *Cumberland*, *Jupiter* and *Royal Victoria*, started a service from Lowestoft to Denmark.

From the beginning the emphasis was on the cattle trade, though passengers and dairy produce were also catered for. An account appearing about this time may be worth quoting to show the general enthusiasm for the new venture. In the *Illustrated Guide Book to Lowestoft*, published in 1854, we read:

> Only a short time has elapsed since oxen became an article of commerce to any extent from abroad. Yet so rapid has been its increase that it now forms one of the principal freights for steamships from the north of Europe to England. And when the nature of the cargo is considered, it becomes no longer a matter of surprise that it should be thought advisable to construct a vessel expressly for its conveyance, and at the same time make such arrangements for passengers as would secure them from any annoyance from the cattle. All this has been done in the *City of Norwich*, for no cattle are carried on the upper deck occupied by passengers.
>
> At first it was thought sufficient to employ old and worn out vessels, very inferior in capacity and speed, for the voyage they had to perform or the freight they had to carry. But a very short experience was sufficient to show that this was a most unprofitable mode of proceeding, for not only did it frequently happen that a large number of cattle were lost or died upon the voyage, but the remaining portion were in so bad a state as to be of very small value in the market.
>
> From this cause, also, arose the great prejudice against foreign cattle which frequently became diseased from the long endurance, close confinement and injury received in the hold of a small vessel.
>
> Self policy, as well as humanity, soon improved the mode of conveyance, and larger and faster vessels were employed. Now, for the first time, a vessel has been built expressly to carry cattle, of such capacity and speed as to ensure both their comfort, safety and rapid transit.
>
> The *City of Norwich* is 700 tons and 200 h.p., and was built by Messrs. Wingate and Company of Glasgow for the Northern Steam Packet Company of which S. M. Peto, Esq., is Chairman. And through the liberal policy and clear foresight of this gentleman, ably seconded and carried out by Captain Andrews, the Managing Director of the Company and harbour master at Lowestoft, the public are indebted for this great improvement in the mode of bringing this very necessary article of food safely and cheaply to this country.
>
> Nor is this a trifling advantage when it is considered that cheap and good meat is almost as important as cheap bread. And it is the opinion of those most conversant with the subject that without our imports of foreign cattle beef, at this moment, would be at least a shilling a pound in the metropolis.
>
> Like the greater part of modern steam vessels, the *City of Norwich* is

constructed of iron, and propelled by two engines on the direct action principle, occupying very little space and making thirty-two revolutions per minute. She has tubular boilers, and patent feathering paddles of beautiful construction and great strength. She has three decks, on the lower of which only the cattle are stowed, no cattle being placed in the hold or on the upper deck.

The between decks are seven feet six inches high and are fitted with stalls and ventilated by means of side ports, as well as large hatchways running fore and aft. By these means a perfect system of ventilation is kept up and the cattle kept cool and comfortable as well as protected from the weather. Large water tanks for the supply of fresh water are fitted in the holds as also stowage for hay and fodder.

Proper men are employed to feed and attend the cattle, independent of the crew, and arrangements are made by which the cattle all walk on board and down below without being slung or lowered down. The ship carries 250 head of oxen between decks, besides having room for 500 sheep on the upper deck if required, and stows 150 tons of heavy goods in the lower hold.

Notwithstanding her comparatively small horse-power for her tonnage, the vessel is of extraordinary speed, averaging 12 knots. On her first voyage from Lowestoft to the Eider she ran the distance, 288 miles, in 24 hours. She is remarkably stiff and steady at sea and a first-rate sea boat.

The *City of Norwich* was a good-looking ship, with an impressive clipper bow, figurehead, and bowsprit. Unlike her sisters, she crossed no yards, but could set useful fore-and-aft sails on her two masts, besides two large head sails. These vessels must have done their job well for the account continues:

It is gratifying to be able to state that the success anticipated, and justly merited, in this spirited undertaking has been fully realized, notwithstanding the difficulties of opening out an entirely new trade from a new port, to what may be called to us an entire new country.

Between April and December 1851, these vessels brought from Denmark, and landed at Lowestoft, 46 passengers, 49 horses, 7,661 oxen, 3,347 sheep, 694 pigs, 818 casks of butter, 976 quarters of oats, besides goods and merchandise of a general character.

These steamers have all excellent accommodation for passengers who are only one night at sea, a great desideratum to the majority of travellers unaccustomed to the motion of a ship. Notwithstanding these great advantages the fares are moderate. A first-class passenger is conveyed from London to Lowestoft in a first-class carriage, and from Lowestoft to Denmark in the chief cabin, for £2 10s.; a second-class passenger for £2; and a third-class passenger £1.

The packets leave Lowestoft every Saturday and commence to run in March to Ballum and Hjerting alternatively. These two ports are situated on the west coast of Jutland and are distant from each other about forty English miles. From these ports across the peninsular of Jutland to the east coast the distance is, from Hjerting forty miles, and from Ballum only twenty-eight miles. This is the narrowest part of the isthmus dividing Jutland from Schleswig and Holstein.

Passing as it does large and safe ports on both sides, viz, Ballum on the west and Apenrade on the east, with a rich, level and well drained country between, this is undoubtedly the most eligible line for a railway to connect the German Ocean with the Cattegat, the Sound and the Baltic Sea.

Cattle arriving by sea were usually in the London markets within a few hours of coming off the ship. Not all the beasts went straight to market, however, many were first put out to graze on nearby marshes, where they spent a few weeks fattening up. On boat day, when the streams of oxen, horses, sheep and pigs came pouring down the gangways, Lowestoft looked more like a market town than a fishing port. There were animals everywhere, in the pens, on the quayside, in the adjoining streets, with a motley crowd of drovers and yelping dogs wrestling to get their charges under control.

This new traffic was of immense benefit to the town and one is reminded of it even now by names like Denmark Road, Tonning Street and Flensburg Street.

The link between the two countries by way of Lowestoft lasted for ten years or so, then it gradually passed to Harwich, the route most people take today. But the harbour continued in constant use by coasters, colliers, timber and grain ships, besides its own considerable fleet of drifters and trawlers.

So amid all the shipping in Lowestoft that Sunday morning, in March 1857, a few people only may have paused to watch the four wherries quietly slip their moorings and head out through the pierheads.

Conditions were perfect; a handsome, whole-sail breeze from the north-west, with a little swell but no broken water. For the first dozen miles they were on familiar ground. They kept close in past Pakefield and Kessingland, rounded Benacre Ness, and bringing Southwold lighthouse abeam, passed into Sole Bay. Here were historic waters and no mistake for wherries to be; where Dutch and English battled it out nearly two centuries before. But as they pushed on towards Dunwich they, too, were making history; they had gone further south than any wherry before them. The red bunting at the mastheads of the *Mahala*, the *Carrow*, the *Accommodation* and the *Number One* was blazing a new trail as they pressed on towards Orford.

The 'admiral' of the group appears to have been Martin Wigg, skipper of the *Mahala*. Although she was the smallest of the four she had the largest crew, because the skipper brought not only his mate, but Mrs. Wigg, their young son Martin, and their daughter Elizabeth, just three months old. Martin, junior lived to a great age, and as recently as 1930 retained the most vivid memories of the whole journey.

They soon put Orford light astern and with the wind freshening made short work of the remaining miles to Harwich. Here they were due to pick up pilots, and they arrived in time to have tea and put the baby to sleep in daylight. The wind got up during the night and blew hard throughout the Monday, Tuesday, Wednesday and Thursday. But they had snug berths and were content to let it blow itself out.

Things quietened down by Thursday evening and the pilots came aboard. It was agreed to make a start at first light if the weather continued to improve.

The young Elizabeth slept soundly, and was still asleep, when her father, the mate and the pilot, each with a scalding mug of tea, went on deck for a look round. It could not have been better; the sea had gone down and a steady breeze was coming out of the north-north-west, and looking as if it would hold.

Within the hour they had all left Landguard point astern and were out in the Rolling Grounds romping away to the southward. The north wind served them well on the long stretch over to the North Foreland when they had the experience no wherry had ever had before, of being out of sight of land. But their pilots knew the way all right and soon after midday they rounded the North Foreland.

Running through the Downs things were just to their liking with a smooth sea and a fine blow on the quarter. By tea-time they were abreast of Dungeness, and with the wind as it was they shipped their tall chimneys and stoked up a good fire. The keen air put an edge on their appetites and everyone, especially young Martin, did ample justice to the Essex beef and Harwich cod.

The baby Elizabeth needed no rocking. The gentle motion of the *Mahala* did all that was required and she lay blissfully content, curled up in her bunk, while her father and the pilot stood in the sternsheets watching Beachey Head light over the starboard bow. It was leading the *Mahala* and her companions into the pages of the history books.

For as they sailed down Channel, in company with the sturdy East Indiamen, the tall clippers, and the many other aristocrats of the London river; with darkness already upon them and only winking, unfamiliar lights for guide, they became the first wherries ever to make a sea-passage by night, and the first to taste salt-water so far from home.

Yet being the men they were, I doubt if they gave it a thought. For them it was just another job of work. Their orders were to sail to Portsmouth, and sail there they would if the pilots knew the way.

On they sailed through the darkness, invisible almost with their black hulls and black sails. But the skippers' eyes were good and they kept together. Midnight came and Beachey Head was astern. In the early hours of Saturday morning the wind fell away and dawn found them still to the east of Selsey Bill. But it rose again with the sun and they bowled along manfully.

And then, within sight of her destination, disaster overtook the *Accommodation*. She was seen to be having difficulty with her steering, and started falling away to leeward, towards the Isle of Wight. It seemed to her companions she had lost her rudder, and this was confirmed soon after when they saw her drive on the beach. Fortunately, the sea was not rough and her crew managed to jump to safety; but the wherry was doomed and eventually became a total loss. She was the first, and last, of her kind to be wrecked at sea, and the accident naturally put a damper on things. But after making sure everyone was safe, the others stood across for Portsmouth and entered harbour during the forenoon.

Lucas Bros. were not deterred at losing the *Accommodation* and four months later, in July, assembled another four craft at Lowestoft. They were the *Star*, 28 tons; the *Dahlia*, 30 tons; the *Wellington*, 36 tons; and the *Norfolk Hero*, 40 tons. This time they met with no trouble of any kind and all reached Portsmouth safely.

Their work entailed quite a lot of sailing in open water, and, wherever possible, this was given to the largest craft, *Number One*, *Norfolk Hero* and *Wellington*. Martin Wigg and his family transferred to the *Number One*, while John Mann sailed the *Wellington*, which he had brought from Lowestoft.

One of the main jobs was fetching breeze and sand from Southampton and Langston, though there were endless trips across to Cowes, and up the river to Newport, after cement. They were kept hard at it for more than a year and amply justified the confidence of the contractors. They ran into no trouble, and once the crews had accustomed themselves to the new conditions, proved just as good as the local men.

By the summer of 1858 most of their work was finished and it was time to think about going home. They had done all they had been sent to do and everyone was looking forward now to returning to their own waters. But the *Carrow* and *Norfolk Hero* never returned. They were sold at Portsmouth and went on working there for a time, until they went round to end their days on the Thames. What they did there nobody seems to know exactly, but I believe they were actually trading for a while.

The *Wellington* and the *Star* were the first to leave, and picking their weather, got back to Lowestoft without incident. That left the *Mahala*, *Dahlia* and *Number One*, and they found plenty to do until the end of September. Then, with the days drawing in and bad weather not far round the corner, Lucas Bros. decided it was time for them to be getting away too. So all three had a good scrub out, looked to their gear, and stood by for a south-west wind.

Soon they were hoisting their black sails for the last time in Portsmouth harbour, and taking final leave of the great men-o'-war, bore away to the east, homeward bound. The trip was planned in three legs, with calls at Newhaven and Harwich, but as things turned out they only visited Newhaven. They put in there the first night, but as the wind still held south-west, were away early the next morning.

The young Elizabeth was now a toddler and needed careful watching, while the boy Martin reckoned himself a fully-grown shellback after his year on the south coast. But it was not so cramped in the *Number One* as it had been in the *Mahala*, they had a bit more room to stretch their legs. And with fine warm weather they were able to sit up on deck and watch the wonderful array of shipping all round them. The Downs were packed with outward-bounders, held up by the wind serving them so well, and they sped through the anchored fleet with a bone in their teeth.

Rounding the Foreland they shaped a course for Harwich intending to spend the night there; but all the way over the wind kept veering and was a little north of west by the time they got there. So to make sure of their passage while the going was good they carried on for Lowestoft and arrived there in the early hours of the morning.

If they attracted little attention when they left, they attracted even less on their return. It was still dark and the Lowestoft folk were all abed; the crews of the luggers slept hard; small whisps of steam climbing into the night sky from Morton Peto's cattle boats, and the circling beam of the lighthouse, were the only signs of life.

The four wherries went to their accustomed moorings and their tired but smiling crews stowed the sails and had a brief mardle. Then they went below to finish the trip in the only way possible—with mugs of steaming hot tea round the cabin stove.

And the little craft rubbed shoulders with the familiar quayside as if they, too, were glad to be home.

CHAPTER EIGHT

Clippers of the Tideway

The glory of the Fawn—*fireside yarning—village greens and homely fun—a boaster laid low—early regattas and races—wherries compete at sea—'things of beauty'—famous names—new champions—a casualty at sea—enough beer to float a battleship—some stirring contests—overboard on Breydon—no surrender of traditions.*

"Well, there I was, giving the little old *Fawn* a mop down and a tidy up, when this strapping great bloke appears on the quayside. I could tell he was a fisherman by his duffle trousers, blue slop and seal-skin hat. Real powerful chap he was, too, and I remember thinking how small that clay pipe of his looked in his mouth, bit like a baby's dummy, if you understand me.

"He stood there for a minute of two, as if he was sizing the *Fawn* up in his mind. I don't think he missed a thing about her. His eagle eyes passed slowly from stem to rudder, from tabernacle to masthead, where they lingered a while, then down again till they came to rest on me. He gazed at me for what seemed like an age, then he spoke.

" 'Is your skipper aboard?'

" 'Yes,' I answered, a bit nervously, wondering what was up, 'he's in the cabin having a mug of tea.'

" 'Then tell him I'd like a word with him, will you?'

"I glanced at him, imagining all manner of terrible things, and then I thought I saw a twinkle come into those clear, almost sky-blue, eyes of his.

" 'Perhaps you'd like to come aboard,' I answered, with a sort of sinking feeling in my stomach, but putting my foot on the bottom rung of the ladder to steady it for him.

"Despite his size he was as nimble as a cat. As soon as he had joined me on the hatches I went aft to call my father. The cabin was as thick as a smugglers' den with tobacco smoke, and from the merry yarn-spinning I caught snatches of it seemed as if a little something had been added to the tea by way of celebration.

"And, mark you, there really was something to celebrate. You see, the *Fawn* had just won another race in the Roads, and done it handsomely, too, showing the *Beaconsfield* a clean pair of heels.

"Needless to say my father, Ophir, was in charge of her, and that's what counted. Never was another man like him, he could get more out of a wherry than what was in her, if you get my meaning. Once he took hold of the tiller you felt nothing was going to beat the *Fawn*, and nothing usually did either. Real master hand he was, and anyone you meet who remembers him will tell you the same.

"But as I was saying, there was this big old fisherman fellow waiting to speak to my father, so I braved the tobacco smoke and poked my head into the cabin, telling him someone wanted to speak to him.

"He appeared at last out of the haze, and the fisherman ambled along the plankway to meet him. He stopped when he was a few paces away, and looked my father up and down, just as he'd done with the *Fawn* a few minutes earlier.

"'Are you the *Fawn*'s skipper?' he asked, after what I thought was a long, and rather ominous, pause. And yet I could have sworn those wonderful blue eyes had got something near a twinkle in them.

"'That's right, old partner,' answered my father, 'and what can I do for you?'

"'What can you do? You've done it already, master,' said the fisherman, 'what no one did afore, and won't do again, if I know anything about it.'

"'And what might that be,' inquired my father, very puzzled, and at a loss to understand what the other was talking about.

"'I reckon you know well enough,' he said, giving his clay a dexterous flick of the tongue which sent it neatly across to the other corner of his mouth, 'but if you don't, then I'll take the liberty of reminding you.'

"My father looked very uncomfortable at this, and seemed about to suggest a drop of something from the cabin to placate the visitor, when he continued, 'it's about this morning I'm referring to, when we were

Green, Bungay

Jack Powley, *Albion*'s skipper for more than twenty years from 1900

Ophir Powley, skipper of the *Fawn*

George Farrow, *Albion*'s skipper, 1939

Elizabeth and *Dora* racing on Wroxham Broad

both of us off racing, reaching for the north buoy. They started the wherries just before the smacks finished, remember?'

" 'Of course I remember, tidy mess there was, too, and no mistake. Why, soon after we got away, we got properly boxed in and the *Fawn* here had to put her best foot forward to get clear of one of you fellows before we could start racing, as you might say.'

" 'I know she did, and I'm the one you went by. But I didn't like the way you did it, no, not by a long chalk I didn't.'

" 'Come now! There was nothing unfair about it, was there?'

" 'No, there wasn't. Nothing unfair about it at all. But when I'm close-hauled, pinching her as close to the wind as she'll go, I don't like a craft that comes up astern, and because she can't get by windward, just slips through my lee, and still fetches the mark I've been making for. You're a sailor, you'll know how I felt. Wondered if I was sailing a ship or a haystack.'

"At this, a wide, mischievous grin spread all over my father's face. Then the smacksman smiled, too, and this time there was no mistaking the twinkle in those wonderful sky-blue eyes.

" 'But even though I didn't like it, I've come along for the pleasure of shaking hands with the man who can play me such a trick,' and so saying, he stretched out his massive arm, and the two of them shook hands, my father, as I could see, very moved by this altogether unexpected compliment. Because, as you know, there wasn't much you could teach a smacksman about handling a ship.

"Well, my father put his free hand on the other's shoulder and nodded aft. They moved off towards the cabin like bosom pals, and then I got on with my mopping-down and tidying-up."

Albert Powley, who had been telling me this yarn, chuckled happily as we sat round his fire. It had all happened sixty years ago, but to him it was just like yesterday.

Mrs. Powley poured us out some more tea and handed round the buns. The wind whipped over the houses on Cobholm Island, where we were, straight off the Breydon flats, and the sound of it in the chimney seemed to conjure up a wealth of memories for Albert.

It was only natural the swift, incomparable little *Fawn* should have taken pride of place in his recollections. She became a legend, along with her famous skipper, Ophir Powley, for her record in the various regattas, at sea and on the broads, had no equal.

The *Fawn* was built by Charles Hall, of Reedham, to the order of his close neighbour, I. J. Wales, the timber merchant. She was launched in 1875. Ophir Powley took her new, and stayed in her till 1896, when he went in the *Olga*. The *Fawn* carried 25 tons and did a lot of work with big logs as well as deals. On one occasion, using her own gear, she loaded a butt weighing seven tons.

She also carried a great many bricks to Yarmouth and a lot of these went into the alterations then being made to the Aquarium. Many a time she left Reedham at midday, did the eight miles to Yarmouth on the last of the ebb, unloaded at Stonecutters' Quay, and sailed back to Reedham in time for a six o'clock tea.

Wales handled the usual builders' supplies beside timber and his wherries were always busy delivering tiles, drain-pipes, billet-wood, barrel staves, fish-trunk ends, pea sticks, hurdles, beams for trawl nets, shruff and wood chips.

The skippers' boys generally had a treat when the wood chips went away as they were bound for the military camp on Yarmouth South Denes. It was an annual occasion and the chips were used for making trench fires. As it usually coincided with the Yarmouth Races it proved a great attraction for the youngsters who were sent ashore to enjoy themselves for the rest of the day after doing no more than a token amount of discharging.

It must be remembered there was very little organized entertainment as we know it now. Firstly, with wages barely enough to buy food, shelter and clothing, people could not afford it, and secondly, they had the ability, now almost lost, of being able to make their own amusements. The maypole, dancing on the green, the harvest-home, Christmas and other festivities, all grew out of the lives of the people and everyone took part in them as a matter of course. In the games, songs, dances, trials of strength and skill, everybody did something, and because of this participation instead of merely looking on, found them that much more rewarding.

The merrymakings in swept-out barns and on the village green had their counterparts in the frolics on the water. The word 'frolic' aptly describes these aquatic occasions, when the riverside dwellers and the watermen took advantage of the summer sun to bare their bodies and sport about in river and broad. They could do it then because the water was clean and wholesome.

These goings-on no doubt originated from some form of pagan ritual, but latterly they became no more than an excuse for some good, honest fun, and to let off a little steam. Swimming and diving contests were always in the bill, along with mock sea-battles in various improvised craft, while pillow-fights, waged with great vigour and no little dexterity, on swaying, greasy poles over the water, appealed to every lad in the village. Sculling and sailing matches were gradually added to the programmes and as time went on became the chief attractions.

They were confined at first to boats entered by the local gentry and some of these, a couple of hundred years ago, were most elaborate affairs. One was put up for sale at Crostwick Hall, in September 1751, which had 'a cabin with ten windows, plate glass, and door the same, a mast and three pairs of oars 18 feet long, one small pleasure boat used in attendance, and a tent.'

Another came on the market in 1756, 'a boat about three years old, 21 feet long, and well built for sailing and standing to the wind. There is a large sprit-sail, stay-sail and jib-sail, a suit of colours with convenience for stowing, a plenty of stores, two pairs of oars, and six small brass guns, all in good order . . .'

The guns, no doubt enabled the owner to participate in the mock battles already mentioned and which were then quite the rage. A notice dated 20 July, 1772, informed all and sundry of a 'Water Frolic on Hickling with a representation of a sea fight. And gentlemen can enter themselves or their boats.'

Back in 1732 there was a very different kind of contest arising out of professional rivalry between two boat-builders. It was sparked off when Richard Lifton, of Gillingham near Beccles, challenged any other boat on the three rivers to row against his own *Fancy*. The sting was in his boast that he had never been apprenticed, was entirely self-taught, but could still build boats as good, or better, than proper tradesmen could. Such a claim amounted then almost to blasphemy and his challenge was soon accepted by the men of Norwich. There were four to a boat, and the race was rowed one November day, from Beccles.

The result is best given in the words of the victors, as it subsequently appeared in a local paper:

> Whereas Mr. Lifton of Gillingham had the strange imagination to advertise that he continued his resolution to row his boat *Fancy* against any other on the three streams leading to Yarmouth; this is to inform the public that on Friday fortnight four Norwich wherrymen did undertake, with Mr. Watts the Dyer's boat, to row against the above incomparable machine. And though Lifton's *Fancy* was supported by a great many boasted and pretended advantages, and several little methods were used that *Fancy* might keep her credit, yet to the great dishonour of the Gillingham artist, and to convince him that *Fancy* is deceitful, the Norwich boat won the wager by a considerable number of miles and left the poor losers time to form some lame excuses for their present shameful defeat and former presumption.

The contestants were, in fact, passenger-carrying wherries, with mast, sail and tilt removed for the occasion, and this was the first wherry race as such of which I can find mention. It was not until about 1870 that sailing wherry races became established, but thereafter they gained steadily in popularity and usually provided the race of the day.

Barton, Oulton Broad, Wroxham and Burgh Castle staged the four most important inland regattas, though the really testing courses were those at sea in the Marine Regattas at Yarmouth, Gorleston and Lowestoft. The Yarmouth Marine Regatta dates back at least to 1828, when powerful, three-masted luggers, setting enormous topsails on each mast, raced in the Roads. There was no match for wherries, however, until 1882. Lowestoft followed with one the following year and Gorleston in 1885.

These early wherry races at sea created great interest because of the smart way each craft was handled and the speed at which they sailed. The wherrymen enjoyed them, too, and there were always big entries. No less than ten came to the line at Lowestoft in 1883, and the same year at Yarmouth there were eight. In 1884 nine turned up at Lowestoft, but for the first match at Gorleston the year following there were only four starters.

The real novelty was in seeing so many wherries at sea all at once, and onlookers gathered in their thousands to watch the progress of the races. Weather conditions dictated the course, though it was always a square or triangular one four to fives miles long, sailed three or four times.

Every craft carried a big crew so there was no problem in handling the extra sails borrowed specially for the event. Some very fast times were returned. At Yarmouth, in 1889, there were three competitors, the *Martham Trader*, *Beaconsfield* and *Fawn*, and they started at 12.30 p.m. to sail a 24-miles course. After a dingdong struggle the *Fawn* took the winning gun at 2.45 p.m., 2 hours 16 minutes for the distance, giving a speed of 9·2 knots.

A race was usually worth £20, the winner taking £10, second £5, third £3 and fourth £2. But no fourth prize was awarded unless five started, no third unless four started, and it took three to make a race.

During the twenty years or so these races continued, entries were confined to quite a small number of wherries, though they were the pick of those afloat. In all this time only fifteen names appear at Yarmouth, and twenty-two at Lowestoft. It was, of course, for the owners to decide whether their craft took part, and while some, like Wales, of Reedham, were enthusiastic and enjoyed a hard-sailed race, others were just the reverse and grudged the lick of paint to smarten them up. They also grudged the loss of freight money while they were being got ready.

As an instance of how keen Wales was, whenever a wherry of his was competing the skipper had to take a basket of pigeons with him and release one at the completion of each round. He wrote out a message giving his position and within a quarter of an hour everybody in Reedham knew how the *Fawn* or the *Olga* was getting on.

In the last few weeks before the races enthusiasm mounted steadily, with arguments in every pub about the merits of this or that craft and the skills of the various skippers. There was plenty of bragging and boasting going on, often enough with wagers laid to give substance to the views expressed. I suspect the following verse had its origin in some such occasion:

> When the gun it was fired for the wherries to start.
> The swift little *Fawn* she was off like a dart;
> Then soon she got out her long spinnaker boom,
> And the sea on the beaches was all of a foam.

> Now the *Fawn* from her masthead she flies the cup colour,
> Which stops all the cackle of Barber and Muller.

No wherry went to the starting line looking anything but her best; the pride each crew took in their craft can be likened to that of the old-time railway driver for his locomotive. The hours they spent scraping, painting, polishing, overhauling gear, oiling blocks and all the rest of it, were never entered on a time sheet; old wherrymen would have laughed at the idea of getting paid for this sort of thing. They had a keen sense of their duties and responsibilities, and high up on the list was the keeping of their charges in first-rate trim. There were plenty of exceptions, of course, men who could not bother to do more than the bare essentials; they kept going only until their craft dropped to pieces under them. But they were wherrymen in name only, the black sheep which exist in every family.

When a wherry like the *Fawn* sailed out of harbour to race she was in every way a thing of beauty; from the fiery red bunting at her masthead and the rich, freshly-dressed black sail, to the dazzling vermilion hatches and glittering tarred hull. The owner spent a few pounds having her hauled out, scraped and tarred, but it was the crew who attended to all the finer details. They dressed the sail, painted blocks and fore-stay, rudder-head and tiller, spen wires and winch, they rove the new sheet and the new halliard, refurbished the vane with enamel and goldleaf, sewed on the new bunting, and, often as not, got down to the back-aching job of polishing the bottom with black-lead.

Mrs. Powley put another shovelful of coal on the fire. Albert leaned forward rubbing his hands in the warmth of the leaping flames.

"Yes," he said, with a note of genuine pride in his voice, "on race days the wherries were really something to write home about, and I believe people enjoyed seeing them more than the other craft. For one thing it was a treat to see all those black sails out at sea, six, seven or eight of them at a time, and for another, well, I think we used to give them value for money.

"And when we started running up foresails and topsails, that really set tongues awagging because we never had them except for racing. Very often there was more wind than we wanted and we couldn't use them, but they were always on board, just in case.

"It was only at sea you were allowed these extra sails; everywhere else you had to be content with your workaday rig. On the broads, too, you started different, sail down on deck and lying to a sinker thrown over the bows. When the gun went there wasn't half some fun seeing who would be first up, I can tell you. Those that weren't hoisting got the sinker in, walking aft all the time to try and give her a bit of a spring ahead.

"One year at sea, Yarmouth I think it was, 1883, a start was tried like this, with sails down, but apart from that once we always had a flying start at sea."

Albert recalled many an exciting match as we sat comfortably round his fire, with the wind piping mournful tunes round the gable-ends, and Mrs. Powley in ever-watchful attendance with teapot and home-made buns. And while he never tired of singing the *Fawn*'s praises, he readily admitted she had some worthy opponents over the years.

Her greatest rival, I learned, was the *Beaconsfield*. They met at Yarmouth four years running, from 1886 to 1889; the first year *Fawn* won with *Beaconsfield* fourth; the second year *Beaconsfield* won with *Fawn* a close second; the third and fourth years *Fawn* was the winner and *Beaconsfield* second.

At Gorleston they met five times running, from 1885 to 1889, when the *Beaconsfield* was much more successful, winning four times to the *Fawn*'s once. In the second race, however, *Fawn* had to retire with a broken gaff when leading by a distance.

But at Lowestoft the *Fawn* was supreme. She took part in every race from 1883 to 1888, and won all of them, even though she had the *Beaconsfield* against her in the last five. Yet this fine wherry was never beaten by much and took second place in the last three races. Altogether these rivals met fifteen times at sea and the final tally was ten wins for the *Fawn*, and five for the *Beaconsfield*.

No other names appear so regularly in the lists of competitors though over the years both had to meet the challenge of some very smart craft. The *Lowestoft Trader* provided strong opposition in the early races, and though never managing to win she always put up stout resistance. The *Volunteer, British Queen, Robert Alfred* and *Elizabeth* often competed, while the *Ellen, Martham Trader, Myth, Leonard, Alma* and *Lady Violet* now and again hoisted racing colours.

When racing at sea was drawing to an end, and the *Fawn* was getting on in years, the *Olga* and *Dora* came into their own. They shared between them the last four races at Lowestoft, each winning twice, while to *Dora* belongs the distinction of having won the last race at sea, in 1902, at Yarmouth.

The *Olga* was launched in May 1896, and the *Dora* in October 1897, from the same yard as the *Fawn*. Wales, of Reedham, who owned the *Fawn*, gave the order for the *Olga*, while the *Dora* belonged to W. C. Bunn, of Yarmouth.

There may be some truth in the saying that there is no sentiment in business; if so, then Wales was not a very good business man. He had any amount of sentiment when it came to wherries, and that alone explains how the race at Lowestoft, in 1896, came about.

It was sailed towards the end of August when the *Olga* had been in service only three months. Ophir Powley had taken her new, parting company with the *Fawn* to do it after twenty-one triumphant years. But the little veteran still had a Powley at the tiller, one of the old man's sons taking his place, so she was still in the family, so to speak. These were the only two that came out to race.

Up to then no craft had ever led the *Fawn* over the finishing line of a Lowestoft race, though the year before, 1895, she had been disqualified for rounding a buoy the wrong way. As the time for starting drew near excitement became intense among the spectators waiting eagerly on the front.

Here was a match to stir the imagination; the gallant, twenty-one year old *Fawn*, defending her reputation against her stable companion, the spanking new *Olga*, just down the ways. Would there be the same touch of magic in the new creation there was in the old? How would the *Fawn* get on without Ophir? Would his sons make the most of her?

These were the questions waiting to be answered; but would there be a race? Only the two of them had gone out but the rules stated clearly that three must start to make a race.

A hurried meeting of the committee was called. The atmosphere grew tense. Then a cheer went up, the rule had been waived.

It was a day made for the occasion with a handsome wind from the north-east. The course was a four-legged one, of a little over four miles, to be sailed four times. The *Olga* was slightly ahead at the gun, but the

Fawn soon picked up and for a while they ran together almost level. Then the *Fawn* got her nose in front and at the end of the first round led by 1 minute 5 seconds. Both wherries were beautifully handled and for all he was behind, old Ophir must have chuckled to himself not only at seeing the *Fawn* in her accustomed position, way out ahead, but how his sons were getting her along.

By the end of the second round the *Olga* had dropped behind 2 minutes 14 seconds, and although she picked up a little at the beginning of the third round, she finished it 2 minutes 36 seconds behind. At this point the *Fawn* appeared to have the race in her pocket and old-timers kept muttering that Ophir must be losing his touch or else the *Olga* was not as good as they had taken her to be.

But what happened in the last round made them whistle a different tune. Almost as if he was out to teach his sons a lesson, and anyone else as well for that matter, he went after the *Fawn* like a railway train, caught her, passed her, and took the gun with 2 minutes 2 seconds to spare. It was a great triumph for the Old Man and he got the reception he deserved when he came in. But the *Fawn*, too, got a big hand for her game struggle; the sons had certainly not disgraced their father.

For a long time afterwards there were arguments about whether the *Fawn* would have won if Ophir had been sailing her; but in the end it was generally agreed that giving away twenty-one years was just too much for her. Wales himself had very mixed feelings over the result. He was naturally pleased his new wherry had shown up so well, but he was sorry the *Fawn* had at last been vanquished. That is probably why he entered both of them again the next year at Lowestoft; he was anxious for her to turn the tables if she could.

For the 1898 event two others joined them, Bunn's *Dora*, from Yarmouth, and Walker's *Eudora*, from Bungay. But over a similar course it developed into a battle between the *Olga* and the *Dora*, which the former won by the narrow margin of 28 seconds. The *Fawn* was third, 2 minutes 37 seconds behind the *Dora*, no mean effort against two brand new craft.

Yet as she sailed back into harbour when it was all over, most people felt it was for the last time; that she would never be seen on salt-water again. And so it was. Wales knew he had a fine wherry in the *Olga* and was content to let the *Fawn* be remembered as she was in her prime. He never entered her to race again.

"But by then, of course, sea racing was almost finished," Albert reminded me. "There was no wherry event at Gorleston after 1892, though they tried to revive it in 1899. But after seven years it didn't arouse much interest and no one entered."

"What about Yarmouth and Lowestoft?" I inquired.

"Let me see, now. The last race at Lowestoft was in August 1901, when the *Dora*, *Maud* and *Bell* turned out. It was a walk-over for the *Dora*, came in twenty minutes ahead of the *Maud* while the *Bell* gave up. The *Dora* was a big, powerful wherry, with the longest gaff on the river, 40 feet 2 inches it was, bigger than the *Wonder*'s.

"She and the *Maud* sailed in the last race at Yarmouth the next year, 1902, and this time the *Maud* did much better and only lost by 2 minutes. That was the last of the races at sea, though they did try to arrange a match at Lowestoft the same year. Your own *Albion* was there, Jimmy Lacey was skipper of her then, and the *Maud* turned up as well, but there was some argument over prize-money and in the end the race was called off. A great pity that was because the *Albion* wasn't much more than three years old then and we all wanted to see what Jimmy Lacey would do in her. Good skipper he was, and he had a good mate, too, Jack Powley. I don't need to tell you that Jack went skipper in her himself soon after and had her for about twenty years. Funny thing, although his name was Powley, he was a different family to ours, and came from Bungay."

"Getting back to that last race at Lowestoft," I quizzed Albert, "weren't you mixed up in it yourself?"

A broad grin spread over Albert's face. He took a large red handkerchief from his pocket and gave his nose a fierce blow as if it was tickling him.

"Well, yes, I suppose I was. Happened to be skipper of the *Dora*, you see. And my old Dad, he had the *Maud*. So it was a proper father and son affair, though the old chap knew he didn't stand much of a chance. As I've told you, the *Dora* was a fine, powerful wherry."

"You didn't give him much chance either, did you, winning by twenty minutes," I said teasingly.

"Of course not!" said Albert chuckling, "had to show him I knew how to sail the blessed thing, didn't I?"

He finished polishing the tip of his nose with one or two circular movements of the handkerchief, and returned it to his pocket. He paused for a moment, gazing into the fire as if the glowing embers held for him a picture of that long-ago tussle with his father. I took the opportunity to fill my pipe and while I was lighting it heard him continue:

"But all this talk about the races ending shouldn't make us forget the exciting days we had before that. And there were some, I can tell you. Take the Lowestoft race of 1883, for instance, first time the *Fawn* entered there. That was a day and no mistake.

"Ten wherries turned up, about as many as ever were in a race so far as I recollect, and if you'd like to know their names I'll give them to you. Besides the *Fawn* there was the *Ellen, Leonard, Lowestoft Trader, Courier, Elizabeth, Ethel, Robert Alfred, British Queen* and *Myth*. With all that lot milling about at the start you needed eyes in the back of your head, but Dad soon got the *Fawn* clear of the others and won easily as it turned out, about five or six minutes ahead of the *Myth*. *Lowestoft Trader* was third.

"Now the *Ellen* in that race had some real bad luck the next year and got sunk. It happened as she and the *Robert Alfred* were beating to windward. Somehow they ran foul of each other and the poor little *Ellen* had most of her planking stove in on the port side. Needless to say, she went down like a log. The chaps in the *Robert Alfred* managed to fish out her crew and brought them back to harbour safe and sound.

"That all happened on the Thursday. By Saturday the tide had washed her in towards the beach, and in the evening they managed to haul her ashore. A proper wreck she was, too.

"But mark this! When the skipper scrambled aboard he made his way to the cabin, and there he found all his money and two watches! Bit of luck that was, though we never fathomed out why they hadn't been washed away.

"There used to be a kind of memorial of this accident in the old Tollhouse Museum. I say used to be, because some of Mr. Hitler's bombs put paid to it, and a whole lot of interesting relics were lost."

"What sort of memorial was it?" I asked.

"Oh, quite a simple little thing, just an inscription in old-fashioned bone lettering. I suppose someone did it as a bit of a novelty because it was such an unheard-of thing for a wherry to get lost at sea. How did it go now? Ah, yes, I remember. It said 'In memory of the WHERRY ELLEN, of Great Yarmouth, which was run down at sea by the *Robert Alfred* whilst sailing a match for ten guineas in the Lowestoft Roads, August 28th, 1884. H. Deacon, master. J. J. Goff, owner.'

"One thing about it I could never understand, though, was why they said the *Ellen* came from Yarmouth when, of course, she belonged to Loddon. The *Robert Alfred* now, she was a Yarmouth craft, Robert Pratt the lime-burner owned her. He had the *Harry and Ethel* too, nice wherries both of them, and well looked after."

From sea regattas we passed to those on the broads, with a special word about Oulton where the *Fawn* first hoisted racing colours, in 1877. She was only two years old then, and the race was sailed in two parts, one for craft not exceeding 25 tons, and one for those over 25 tons. The *Fawn* just qualified for the smaller class.

Ophir Powley, after being in her a couple of years, had no doubt discovered she was pretty smart and advised Wales to enter her. But for this first trial of strength she had five craft against her all with a good turn of speed and sailed by some of the best skippers on the river. They were the *Jenny Morgan, British Queen, Zephyr, Samuel* and *Volunteer*.

As the gun was about to fire all six lay to their sinkers on the line, gaff and sail resting on the hatches. Four men, two to a handle, were poised ready at the winch. At the first sound, handles went flying round, sails streaked aloft, sinkers came tumbling inboard: in a matter of seconds every craft was under way with each sheetman and skipper using all the cunning he had to steal a march on his rivals.

With a fine, steady wind from the N.N.E. it proved the close race predicted, keeping the crowd on its feet throughout all six rounds of the three-mile course. The first four rounds saw the *Fawn, Jenny Morgan* and *British Queen* sailing absolutely level, with each skipper trying his best and using every trick of the trade to work out ahead. But after twelve miles, and with only two rounds to go, it was still level-pegging.

Then, half-way through the fifth round, a cheer went up when it was seen the *Fawn* had edged her nose in front. But the other two were giving nothing away and hung on grimly so that they were no more than a length behind at the end of the round. The battle-royal continued for the whole of the last round, but the *Fawn* and Ophir proved just that bit too good, and ended by winning fairly comfortably. It was a taste of all that was in store during the next twenty years.

She took part at Oulton the following year and won again, but of the five she had previously beaten, only the *Jenny Morgan* came to the line. They were joined by the *Enfield, Leonard, Theodore* and *Maria*, though the last named sprang her mast just before the race and could not start.

The course was the same as before. Getting a good start the *Jenny Morgan* worked out a substantial lead by the end of the first round, with the *Enfield* second and *Fawn* third. They held these positions till the third round when, in squally weather with heavy showers of rain, the *Fawn* began to close the gap. Then the *Enfield* started overhauling *Jenny Morgan*, passed her and took the lead. *Fawn*, romping up, drew level with *Jenny Morgan*, providing once more the spectacle of three wherries separated by only a few feet after ten miles.

But after this there was no stopping the *Fawn* and she went on to win easily, with the game little *Enfield* of only 18 tons, second. *Jenny Morgan* was third, *Theodore* fourth and *Leonard* fifth. Only 6 minutes 30 seconds difference in the times of the first and last wherry, for a distance of eighteen miles, shows how close the racing was.

"But quite apart from the racing," said Albert, "regatta days were always a bit of fun for the wherrymen's families. Wives, children, friends, relations, they were all packed away down in the cabin and in the hold, while the skipper's missus took charge of the tea-making. For no matter how close a race might be, there was always time to knock back a mug or two.

"And at the end of the day when it was all over, everyone made their way to the local. There the races were sailed again and again, with this move and that move coming under fire, and each skipper being criticized for what he did do and what he didn't do, and what a different result there'd have been if so-and-so had done such-and-such. The beer and stout, of course, flowed steadily into the great quart mugs, enough of it to float a battleship, for they knew how to drink in those days, take my word for it. There was the prize money, you see, knocking around, and that made a world of difference. Oh yes," murmured Albert with an appreciative sigh, "we had some merry old nights, that we did, singing, dancing, yarn-spinning, and always a full pot at your elbow."

We had a night rather like that after the last Oulton Broad wherry race in 1950. The *Albion* was paying a courtesy visit to Lowestoft over Whitsun and a race was got up between her and the three pleasure wherries *Ardea*, *Claudian* and *Bramble*. Some sixty years had passed since the last one, and as the day proved fine and warm with a fresh north-westerly, the world and his wife turned out to watch.

They saw little to get excited about in the way of racing, except Jack Cates' handling of the *Albion*, but being accustomed to small yacht racing, they found a real holiday treat in seeing these four heavyweights turning up and down the Broad. The result had been a foregone conclusion and the *Albion* won as she pleased, but it was a sporting gesture from the others to turn out and make a race at all.

That night, along with Jack and his brothers, all their wives, innumerable relations and the crews of the other competitiors, we drank immense quantities of beer in the Lady of the Lake. This pub stands within a stone's-throw of where the *Albion* had been built fifty-two years before, and in the sentimental way of sailors, we toasted not only her win, but her still being alive and kicking after all this time.

It was the first race she took part in, but all of us wished we could have put the clock back fifty years and seen her matched against such flyers as the *Fawn*, *Beaconsfield*, *Olga* and *Dora*.

Later that summer we took the *Albion* to Barton and once again three pleasure wherries turned out to make a race, the *Claudian* and *Ardea* being joined by the *Dragon*. They stood little chance and as expected she got home by a distance, but the race proved the high spot of the regatta reviving many memories of when such races were regular events in the Barton programme.

Regattas have been held here since as far back as the eighteen-thirties if not before, though there seems to have been no wherry racing earlier than 1874. In that year four craft put in an appearance, the *Swift*, *Elizabeth*, *Samuel* and *Industry*. It was the usual start, from moorings with sails down, but the moment they got into position a violent thunderstorm broke over the broad, with gale-force gusts of wind and torrential rain. The Commodore rightly refused to start them, though they spent an uncomfortable hour trying to hang on to their weights and avoid being swept into the reeds. But it was soon over, the sun came out, and in a nice breeze they went away for a good race which the *Samuel* won.

This smart little craft was owned by Clarke, of Ludham, and repeated her success the following year. But good as she was against other north river wherries she was no match, as we have seen, for the *Fawn*, *Jenny Morgan* or *British Queen* on the one occasion they met, at Oulton in 1877.

She raced again at Barton, in 1881, against the *Dilham Trader*, *Harriet*, *Industry*, *Lucy* and *Elizabeth*, but could only manage fourth place. She made one more appearance, in 1883, against the *Alma*, *Dilham Trader* and *Elizabeth* but had to give up, and after that she never raced again.

One of the most regular starters and consistent performers at the regattas was the *Elizabeth*, owned by Press Bros. She still survives as a houseboat though now nearly a hundred and twenty years old. She is quite small, only 18 tons, and has a square stern and slightly raking stem. She always did best in a hard blow and when conditions were to her liking was very hard to beat.

She took part in all the early races at Barton winning there in 1891 and 1892, and on her last appearance in 1901. Her name appears in the list of Wroxham competitors as far back as 1852, when she won out of a field of nine. The others were the *Two Brothers* and *Mary Ann*, both of Horning, the *Emma* of Norwich, the *Prince of Wales* of Aylsham, the *Harvest* of Salhouse, the *Maria* of Horning, the *Henry* of Wroxham, and the *Mayflower* of Sutton.

The *Elizabeth*'s prize on that occasion was not money, but a pair of silver-mounted drinking horns. They were very much in keeping with the spirit of the times for regattas had not then lost the atmosphere of the old-fashioned water frolics. An observer has described how spectators gathered aboard the larger wherries, moored to form floating grandstands, in great numbers, 'where mountains of comestibles and oceans of beer were provided for all comers'. So no doubt the victorious crew of the *Elizabeth* had an early opportunity to christen their trophies.

Several features grew up at the different regattas which became firmly established traditions. A wherry, for instance, always served as committee-boat, and the custom did not die out at Barton till 1927. The year before another happy tradition had come to an end. The Stalham Town Band, assembled on a lighter amongst the reeds, played, for the last time, 'See, the Conquering Hero Comes' as the *Hilda* took the winning gun. For years this piece had greeted the victorious wherry, and the sound of it ringing out over the waters gave a dramatic touch to the proceedings. It was not confined to Barton but was heard wherever a band was in attendance.

Stalham not only provided Barton Regatta with its band but also its boiled beef. Luncheon aboard the committee wherry was very much of an occasion, presided over by Tom Goodwin, a waiter of the old school. The joint he dispensed was always of superb quality, and the 'Stalham beef' of Barton became almost as famous as the regatta.

The *Fawn* was never able to race at Barton as she was too wide in the beam to go through old Ludham Bridge. But Wroxham often saw her after her first appearance on the broad in 1890, when she sailed against the *Elizabeth, Eva Rosa, Martham Trader* and *Helen*. It was the customary start from moorings and the *Elizabeth* got away smartly with the *Fawn* close on her heels. *Elizabeth* kept her advantage during the first round though there was only 10 seconds in it. In the second round *Fawn* overhauled her and took a lead of 30 seconds. Thereafter it became a procession, *Fawn* increasing her lead every round, till she crossed the line 7 minutes ahead.

She missed the 1891 race but turned out again in 1892 against the *Eva Rosa, Surprise, Elizabeth* and *Robert and Henry*. This time she got away ahead of the *Elizabeth* and was never challenged, winning by 10 minutes. In 1893 she sailed against the *Elizabeth* once more, and the *Dauntless*, beating the former by 7 minutes, but the 1894 event was marred by tragedy.

Three competitors were sailing to Wroxham on the morning of the race when a young man, taking passage in one of them, slipped overboard. He did not come up again, and although the search went on for a long time, they found no trace of him. Apparently he went in feet-first and sank so far in the mud that he was held fast. The body was not recovered till three hours afterwards when it was identified as Buck, the Ludham postman.

There was little inclination to race after such an accident and when the three wherries at last reached the broad they found the *Elizabeth* had already sailed over for the prize.

But there was a different story the following year when no less than six entries were received. The number alone promised plenty of excitement, but what stirred most people's imagination was the prospect of a do-or-die struggle between those great rivals, *Fawn* and *Beaconsfield*. Their battles at sea were still fresh in the memory, so that August day, 1895, all roads led to Wroxham.

The draw for places gave *Britannia* the windward berth, followed by *Ethnie, Eva Rosa, Fawn, Elizabeth* and *Beaconsfield*. *Elizabeth* made another splendid start, her huge mainsail going up at tremendous speed, but *Britannia* lost all the advantage of her station and was last away. *Eva Rosa* showed she had nothing to learn about hoisting sail smartly and did so well she took an early lead. As the round progressed she added to it steadily and worked out a handsome advantage over the favourites.

While this was exciting and unexpected, even more unexpected was the poor showing of the *Beaconsfield*, trailing along last. In the second round she did a bit better and passed *Britannia*, but *Eva Rosa* was going great guns though chased hard by *Elizabeth*. She in turn was being hotly pursued by *Ethnie* and *Fawn*, a very unaccustomed position for Ophir Powley to find himself in. It must have seemed as if the other wherries had only one aim, to beat the *Fawn*. But Ophir had his own ideas about this and before the end of the second round he tucked the *Ethnie* astern and made tracks after *Elizabeth*.

As the third round started the skies darkened over and the broad was enveloped in a downpour of rain. But it did not last long enough to dampen the spirits of crews or spectators, who were having the time of their lives. Only an earthquake would have stopped them seeing the end of the race.

For Ophir, do as he would with the *Fawn*, could make no impression on *Elizabeth* and *Eva Rosa*, and when the final round began it looked an odds-on chance the *Fawn* would be well and truly beaten.

Then, as the clouds rolled away and the sun came out, excitement grew. The course was a two-legged one, up and down the broad, and on the first of these two last legs, *Fawn* managed to get up with *Elizabeth* and pass her. She was now close behind *Eva Rosa* and soon the two craft were running stem to stem for the final buoy. They rounded it, still together, but *Fawn* was a fraction smarter filling away and romped home to take the gun 1 minute 17 seconds ahead of her rival. As she crossed the line the long-familiar strains of 'See, the Conquering Hero Comes' rang out in salute.

The battle anticipated between her and the *Beaconsfield* failed to materialize; but Billy Brighton's *Eva Rosa*, built when a lad of only seventeen, had given her a run for her money, and made a race that was never forgotten by those who saw it. The *Beaconsfield* finished last but one, a sad position for such a famous flyer. But the years were already weighing heavily on her and she never raced again.

"Oh yes, the *Beaconsfield* was a good 'un, and no mistake," said Albert, paying tribute to an old and respected rival, "but like the rest of us, you couldn't expect her to go on for ever. No more you could the *Fawn*, and it wasn't any surprise when the *Olga* beat her at Wroxham in 1896, and the *Dora* two years after, in 1898. She was well over twenty years old then while they were brand-new. But she didn't do too badly at Wroxham for an old lady, as out of her six races there, as a trading wherry I mean, she won four and came second the other two.

"After that, as you know, Mr. Wales sold her to Bullen, of Oulton Broad, where she was turned into a pleasure craft. Nice job, too, they made of her, though what we never stopped arguing about at the time, was how she would fare after all the alterations had been done.

"Well, we didn't have long to wait to find out, because in 1900 they entered her in the race for pleasure wherries at Wroxham. They'd had a race there of this kind since 1887, but for that first race only two pleasuring craft turned up, the *Heron* and the *Bertha*. They always had their holiday parties on board when they were racing, so you can imagine they were pretty light-hearted affairs. But that doesn't mean skippers didn't go all out to win, because they did. And, of course, there were the passengers urging them on all the time! Take it from me, they wanted to win all right!"

In her first race as a pleasure wherry the *Fawn* was up against an old opponent from trading days, the *British Queen*, together with the *Claudian*, *Industry*, *Britannia* and *Rambler*. The day was fine with plenty of wind, and the start made a wonderful picture with all six getting away together. It set the pattern for the whole race, all craft keeping close up with one another, though *Fawn* managed to edge herself into the lead soon after the gun. But *Industry* kept close on her tail, with *British Queen* challenging strongly for second place. In the second round *Rambler* fouled a buoy and retired.

Positions remained unchanged to the end, which meant victory for the *Fawn*, though she only had 1 minute 9 seconds to spare over *Industry*. *British Queen* came in a good third, with *Claudian* fourth. So, even in her new guise, the *Fawn* was successful; but whether it was the alterations, or having a new hand at the helm, she never really got into her stride. She made heavy weather of a race, which, in the old days, she would have won as she pleased.

The next year's race was a fiasco. There were two entries only, *Fawn* and *Dauntless*, but at the gun the latter was cruising about the broad as if unaware of the time. Although she came down and crossed the line, *Fawn* was miles ahead and won by a quarter of an hour.

The following year, 1902, saw the *Fawn* hoist racing colours for the last time. But though she started she never finished, having to retire after fouling a buoy. At the time she was, as so often in the past, way out ahead; yet it was only becoming of such an aristocrat that, having offended against the rules, she should gracefully withdraw. And so ended her wonderful twenty-five years of racing.

In that quarter of a century she reigned supreme and her disappearance left a gap that could never be filled. I said earlier there must have been some magic went into her building, and that is really the only word that describes it. The few old-timers who remember her all agree 'there was never another like her', and as wherrymen, look upon her much as blue-water sailormen do the *Cutty Sark*.

Although wherry racing continued well on into the present century, chiefly at Barton and Wroxham, interest in it gradually waned as more and more people bought yachts to race in themselves. In addition, the wherry fleets were thinning out, no new craft were being built, so it was left to the veterans to go on hammering away at each other year after year.

"But don't forget, there were other races we haven't talked about," Albert reminded me, "like the Burgh Castle frolic held on Breydon Water. I reckon that must be the oldest of all the regattas, and we generally had some good sport there.

"You find the same names cropping up as at all the other races, the *Fawn* and *Beaconsfield* as you might expect, and the little *Elizabeth*, she could always be relied on, along with the *Dauntless* and *British Queen*. Then we used to see the *Ellen*, the one that got sunk at Lowestoft, in fact all the regular racers used to turn up if they got the chance.

"We had quite a do in 1893 when four of us were taking part, the *Fawn*, *Beaconsfield*, *Dauntless* and *Elizabeth*. The *Fawn* got away to a good start, but on the run down *Elizabeth* went on the mud. That isn't very hard to do on Breydon, as you know, and there she had to stay till the flood made. The *Beaconsfield* and *Dauntless* weren't much astern of the *Fawn* when we rounded the bottom buoy, and the wind being as it was we had to gybe. But as the *Dauntless* gybed, poor old Jack Benns got clouted by the sail and went in the drink.

"As luck would have it, he was a good swimmer, and the last thing he wanted was the *Dauntless*, or any of the others, to spoil the race picking him up. So he waves his skipper on, and cool as a cucumber paddles away to one of those posts marking the channel. Then he puts his arms round it, as if he was cuddling some young party, and waits for a pleasure steamer to pick him up.

"Of course, it all made a bit of a frap because the *Dauntless* and *Beaconsfield* were so close together when it happened. There was a proper mix-up for a few minutes, but they soon sorted themselves out, and it ended up with the pair of them making a good race of it for second place. The *Beaconsfield* won, but by that time the *Fawn* was stowed up and we were all having a mug of tea."

The Burgh Castle Water Frolic originated in a 'beating of the bounds' ceremony. Members of the Yarmouth Corporation used to process by water up to Hardley Cross, the limit of their jurisdiction on the River Yare, where they met officials from the Norwich Corporation. After an exchange of civic courtesies, the Yarmouth contingent returned to Breydon for a day's merrymaking. A contemporary observer has aptly described the scene, and I cannot do better than quote it:

Annually in July the Mayors of Norwich and Yarmouth meet in their state barges on the River Yare at Hardley Cross, which separates their respective jurisdictions, and in the afternoon fall down into Breydon.

This is a broad expanse of water which receives three tributary streams, the Waveney, the Yare and the Bure. All the many pleasure boats kept on these rivers assemble; the commercial craft are in requisition to stow spectators, to waft music, to vend refreshments. Such of the shipping as ascends above Yarmouth drawbridge is moored within ken.

There are sailing matches, rowing matches, and spontaneous evolutions of vessels of all sorts, a dance of ships, their streamers flying and their canvas spread. It is a fair afloat, where the voice of revelry resounds from every gliding tent.

And when the tide begins to fall, and to condense this various fleet into the narrower waters, and the bridge and quays and balconies and windows of Yarmouth are thronged with innumerable spectators—and boys have climbed the masts and rigging of the moored ships, adding to the crowd ashore a rocking crowd above—and the gathering boats mingle their separate concerts in one chorus of jollity—and guns fire—and loyalty and liberty shout with rival glee—and the setting sun inflames the whole lake—the scene becomes surpassingly impressive, exhilarating and magnificent.

These official junketings were brought to an end by the Municipal Corporations Act of 1835, which forbade the use of borough funds for such purposes, but local enthusiasm kept it going, on a diminished scale, till about the turn of this century.

Breydon was thus quite an appropriate setting for the last of all the wherry races, in 1952, when the *Albion* broke her mast. It is unlikely there will ever be another because, although one or two pleasure craft are still afloat, there are no longer the men to sail them. On top of this, there is a widespread feeling that craft of this kind interfere with the yacht racing, which most clubs exist to foster.

Yet we can take comfort in the thought that right to the end wherry racing retained its traditional form. There was no attempt to 'pep it up', to debase it by artificial additions; no adoption of freak rigs; no atmosphere of blatant commercial exploitation such as now surrounds the Thames barge race, for instance. The appalling spectacle of these once splendid craft, decked out with bermuda mizzens, striped spinnakers, sickly-white mainsails, and fussy, exaggerated paintwork, makes us thankful that Norfolk's black-sailed traders were spared any comparable humiliation. Can it be the folk on the Yare have more pride in tradition than those on the Thames?

Albert went on to tell me about wherry races held in out-of-the-way and rather unexpected places. Horsey Mere, for instance, was several times the scene of quite a sizeable regatta, with events for open boats and wherries in the sailing section, besides rowing and quanting races. In 1882, four wherries competed, the *Dilham Trader, Elizabeth, Violet* and *Sarah Ann*, but they spent most of their time whistling for a breeze. After drifting for about five miles round the course, *Dilham Trader* was declared the winner and received the prize of £2.

At Beccles, too, they were racing wherries as early as 1846, for a first prize of £5, second £1 10s., and third £1. Beccles, in fact, must have been one of the first centres to arrange such events, though from the width of the Waveney, only small wherries could have taken part. This is suggested by the rules, which allowed only the skipper and mate to be on board, permitted only two quants to be carried, and demanded four to enter or no race. The entrance fee was 5s. and each craft was required to have a distinguishing colour at her masthead. It is a pity no records seem to have survived, either of competitors or results, indeed, there is nothing to show how long these races continued. But by 1846, wherries working up to Beccles were growing rapidly in size, and racing them there would have been a bit hazardous. It may well have been such events died out during the eighteen-fifties.

"The trouble is, once you start yarning about the old days, you can go on for ever," said Albert, prodding a few unburned pieces of coal into a last, fitful blaze.

His words reminded me it was getting late, and that I was probably keeping him and his wife from bed.

I said good-bye to Mrs. Powley, very reluctantly I do not mind admitting, and then Albert showed me to the door. When he opened it, the wind off Breydon caught us full in the face, charged with the wild tang of the mudflats. We both took deep breaths of it.

"Nice sailing breeze," I said, grasping his hand, "just right for the *Fawn*, eh?"

He took another sniff and cocked an eye aloft, as if instinctively looking for the dim outline of her vane against the night sky; as he used to do when only a slip of a lad in knickerbockers.

"Lovely," he answered, "just how she liked it."

He spoke rather slowly and with a trace of sadness in his voice. Did he, I wondered, feel he was now a man out of his time? That the present-day world was one he would never understand, with its changed ways and different standards? Perhaps it was all bound up with the realization that the times we had been talking about, the frolics and races, the good-natured rivalry, the homely fun, and the manly work of sailing a ship to earn a living, were gone for ever, and lived on only in the memories of old men like himself.

But he was cheerful enough when he said, "You know, you ought to write a book about those wherries of ours, proper little clippers they were, make no mistake about it."

We said good night and as he closed the door I made off towards the harbour.

Going over the Haven bridge I pulled my collar up for the wind was raw. Downstream I could just make out the *Albion*, laden with timber, asleep against the quay.

Tomorrow, I knew she would be bound up to Norwich with deals for council houses, portable garages and chicken sheds. Those who used that wood would neither know nor care that it had come to them by wherry, as it had done for the past three hundred years.

The thought made me pause a while, despite the bitter sea-wind round my ears, and it struck me how the *Albion*, too, was something out of her time; an anachronism in this age of speed, space-rockets and ulcerated stomachs.

I moved on thinking how lucky it was there were still men like Albert Powley left to tell me about those other days.

CHAPTER NINE

Tavern Tales and Spun Yarns

A long drink—the reward of suspicion—the sign of the wherry—a dead Dragoon—smuggling and the defeat of justice—'apostles of democarcy'—the oldest profession—dress and dancing—charity—military manoeuvres—collisions and tragedies—a well-taught lesson—a floating power station—the end of it all.

"AND without a word of a lie, there was weed growing on the *Widgeon*'s bottom a yard long. That's a fact all right, because I saw it with my own eyes."

"After you'd had a pint too many, Walter, and didn't rightly know what you were looking at," commented one of the younger, and less credulous, wherrymen leaning against the bar. "How could weed that length grow on a wherry's bottom unless she was moored up, and left lying, and never did any work?"

"That's just how it was, Martin my boy, just how it was," replied Walter, "only you won't seem to listen. Old Billy, as I've said before, had picked up a freight of stones for Norton, in the way of a godsend, too, it was, because he found work pretty hard to get then. Anyhow, he sails off down the river, delivers his stones, picks up the freight money, and on his way back throws a line ashore here, and drops in for a quick one.

"Now, even the way Billy could spin things out, that shouldn't have taken him much above an hour, but by the time he'd finished one, he felt like another, and so it went on.

"I suppose it was the feel of all those shillings in his pocket gave him a thirst; it was rare enough for Billy to have hold of a bit of silver.

"Anyway, to cut a long story short, instead of popping in, having a quick one, and getting off up to Norwich after another freight, he just stays here drinking. That's right enough what I'm telling you."

Walter took a long pull from his mug, all the while peering over the rim as if challenging contradiction.

"How long did he stay then, till next morning?" queried another member of the company, his half-leather jacket and cheese-cutter cap just visible in the dim light and thick haze of tobacco smoke.

"Oh yes, he stayed till morning all right," said the publican, taking up the story, though continuing all the while his task of polishing a dozen or so pink and blue beer pots. He never lavished such attention on the glass variety which, he used to say, 'didn't repay much doing to', and held them in reserve only against the visits of city gents. They found his house conveniently situated to bring their young secretaries to after a tiring day in the office, and they liked to sip their pale ale and stout from glasses.

But the locals, who mostly worked on the land, and the wherrymen, whom he regarded as amphibious animals endowed by God or hard labour with prodigious thirsts, were not the sipping kind. They swallowed their drink whole, so to speak, and only quart pots would satisfy them.

"He stayed till morning all right," he said once again, giving all the occupants of the bar a knowing smile, "and the next, and the next, and the one after that. In fact, he made a real proper stay of it, that he did. And you needn't take my word for it alone."

He turned his glance towards a gnarled and toothless old chap sitting on a bench near the fire. You could tell he had once been an active, powerful man, and even now belied the nickname 'Slushy' he had carried for close on four-score years. He had worked on the land and he had worked in the wherries, he had cut reeds off the ronds and he had been fishing on the North Sea. Slushy had done a lot of things in his time, but his favourite employment had always been sitting on that particular bench by the fire, sampling the wares of the Norwich brewery which owned the house.

'Sampling' is an apt description, for whenever he was asked to have a drink, which he frequently was, especially when the city gents and their young secretaries were present, he always replied with, "Thank you, I'll try a pint of mild." The word 'try' should be noted, because he delivered it with a chanting, upward inflexion, as if anticipating a unique and novel experience.

There was an artistry about the whole thing which made the city gent feel immensely good. It enabled him to turn, smiling, to his rather tired young secretary, as if to say: "Just see how happy I've made that old fellow, I'm human, you know, I can unbend and be a man of the people, and I should like to make you happy, too, if only you'd forget, just for tonight, that I'm your boss, because ever since you've been in the office I've thought how extraordinarily attractive you are..." and so on, and so on, till they became so engrossed they failed to hear the respectful, "Your health master, and m-m-madam," with which Slushy invariably saluted his benefactors. But it must be admitted he sometimes stumbled a little when coupling the lady in his toast, due to a certain indecision whether the word should be 'madam', 'miss' or 'mistress'. For Slushy was a man of the world and knew about such things, though never a word was breathed till the door had safely closed on the gent and his lady, or whatever she was.

Even then a sentence sufficed to express the views of all present; and it was usually Slushy, as the chief recipient of the hospitality dispensed, who voiced them. As the sound of the car's self-starter came to them, he would say with a grin that still had bundles of mischief in it: "Well, she didn't look the sort to need all that persuading, did she?" And after a general murmur of assent, they resumed their respective arguments and discussions.

As the oldest inhabitant of the bar Slushy could always be appealed to about events that happened before most of the others were born; for like the majority of old people he remembered things that took place sixty or seventy years ago much more clearly than he did those of last week or last year. He could put a date to floods, droughts, tempests, births and deaths long before this century was in; but ask him what he had for yesterday's tea and he could not remember.

If you inquired about the giant pike, sleeping dreamily in its glass case over the fireplace, Slushy would tell you the day, month and year when 'Nails' hauled it in on a spinner he had been trailing astern since Cantley; and if you mentioned wildfowling, he would tell you the exact morning 'Scientific' brought down five mallard with two barrels.

As with so many who dwell close to the soil his long and accurate memory was allied to much homely wisdom. A young lad once came into the bar with a basket of fine lettuces which he started showing, very proudly, to all and sundry. He held one out to Slushy saying, "Don't you think these are good 'uns? Grew 'em myself I did."

Slushy looked at them with great admiration.

"Grew 'em yourself, you say?"

"Yes, I did an' all."

"You didn't young fellow me lad, you didn't grow 'em, you know."

"That I did, Slushy, on that patch next the cesspit, that's why they're so big."

Slushy looked at the beaming face of the youngster, then laid his hand on his shoulder and said kindly: "No, no, you sowed 'em son; but God grew 'em for you."

There was a rare wit, too, about many of his observations on society which he delighted in throwing at the hordes of holidaymakers who invaded the sanctity of the bar in summertime. On one occasion some semi-nude females and their hairy-legged companions, proud hirers of a mammoth, box-like cruiser, engaged Slushy in conversation, telling him how lovely it was to be on holiday because they worked so hard the rest of the year.

Then one of the semi-nudes, who was wearing a shirt-like garment printed over with vermouth-bottle labels, and spoke with a nasal drawl simulating the American, asked innocently what work he did.

"What work do I do?" repeated Slushy, eyeing the spokeswoman very intently, and not missing one of her infinite variety of curves for all his four-score years, "I don't do any work, missy, and I'll tell you for why; you see, this world is divided into two. Now one half is quite willing to work, and that's the half you're in; but the other half is just as willing to let 'em, and that's the half I'm in."

Thereupon Slushy turned contentedly to one of the hairy-legs and in response to his pressing invitation, replied with the inevitable words: "Thank you, I'll try a pint of mild." For, as he was often heard to say, why should anyone work, who doesn't want to, when those that do want to, are willing to buy them their beer?

In seeking Slushy's confirmation of the length of Billy's stay, the publican was thus appealing to no mean oracle. It was long enough ago for him to remember it clearly, and he nodded in the direction of Walter.

"What he says is true enough, there was weed as long as your arm all along the waterline, that thin stuff like green ribbon, looking as how Billy was getting ahead with his Christmas decorations. Never saw such a sight in all my life and that's a fact."

"You're not going to tell me anything could grow that length in a matter of days," said Martin, assuming the role of a real doubting Thomas.

"Matter of days!" mocked Slushy, "it wasn't a matter of days, my boy, nor yet weeks. It was months!"

"Months!" shouted Martin in genuine disbelief, "that be damned for a tale."

"Be damned or no, that's how long he stayed, two months and two days. About the longest any man took having a quick one, if you ask me. And when all those shillings at last came to an end, and he had to push off, you ought to have seen those weeds streaming out astern of him. But he didn't bother, not Billy, you all know what he was like."

They certainly did know, from personal experience and riverside gossip, for Billy was a character in every sense of the word. The *Widgeon* belonged to him and he made it his home, taking a few freights now and again to earn the price of a loaf of bread and a jug of beer. Because of his simple life he never hurried and was never put out by anything.

You could better describe him as about the last of the Norfolk 'primitives', men who lived their whole life cheek by jowl with nature, spurning the time-wasting, nerve-fraying complications of modern life, and preferring their own skill with gun, net or sail, to keep body and soul together. These men had a great, if simple, dignity and great independence of spirit. Independent admirably describes Billy Tooley.

"There was that time, too, when he had twenty-five ton of coal in the *Widgeon* for that farmer up yonder. Remember that little lark?" said Walter rolling himself a cigarette.

"What was Billy up to then?" asked Martin.

"Slushy'll bear out the tale because he was working round the dyke at the time, good old laugh we had over it afterwards, didn't we Slushy?"

"We did an' all, old partner, proper caution that was, do you tell 'em about it."

"Well, it was like this," said Walter settling himself down and drawing his pot a bit closer, "for some reason or other this farmer chap had what you might call his suspicions about Billy; thought he took a bag or two of coal now and again for the cabin stove, or something of the sort. Kept hearing the word 'pilfer', so I guessed that's what it was.

"Anyway, it ended up with this farmer—and I'm not mentioning no names because you all know who I'm speaking of—coming up to Billy the moment he'd got the hatches off, and saying to him real offensive like: "You're supposed to have twenty-five ton of coal in there for me, have you got it?"

" 'Twenty-five ton it is,' replied Billy.

" 'That's what you say, but I'm going to make sure it is twenty-five ton and nothing under,' said the farmer with a nasty, venomous look on his face, for all the world like one of those viper snakes preparing to strike, 'that's what these scales are for,' and he pointed to the machine they had for weighing up potatoes. 'I mean to weigh every bag as it's landed; and if you're short, master Billy, so much the worse for you. I'll have the law on you.' And with that he turned to his men, gave them some instructions, and stumped off, a horrible black scowl all over his face.

"Of course, as you can guess, the men didn't relish the job, but they had to do as they were told. Each bag was weighed as it came out of the *Widgeon*, and there was one chap sitting at the scales doing nothing but keep a tally.

"By the time the last bag was landed the farmer came back and stood by this tally chap. Billy emerged from the cabin wiping his mouth with the back of his hand, because all this time he'd been down below having a bite to eat, and a bit of a snooze, taking no notice whatever of what was going on.

" 'What's the total,' rapped out the farmer with a gloating tone in his voice.

"The man worked away with his pencil, doing little sums at the bottom of each column, then looked up and said in a cheery tone of voice: 'Twenty-six ton, three hundredweight.'

"The farmer looked proper crestfallen and repeated slowly, 'Twenty-six ton, three hundredweight, are you sure?'

" 'That's what it is,' said the chap, 'no more, and no less.'

"We could all see the farmer was absolutely dumbfounded, but realizing we were standing staring at him, and grinning, too, some of us, he tried to put a bold face on things.

" 'Well, I'm glad to see you've brought me a full load after all,' he said turning to Billy, and putting a hand in his pocket took out a sovereign and five shillings, the freight money at a shilling a ton.

"But there Billy sat on the cabin, stuffing shag into his clay pipe, and making no effort at all to take the farmer's money.

" 'Here you are, man, here's your freight money,' said the farmer, all nasty and peevish, 'you know I'm the sort who always pays on the nail.'

"At that Billy looks at him, with the kind of look that made the farmer wish a great hole would open up at his feet and swallow him.

" 'Pay on the nail?' said Billy slowly, his face brimming over with contempt, 'pay on the nail? That's just what you aren't doing, if you think you are.'

" 'How do you make that out?' asked the farmer getting more and more uncomfortable, 'you brought me twenty-five ton of coal, at a shilling a ton, that's twenty-five shillings unless I'm very much mistaken.'

" 'But you are mistaken, mister,' responded Billy putting a match to his pipe, and fixing the farmer with that piercing gaze of his, 'very much mistaken.'

" 'I'm afraid I don't follow you,' said the farmer who was getting so ratty now he kept kicking the ground and swearing under his breath.

" 'Then you must be denser than I took you for. You ordered twenty-five ton all right, and it's twenty-five ton I've brought you. But you thought I hadn't. Imagined I'd done a little bit of pilfering on the way, didn't you? Took me for a common thief and no better. Wanted to weigh the whole perishing freight just to prove it against me, didn't you?

" 'All right, mister. It was your idea not mine. But what you've found out by doing it, you're going to pay for, and on top of the freight money. So besides that twenty-five shillings of yours, you're going to pay me for the twenty-three hundredweights of coal you've got, over and above your order. At two shillings a hundredweight that comes to two pounds six shillings, and I'll thank you to hand the lot over so I can be getting away up to Norwich.'

"For a moment we all thought the farmer was going to explode or throw a fit, but he pulled himself together as he must have realized what Billy said was true. If he hadn't have weighed it, no one would have been any the wiser, and he'd have got the extra for nothing. As it was, Billy meant to make him pay, and pay he did."

A merry laugh went round the bar and then Slushy said: "And serve him right, too. Billy was a rum 'un, sure enough, with some rare funny ways; but he was as straight as a pine-tree. Anyone who called him a thief didn't know their man, and deserved all they got for doing it."

This summing up was met with murmurs of agreement, and as pots were pushed forward to be filled again, conversation passed to other topics.

There used to be inns like this, with men of similar stamp for patrons, all along the rivers of Norfolk and Suffolk. The price of a pint of beer entitled you to eavesdrop on all their homely gossiping, different from the ordinary run of gossip in that most of it was true, or at least founded on fact.

From Yarmouth, all the way up the Yare, the Bure and the Waveney, there were these ports of call where wherrymen could moor up for a spell, take a pint and have a yarn; where they could stretch their legs, eat a plate of victuals, make eyes at the landlord's daughter, and pass on news of what ships were in, what freights would be offering, if the smacks were needing ice, and whether little Jimmy would ever make a wherryman. They were the clearing houses for all that happened on the river and had a lot in common with the coffee-houses of London where sea captains once congregated to exchange views and seek information.

It was, perhaps, only natural that many of these houses should adopt the wherry as their sign, or if not specifically a wherry, a name showing their close connection with the river trade such as the Day-Barge or the Waterman. The majority have now disappeared or changed their names, but six still remain. In King Street, Norwich, we find the Keel and Wherry which, although it lacks a signboard, has the name in very elegant raised lettering done with gold-leaf. But I always feel the brewers have missed a wonderful opportunity of displaying these two Norfolk craft in all their glory. It would help to relieve the rather drab character of this part of King Street and would be in keeping with the situation of the house, right opposite Carrow bridge over the River Yare. There are three others in Norfolk called the Wherry: at Paston, on the old Dilham–Antingham canal; at Geldeston, on the Beccles–Bungay navigation; and at Langley, on the River Yare. Suffolk has two, the Wherry Hotel at Oulton Broad, and the Wherry Inn, Halesworth, built about the time the Blyth Navigation was opened. All of them, except Oulton Broad, have signboards outside depicting wherries, though executed with varying degrees of skill. The best is probably at Halesworth, followed by Geldestone which, as I mentioned earlier, was painted from a photograph of the *Eudora*, taken about 1900.

In days gone by, wherever you had a lonely inn close to the water, you were pretty sure to find smuggling going on. Tea, gin, brandy, tobacco and silks were the things most in demand, because the high duty they carried when imported legally put them beyond the reach of ordinary people. Smuggled goods found a ready sale on account of their cheapness.

Enormous shipments were brought across from Holland and France, and landed on the Norfolk and Suffolk coasts. By devious routes they found their way to Norwich and Ipswich, chiefly by wagon. But in Norfolk a lot went by wherry, and in the small barges used for carrying reeds.

A favourite method was to make a landing at Horsey, carry the tubs and cases to the Mere, and load them into a waiting wherry; then, under cover of darkness, sail them down the Thurne and up the Bure to Wroxham, where they were transferred to wagons for the last stage of their journey to Norwich. To avoid detection, wherries and barges would lay up in some lonely spot during the hours of daylight, and conceal themselves among the reeds.

Smugglers and excisemen were always coming into conflict, and some fierce skirmishes took place on the beaches in the early-morning hours, when most honest folk were asleep. If the preventive men thought they were likely to be outnumbered they called in the troops, but this nearly always led to bloodshed. An incident of this kind is recorded

The start, Barton Regatta

Under way, Barton Regatta: (left) *Lady Violet*, (centre) *Despatch*, (right) *Hilda*

Humphrey Boardman, Esq., Queen Street, Norwich

Breydon Wherry Race, 31st August, 1952. The *Albion* a few seconds before breaking her mast

on a tombstone in a quiet Norfolk churchyard, within sound of the sea:

> I am not dead, but sleepeth here,
> And when the trumpet sound I will appear;
> Four balls through me pierced their way,
> Hard it was I had no time to pray.
> This stone that here you do see
> My comrades erected for the sake of me.

The penalties for smuggling were severe, imprisonment, transportation, service in the fleet, and the confiscation and destruction of any craft found engaging in it. But for all this, the 'free trade' flourished. There was never lack of men with wit and courage enough to carry it on, and there was the incentive of knowing they could dispose of everything they were able to run. Their customers came by no means from the poorer classes alone, but included everyone, from the lord of the manor and the parson, downward. The gentry were always in the market for 'moonshine', as smuggled liquor was called, and for anything else the 'gentlemen' had to offer. They found no difficulty in reconciling such dealing with their positions as magistrates and ministers.

Very often, indeed, when a smuggler had the misfortune to appear before them, the case was dismissed on some pretext to other, to ensure there should be no interruption in the steady supply of these much-valued goods.

It may well have been an excess of moonshine that led the lord of the manor of Martham to an act which years afterwards, caused the setting up of, perhaps, the most remarkable memorial slab in any English church. Martham stands right on the route I have just described, from Horsey to Norwich, so plentiful supplies of gin and brandy were always going by. But first, let me give the inscription on this slab, then I will tell the story behind it:

> Here Lyeth the Body of
> CHRISTOPHER BUNAWAY
> Who departed this life
> ye 18th day of October, anno domini,
> 1730
> Aged 59 Years

> And there Lyeth
> ALICE
> Who by her life was my Sister,
> my Mistress, my Mother
> and my Wife.
> Dyed February 12th, 1729.
> Aged 76 Years

On the face of it one would say, impossible, but this is how it came about. The Lord of the manor had a daughter named Alice who, at the age of seventeen, gave birth to a son after incestuous intercourse with him. To hide the disgrace and prevent a scandal, the child was secretly taken away and placed in a foundling hospital.

When old enough to leave the institution he started work on the land, and after some years wandering from one place to another, chance led him one day to Martham. With her father and mother both dead, Alice was now owner of the estate, and needing a labourer engaged him when he applied for work.

He proved a person of excellent character and great industry, and in time rose from a common labourer to farm bailiff. His successful management of affairs so impressed Alice that she was persuaded to become his wife, not knowing, of course, that she was already his mother and his sister.

They were very happy till one day when he was undressing she happened to notice a peculiar birthmark on his shoulder. She then realized in a flash that her husband was also her son, and the horror of the discovery so affected her that she fell into a coma. In a period of consciousness she was able to explain the position to him, but soon after died.

The husband was no less affected and, as the inscription records, followed her to the grave the next year. And he left instructions that the slab should be placed in the church to mark their resting-places, and the circumstances which brought about their ends.

Wherrymen had plenty of opportunities for a little smuggling with their constant visits to ships at Yarmouth. A tub of gin and a few packs of tobacco could be slipped aboard without anyone being the wiser, and once up the river there was little to fear from the preventive men.

The *Little Georgie*, owned by George Griffin, of Ludham, was quite a notorious smuggler. She was nick-named the 'cabbage Wherry', because she mostly brought garden produce to Yarmouth market; but often as not she had other things under her hatches. After a good run for her money she was eventually seized and her owner, together with the landlord of the White Swan, at Yarmouth, received a stiff prison sentence.

I remember hearing a tale one winter's night in a certain pub which had all the atmosphere of an old smuggler's den. A cold wind from the sea sent the sparks leaping up the chimney; the ceiling was brown as treacle from the generations who had smoked their Irish twist and Dutch hard-cake there; a small oil-lamp cast a fitful, mysterious gloom over everything; my only wonder was that a group of riding officers or a posse of dragoons did not fling open the door and drag us all to Norwich gaol. But perhaps that was just a guilty conscience after a recent visit to Holland.

The weather outside made you draw your chair instinctively towards the fire, where an armful of blazing, crackling pine logs set weird shadows dancing round the walls. The warmth and ruddy glow of the flames, the glimmer of the lamp, all seemed to make it inevitable that sooner or later someone would start telling a yarn. I was content just to sit and let life return to my numbed feet and legs, while fortifying my inner regions with a peg of rum mixed with boiling water, two lumps of sugar, and a generous squeeze of lemon.

As I slowly thawed out I kept thinking of all the stories that treacle-brown ceiling could tell if it had the gift of speech; and my gaze had wandered to a primitive, but lively, painting of a Yarmouth lugger shooting her nets, when I became aware that the most talkative of the little blue-jerseyed group was embarking on a tale of much promise. There had been a few anecdotes about the ways of smacksmen in deceiving the customs, and of how they never seemed short of a fill of baccy or a tot of rum, so I reckoned we were in for a smuggling yarn.

"As we all know," said the blue-clad figure settling himself into the chair with a sailor-like precision, so that his weight was shared comfortably between the buttocks and back, "Grubb's Haven was a very different place in those days to what it is now."

There were mutters of assent. The road from Yarmouth to Caister now passes over where Grubb's Haven used to be, almost the whole area has been built on, and few travellers would realize it was once an outlet from the Bure to the sea.

"It was a lonely spot then all right, for all it was so close to Yarmouth, and many's the boat-load of stuff that's been smuggled ashore there. As you know, the beach chaps used to go off a mile or so and take it out of the Dutch or French luggers, then, when it was safe ashore, they loaded it on wagons and took it to different hiding places inland. Of course, all this happened at night, but come the morning no one would have guessed at the goings on because they drove sheep over the sand to cover up the marks of wheels and horses' hooves.

"But the time I'm going to tell you about, that is, if you've a mind to hear it, was when they had a bit of trouble of some sort getting hold of a wagon. It seems all the stuff coming in was bound for Norwich, so they got round it by using a wherry. Probably wasn't the first time, either, but anyhow, on the appointed night there she lay nice and snug against the bank waiting to be loaded up. Being a dark night, and not meeting any interference, they made a good run and put about two wagon-loads into the wherry, the usual things, tobacco, cigars, brandy, gin, wine, and all the rest of it.

"So on went the hatches and the wherry slipped quietly downstream till she reached Breydon. With a smart breeze easterly they squared her off and counted on a quick trip to Norwich.

"There were three brothers for crew, sons of old Christopher Royall, and as good wherrymen as you ever wanted to see.

"When they got to the Dickey Works—you know where they are, top end of Breydon—one of them noticed something a bit suspicious astern. They gazed at it a while, then all agreed it must be a sail; but even in the dark they could see it wasn't a wherry but the custom house cutter. Somehow or other the preventive chaps had got wind of the run, and were now out to catch the Royalls red-handed with all the stuff on board.

"We've all heard about the chases out at sea between the revenue boats and the smugglers; I reckon this was about the first one on the River Yare. It was really just the same as being at sea, though, keeping going and seeing if one could catch the other. For those Royalls had no intention of giving themselves up, not on your life; if the customs wanted them they could come and get them.

"So on and on the two craft went through the darkness, the brothers doing all they knew to out-sail their pursuers, and the revenue chaps doing all they could to catch up with them. But they couldn't do it, the wherry was too fleet, and they had to content themselves seeing her black sail gliding along like a big shadow over the night sky ahead of them. It never got any nearer and their only chance was to hang on and hope for the best.

"They knew it was very different from being at sea; the wherry couldn't give them the slip. Sooner or later she would have to stop, then they could pounce, if they were close enough up to her.

"And that's just what happened. By the time they'd got to Thorpe, the brothers realized the game was up, so they downed sail and moored hard by the church. With the customs chaps right on their heels there was precious little chance to escape; they were arrested, charged with smuggling, and had to serve a twelve-month sentence in Norwich Castle gaol."

There was a pause while our storyteller took a well-earned swig from his pot. The landlord took his cue and appeared from behind the bar with an armful of logs. The glowing embers kindled them into wild cascades of sparks till they burst at last into flames of rich yellow, inviting us to rub our palms in their welcome warmth. The landlord gathered up the empty mugs for replenishment, and prepared me another rum, with boiling water, sugar and lemon.

When all our wants had been satisfied, pipes re-filled and lit, and some of us had edged an inch or two nearer the flames, the story was resumed. This surprised me at the time as I imagined there could be no more to tell, with the guilty ones brought to justice and put safely behind bars. Naturally, I was all ears for what was to follow.

"I dare say you all know that being locked up was only part of the punishment for smugglers; their boats were taken as well, the usual thing being to burn them. That was really the worst of all because it took away a chap's living after he came out. It was a harsh law right enough, but that's how it was; and that was what they had in store for the Royall's wherry after they had taken out all the contraband.

"So as soon as the brothers had been carted off, the customs chaps set about unloading all those lovely cigars and all that beautiful tobacco—breaks your heart to think about it, doesn't it! And in the way of these government blokes, it was all done very methodical like; each item was written down as it was landed, checked once and checked again, and then the lot was sent off to bond. Took a fair bit of time, as you can imagine, with two wagon-loads to account for, and when it was finished they felt the need of something to slake their thirsts.

"So off they go to the inn nearby and spent a pleasant half-hour sampling the local brew and patting each other's backs for a good night's work. Shouldn't be surprised if they started figuring out what their reward would be, and whether a bit of promotion might not come their way for being such good boys.

"Anyway, they had a nice little spell, drinking and day-dreaming. But what a horrible shock was in store for them when they came out. The wherry they meant to burn had—well—disappeared!"

We all stared in astonishment. "Disappeared?" someone said, "blast, wherries don't just disappear! Had she sunk, or something?"

"No, she hadn't sunk. Far from it. Not yet, anyway. What had happened was this. The Royalls, as you know, had plenty of friends up and down the river, and you only find out who your real friends are when you're in trouble. Oh yes, when things are going nice and smooth and all that, a man may have plenty of what he's pleased to call friends; but when the going's a bit rough, and he needs a helping hand, watch how they fade away! It's at times like that, as I say, when you find who're your proper friends.

"That's how the Royalls were, up to their necks in trouble, and badly wanting a bit of help. I'm glad to say they got it.

"While the customs fellows were in the pub, drinking and counting their chickens, as you might say, one or two of the Royalls' pals were strolling about idly, or so it seemed, with hands in pockets and such innocent expressions on their faces you wouldn't have thought butter could melt in their mouths. But they were really keeping careful watch for the chance to put a little plan of theirs into operation, and it came when the revenue men went off to have a quick one. Like a flash, these pals of the Royalls slipped aboard the wherry, hoisted sail and made off down the river.

"As I say, the government blokes were properly flabbergasted when they came out again, for all they could see was her peak disappearing among the trees. They rushed across the quay, jumped into the cutter, and had every intention of giving chase for the second time. But they weren't able to. Why? Well, when they went to hoist sail, they found there was no halliard; and looking a bit closer, they saw there was no mainsheet either! Funny, that, wasn't it? So there they had to stay, watching the wherry's sail fading into the distance, and all their hopes of promotion along with it.

"And the strange part of it all is that the wherry did disappear; vanished, so to speak, into thin air. They searched for her high and low, but never set eyes on her again, nor did anyone else for that matter. Not for a twelve-month, that is; when, as you'll recollect, the brothers were due to come out of gaol.

"Then one fine day, bold as brass, there they were sailing through Thorpe with a freight of deals for Norwich. That made us all gape, I can tell you, but it wasn't for some time we heard the story of what had happened.

"It seems those friends of the Royalls knew quite well the wherry would be burned; so they made up their minds to cut her out, just as our old Nelson would have done if he'd been there, and take her away and hide her. But where? That was the problem. You can't make a wherry just disappear, as you said a moment ago.

"Then someone had a brain-wave: 'Let's sink her,' he said. 'No one will find her on the bottom, that's a sure thing.'

"And that's what they did. Took all the gear out of her, stowed it away where no questions were asked, lowered the mast and secured it to the horsa, then finding a nice, quiet stretch of broad, with just enough depth of water, undid the keel bolts and let her go down.

"For a year she lay there, taking less harm, I suppose, than if she'd been afloat. But when the brothers came out they fished her up, cleaned out the mud, slapped on some tar and paint, and shipped back all the gear. Soon after, as I say, we all saw them, large as life, freighting deals up to Norwich."

I suppose there is a bit of the Robin Hood in all of us, which may be why our little group hailed, as it certainly did, the defeat of justice with so much approval. In all true hearts there is sympathy for the under-dog; and on the rare occasions when he triumphs, if it be by wit rather than malice, then it is a stern nature indeed that can suppress a cheer.

Triumph, of a rather different kind, has always been the quest of politicians; in olden times, perhaps more than now, they stopped at nothing to achieve it. Rewards were great, in terms of money and influence, and the saying in local affairs, was 'get on the council and get on'. Few failed to feather their own nests very satisfactorily, and competition for places was, therefore, of the keenest. No trick was too low, mean or contemptible, if it led to a seat in the chamber.

In Norfolk early last century the usual thing was to bribe the electorate. The wealthier you were, the more votes you could buy, so victory generally went to the one with the longest stocking. Buying votes was fairly easy in a poverty-stricken countryside, but now and again, for one reason or another, it could not be done, then more drastic measures were necessary to ensure success.

A popular method was to round up all those likely to vote against you, and carry them off to some lonely spot where they would be out of the way till after the election. The important thing was that they should not be able to escape, nor call for assistance. Finding a suitable 'prison' was the key to success, and it did not take these apostles of democracy long to realize the eminent suitability of a wherry. She had plenty of room, could be anchored in the middle of a broad when escape would be impossible, and any cries for help would remain unanswered.

When the Norwich Municipal Commission was held in 1833, a certain Robert Alden gave evidence that he had been 'cooped', as he put it, along with others, in a wherry moored in the middle of Ranworth broad. All those who proved 'truculent' were deprived of their boots, in case they managed to swim ashore; they could then be easily recaptured.

As elections then lasted several days, food and drink had to be provided; there were ample supplies of beer, spirits, bread, meat and tobacco on board. A strong guard was also in evidence, made up of men armed with scythes, weapons calculated to deter the bravest would-be rescuer. An attempt at rescue was always on the cards and this time another wherry did sail up to see what could be done. But in face of the flashing scythe-blades, and being told that anyone setting foot on board would be cut down, she made off, leaving the imprisoned victims to their fate.

And it was not a very pleasant one as they were confined in the hold for a week, spending most of it at anchor in the middle of Horsey Mere. They had sailed there to be free of any more rescue attempts, and did not return to Ranworth till the election was safely over. Her reluctant passengers were then given their freedom.

Among the many other strange tasks wherries undertook, one of the strangest was acting as a hearse. It often happened that the only way of getting a coffin from a lonely farmhouse in the marshes to the church, was by water. It was then some wherryman, known to the family, would be called upon to help. The coffin was placed on trestles in the hold, strewn with flowers, and accompanied by the mourners. Looking up as the wherry moved slowly along, they must have thought how appropriate her black sail was.

A much more gruesome duty was performed in 1781, after the notorious Pirate Payne had been captured. He was tried in London, found guilty and hanged. Perhaps the authorities thought it would be best to exhibit him somewhere near the sea, so he was cut down, sent to Norwich by wagon, and from there to Yarmouth by wherry. Then, in a suitable place on the Denes, where everyone could see, the corpse was strung up in chains till rot, and the ravening beaks of sea-birds, left only the bones to swing and rattle in the breeze.

The promoters of the Norwich and Lowestoft Navigation must have had this sort of traffic in mind when they drew up their table of rates. A charge of twenty-one shillings was levied on every corpse carried along the waterway and it was the highest-rated item in the list, exceeding by one shilling the amount payable on an organ. These sums seem rather high bearing in mind that only seven shillings was levied on a four-wheeled carriage, the same on a horse, while five shillings sufficed for a pianoforte, harpsichord, harp or bass viol.

I always find these lists of dues interesting because of the different measures they contain. But you really need to study them with a dictionary in front of you, unless you are exceptionally knowledgeable in such matters, otherwise you may find yourself lost among the bundles, kilderkins, puncheons, chests, butts, hogsheads, pipes, firkins and weys. The reproduction of the table of rates for Southwold in 1789 contains several other curious measures.

Of all the river-folk years ago the women were probably the most striking. Usually they were the wives, but often merely the companions, of the skippers, yet they could handle a wherry with the skill of a man. Quite a few were big, powerful women, topping the six feet mark, and their invariable dress was a blue and white wrapper-handkerchief over the head, with apron to match.

Frank Etheridge was a skipper of the old school who more than once came on board the worse for drink. Lucky for him he took his wife as she would let go the moorings, hoist sail and work the wherry herself, till Frank had sobered-up. Then he took over while she went below to do the cooking—a wonderful recipe for married bliss.

These wherrywomen thought nothing of raising and lowering sail, quanting, stacking hatches, working cargo, and steering, even though they might have two or three children to look after as well. But it was a healthy life, and with no mate to pay, there were always a few extra shillings to spend on food. It was probably economic necessity that drove these women on to the water in the first place, but once there few wanted a return to life on shore.

Needless to say there were women of the other kind, too, who, although possessed of no skill in working the wherries, plied their own particular trade with marked attention to the needs of the men who did. They well understood how uncertain were the wherries' movements, how dependent they were on wind and tide, and might be loading or discharging at all hours of the day or night; so, as the wherrymen often could not go to them, they went to the wherrymen instead.

I heard a tale about this when I was yarning with an old wherryman not long back on the quayside at Norwich. We were standing about half-way between Foundry bridge and Carrow bridge, distant from each other roughly half a mile. This should be borne in mind, together with the fact that a wherry can be quanted from one to the other in ten minutes; what he told me will then be seen in its proper perspective.

It was about a wherry quanting through the city many years ago on her way to Yarmouth. Both skipper and mate were at work, walking each side in turn to keep her in the middle of the stream. The rudder was hardly used at all till they were approaching Foundry bridge, when the skipper gave a touch to the tiller which sheered her in towards the bank. Waiting her opportunity, a woman of the kind we are discussing, made a neat leap and landed safely on board. The skipper was obviously expecting her, as he immediately laid down his quant and accompanied her below, leaving the mate to get the wherry along by himself. He did not seem to mind doing this in the least, said my informant, indeed, he looked in the best of spirits about it.

His good humour was soon accounted for, as just past the bend, or about midway between the two bridges, the skipper emerged from the cabin, and without a word, resumed quanting. This was the signal the mate had been waiting for; he laid down his quant and lost no time getting below to sample the charms which had so speedily satisfied his skipper. Then, just before reaching Carrow bridge, he, too, appeared as if timed by a clock, and with another touch on the tiller the wherry sheered into the bank, the lady hopped ashore, and the trip to Yarmouth, which had never been interrupted, proceeded normally.

"And what did the young lady do then?" I inquired.

"Oh, she just walked back to Foundry bridge along the tow-path, jingling eightpence in her apron pocket, to wait for the next one through."

"Eightpence?" I murmured rather doubtfully.

"Yes," he said, "fourpence a time, that's all she charged. I tell you the cost of living then was nothing like it is now." He chuckled merrily as he said it and from the impish smile that flickered across his face I would have sworn his knowledge of this little episode was got at first hand.

Wherrymen were dressed as distinctively as wherrywomen, often sporting a bowler hat after the manner of coasting skippers, though many preferred the seal-skin cap of the smacksmen. In winter they wore leather crutch-boots, so-called because they came up the full length of the thigh; they were hand-made by local cobblers and cost a sovereign a pair. In summer they had ordinary boots, and trousers tied under the knee with string, a dodge probably picked up from the farm labourers. In one particular they nearly all dressed the same, wearing the 'North End silk' round their necks. How it got that name I do not know as it certainly was not silk but an ordinary red twill wrapper, or handkerchief. It was knotted at the front and tucked in the collar of the shirt, being intended as a sweat-rag as well as to keep out wind and rain.

Whether they ever danced in crutch-boots is extremely doubtful, as their favourite pastime was to stand on a table facing each other and step to the accompaniment of concertina or fiddle. It was really a competition, and before mounting the table each of the two contestants bought a pint and stood it on the counter. Then they went into a heel-and-toe step-dance and continued at it till one was so exhausted he had to give up. The other became the winner and entitled to both pints of beer.

These step-dances, which are done in a space about eighteen inches square, hence the use of a table-top, were once common among sailors. They are supposed to have originated in the long hours spent on deck with little to do except keep a look-out. As time began to drag they started shuffling from one foot to the other, then tapping their toes and heels, till gradually they built up a pattern which in time developed into a dance sequence. Very few are left now who can do these dances, or who can play the right music, but now and again you come across an old-timer willing to show you a step or two.

Many wherrymen were as good with their fists as with their feet, and in the eighteenth century several achieved local fame as pugilists. The most notorious was one by the name of Haylet who took part in many bouts just for the fun of it. Then his fame began to spread and a proper match was arranged at Horning, in 1774, against another of the fancy called Hindry. It was a bare fist contest and lasted no less then forty minutes, when Hindry collapsed, battered, bruised and bleeding.

Haylet's prowess soon became talked about in Norwich and one of the weavers, named Thomas Skoyles, thought to teach him a lesson. The result was a match for 20 guineas arranged to take place at Trowse. Skoyles proved a game customer lasting out for an hour and eighteen minutes, but at the end of it Haylet had hammered him almost insensible. So the wherryman walked off with the purse, which it would have taken him a year's work to earn in the ordinary way.

Climbing a greasy pole was always popular at country events, but for riverside sports a wherry's mast was often pressed into use. It was a bit thick for the job, giving too much purchase for arms and legs, but it caused plenty of amusement.

None of the bygone regattas would have been complete without the attendance of wherries for all sorts of purposes, quite apart from racing. Most important, perhaps, was to provide a bandstand. Music was an essential part of the proceedings and the ideal place for a band was on a staging over a wherry's hold. The *Star* served in this way at the Acle regatta of 1888, when the Carrow Band played aboard, and similar arrangements were made at Barton, Wroxham and Burgh Castle.

They were also in demand as floating beerhouses so that anyone who wanted, onlookers or contestants, could row up and quench their thirsts. Some had trestle-tables in the hold piled high with cold meats, pickled onions and red cabbage, cheese, home-made bread and farm butter, either eaten on board or taken away in baskets, while others sold sweetmeats, toffee-apples, fruit, lemonade and pop for the youngsters.

But there was not always plenty like this, especially in Norwich when there was a bad winter. Really hard frosts could bring hunger and destitution to the river-workers, as in January 1768, when the Yare was impassable as far down as Breydon. There was no form of assistance then for the watermen and their families and things got so bad on one occasion they were forced to parade the city streets carrying a miniature keel into which passers-by were invited to throw pennies.

Later on benevolent societies came into being to help out when things got desperate. One of these was the Norwich Soup and Provident Coal Society which provided food and fuel where it was urgently needed. Thousands in their time benefited from the soup-kitchen in Fishgate Street and just as many were saved from freezing to death round an empty grate by the timely gift of a bag of coal. This came up to Norwich in two wherries owned by the Society, the *Theobald*, 28 tons, and the *Integrity*, 34 tons. They were sailed for many years by Gill Lanham and his son. In 1877 the wherrymen themselves were remembered with a tea specially arranged on their behalf in the St. Julian's School Mission Room.

As we have seen, wherries did an almost infinite variety of jobs, carrying every description of cargo, and serving a multitude of purposes from bandstand and beerhouses to market-stall and prison. But the following newspaper accounts describe two further unusual services. The first says: 'On Thursday last, the Society of the Ancient and Honourable Order of Gregorians, preceded by a band of music in wherries and boats, made a very splendid appearance on the water, in procession to hold their annual venison feast at Postwick Grove, where His Majesty's and other loyal healths were drunk under a discharge of cannon.' That was in 1755. Fifty years later, just before Nelson humbled the might of France and Spain, another report says: 'The Royal Artillery, two troops of the 1st Dragoons, 24th Regiment of Foot, Colonel Patteson's battalion, the City of Norwich Regiment of Volunteers (on permanent duty), and the Rifle Corps, had a sham fight at Bramerton. One party (as English) marched by Trowse, and the other (as French) by Thorpe, to Postwick Grove, and crossed the Yare on floating bridges formed by wherries placed alongside each other and planked over.' So, if only indirectly, we can link the inland sailors of Norfolk with Wellington's victory at Waterloo.

A more joyous occasion was witnessed midway between these two events, on Wednesday, 31 May, 1775, to be precise, when the peal of twelve bells for St. Peter Mancroft arrived in the city. They had been cast in London and were brought by sea to Yarmouth; there they were carefully loaded into keels and conveyed to Norwich. Teams of horses hauling waggons took them safely to the great church overlooking the market-place, their journey through the streets arousing much excitement and interest. As already mentioned, these same bells were rung sixty years later to celebrate the opening of the Navigation between Norwich and Lowestoft.

But to dwell longer on these romantic episodes would tend to obscure the fact that for most of the time the life of a keelman and wherryman was tough and strenuous. It was never free from hazard, and although bad weather accounted for less damage than it did at sea, every gale brought its casualties. The following incident shows the sort of thing that happened.

In Novemember 1774 a wherry with coals, salt and other goods for Bungay, left Yarmouth in a very strong easterly blow. The weather got worse as she crossed Breydon till it looked like the open sea rather than an inland waterway. Just before reaching the Waveney she broached-to and sank, drowning both her crew. She was being followed by a keel bound up to Norwich, but the violence of the weather made it impossible for her to give any help. She reached the Yare safely and drove up as far as Coldham Hall, when her skipper, William Bell, was drowned. He had hold of the bowline as a tremendous gust of wind struck the vessel, tearing the sail to shreds and dragging him into the water. That same night sixteen ships were cast ashore on the coast with the loss of more than a hundred lives.

Sometimes death was not accidental like this but premeditated, as in the case of Benjamin Playford, a Norwich keelman. One night, in 1772, he went to the Tuns tavern, hard by the castle, and asked for a bed. He was given one, but when food was sent up to him later, he was found hanging from a bedpost by a cord, fastened round his neck in a running bowline.

Two years later a young woman called Anne Gelly, who must have been rather tired of life, threw herself into the river at Water Lane Staithe, Norwich. A keelman in his cabin heard the splash and calling for assistance went after her in his small boat. Two men ran from an adjoining malthouse and the three together managed to bring her ashore. But she was in a poor way so they took her to an inn where a warm bed was provided. She fully recovered and some time later a public subscription was opened to reward the keelman and his two helpers.

In several churchyards there are gravestones put up in memory of those drowned in the river. Thurlton has one, with a wherry beautifully worked in relief at the top, and the following inscription:

> Sacred to the memory of Joseph Bexfield who was unfortunately drowned on the 11th of August 1809 in ye 38th year of his age leaving a disconsolate widow and two children to deplore his loss.
> O cruel death that would not spare
> A father kind and husband dear
> Great is ye loss to ye three he left behind
> But he they hope will greater comfort find.

Sudden, strong gusts of wind, like that which took the sail out of the keel at Coldham Hall, are known locally as 'Rogers'. They strike, usually without any warning, and for twenty or thirty seconds blow with almost hurricane force. They are rather like the 'williwaws' in the Straits of Magellan though not so ferocious. But they have torn down windmill sails, stripped off thatched roofs, capsized haystacks and taken a wherry's canvas out of the bolt-ropes.

By keeping their eyes open wherrymen could get a few seconds' warning when one was coming, and if they were quick enough letting go the sheet and downing the tiller, usually came to no harm. But on one occasion five wherries were crossing Breydon together in a gentle breeze when a Roger struck them. They heeled over at a terrifying angle sending quants, boathooks, buckets, brooms and all the other loose gear over the side. Four got through safely, but the fifth, the *Five Brothers*, of Yarmouth, lost her sail and drove up on the mud.

The *Nymph*, of Norwich, had a very different experience, though only quick action saved her from being sunk. She was very deeply laden with deals for Ranson, but having a head wind, threw a rope to a steamer and was enjoying a comfortable tow. Earlier on there had been a great deal of rain causing a bigger run of fresh-water than usual in the upper reaches, and suddenly the *Nymph* passed into this. Being loaded in salt-water, she promptly began to sink through the lessened buoyancy, and the crew shouted out to the steamer to let go their rope. Luckily the mate had just walked to the stern, and seeing the wherry in danger of being towed under, cut her adrift. It remained touch-and-go even then whether she would stay afloat, but eventually a very thankful skipper and mate quanted her alongside Ranson's quay.

Considering all the traffic on the rivers, collisions were very few and far between. Of those that did occur, most were due to steamships getting out of control in the shallows and round some of the sharper bends, many skippers being pretty raw hands at working in confined waters. When Albert Powley had the *Bell* he was run into by the s.s. *Active* at Surlingham, but got off without any serious damage. The *Ursa Minor*, belonging to Woods, Sadd & Moore, of Loddon, was less fortunate when run down by the s.s. *Microphone*, in 1904. She sustained damage amounting to £15 which the owners of the *Microphone* had to pay. Three years later the *Vega*, also owned by Woods, Sadd & Moore, was in collision with a vessel called the *White Heather*, and received £1 10s. by way of damages.

From James Stark's 'Scenery of the Rivers of Norfolk'
Wherry-building on the banks of the River Wensum at Norwich, 1830s

Wherry woman at tiller
'Usually they were the wives, but often merely the companions of the skippers—'

Ford Jenkins, Pier Terrace, Lowestoft

Lowestoft in the Golden Age of sail–Scandinavian timber barques, wherries and a Thames Barge

A tragic accident happened in 1926 on board the wherry *Crystal* when the skipper's seventeen-year-old son was killed. She had dropped through Yarmouth Haven bridge with her chains and was getting up the mast when the spring-stay fouled. The son called to his father to pull it down again, and when he had cleared it his father shouted out, "Are you ready?" Getting the reply "Yes", he thought it meant the mast could go up again, so he let it go. But it stuck for the second time and he went forward to see what the trouble was. To his horror he found his son lying in the bottom of the forepeak, bleeding and unconscious. He died ten minutes after being admitted to hospital.

Witnesses said at the inquest that in all the time they had worked on the river, in some cases forty years, they had never known such a thing happen. It appears the son hopped into the forepeak to clear some additional obstruction he had noticed, and before he could get out again was crushed by the descending balance-weight. It was a foolish thing to have done though it was certainly not due to inexperience; the boy had sailed in wherries since he was eight, and had worked in them from the time he was thirteen.

Another grim occurrence was during the Burgh Castle Water Frolic in 1863, when two men slipped off the hatches of the wherry *Rigby* and had their heads almost severed from their bodies. They were laid out in a shed adjoining the Berney Arms Inn, and an old wherryman who saw them said they were a terrible sight.

Sudden and violent deaths of this kind, however, apart from the occasional suicide, were not common. Drowning claimed by far the most victims and there is a long list of those who met their end like this. It includes wherrywomen as well as wherrymen, for besides the natural hazards of their calling, there was the additional one of excessive drinking. It could happen so easily, a few convivial hours in the local, a pitch-black night outside, an unsteady step from the quay-heading, a gentle splash, and they were gone. If anybody happened to be around and fished them out, so well and good; otherwise it was the end of them.

One keelman was taken out of Yarmouth harbour in 1739 who had been such a short time in the water that letters in his pocket were still dry.

Gybing in the keels seems to have been especially dangerous as there are many instances of crews being knocked overboard. There were fewer accidents of this kind in wherries although a passenger was lost like this in 1776 when travelling from Yarmouth to Norwich.

An involuntary trip over the side was once taken advantage of to teach the victim a much-needed lesson. The mate of a certain wherry had his life made a misery by an exceedingly drunken skipper, and after one protracted session at a riverside inn, this worthy lurched on board and told him to be getting under way. So the mate hoisted sail, cast off and took the tiller, while his befuddled and dazed superior staggered on to the plankway to relieve himself. Missing his foothold, he toppled over the side, but as he went had sufficient presence of mind to grab a mooring rope still turned up on the timber-head. The mate saw it all happen, but finding the skipper had a firm hold, sailed innocently on towards Yarmouth.

After about a mile, and in response to many gurgles and shouts, he nonchalantly looked over the quarter to see him streaming out like a fish on the end of a line. With all the feigned surprise he could muster he called out: "What you over the side, Skipper? Hold you on, now, I'll haul you in. Don't worry old partner, steady now, up you come," and with a great heave he dumped the sodden figure on the hatches. "Funny I never heard you go, been in long, have you?" he asked, "lucky you took hold of that rope. Better get below after a dry shift, won't do any good at your age larking about in the water weather like this," and so saying he went back to his place at the tiller.

The skipper soon followed, and with the shock and the cold he was now completely sober. As he groped his way down into the cabin he kept mumbling that strong drink would never again pass his lips; and to the mate's everlasting peace of mind, it never did.

Incidents like this, along with all the other happenings on the river, soon became toothsome morsels to chew over in the four-ale bars. They were relished for a week or two, repeated to any newcomers who might not have heard them, then gradually made way for more up-to-date pieces of gossip. "Do you hear about old so-and-so?" or "What price the little old what's-her-name?" was the usual commencement, and with numerous interjections like "Darn that for a tale," or "Blast, bor, that's her thirteenth, in't it?" the story would be unfolded to the obvious delight of all the company.

"Do you hear about what the old *Accommodation* is up to now?" said a new arrival one night, looking in for an hour till the tide made. "No, what's that then, Stiff'un?" he was asked. But Stiff'un declined any further amplification till he had taken a long, thankful pull from his pot; then, wiping his mouth with the back of his grimy hand, said casually: "Turned her into an 'ospital."

"'Ospital?" everyone echoed, eyeing him with ill-concealed disbelief, "'ospital?"

"That's right," said the bearer of these remarkable tidings going to the fire, lighting a taper and putting the flame to his pipe. "Icerlation 'ospital or something like that they call it. Been a bad do with the smallpox down in Lowestoft, so they've moored her out in the Broad so it can't spread."

"An' how's mooring the *Accommodation* in Oulton Broad going to do that?" said someone rather sarcastically.

Stiff'un directed a look of the deepest sympathy at the questioner as if making full allowance for his never having been very bright up top. "How?" he repeated slowly, taking another rewarding pull from his pot, "why, I've just told you. She's an 'ospital; they've put everybody into her what they think has got the disease, and there they're going to stay till it's blown over." He looked at the company knitting his eyebrows: "So the lot of you best look out you don't catch it, else that's where you'll be for," then in more confidential tones, "and they tell me there's no beer on board!"

The horror of such a situation caused everyone to reach for his pot and drink eagerly, with many a sorrowing word for those unfortunates incarcerated aboard the wherry.

They talked long of the whole business, for wherries were not turned into hospitals every day of the year, and the tide had made a good two hours before Stiff'un was able to hoist sail again. But from that night onwards the *Accommodation* was never called anything else but 'The Hospital Ship'.

Another craft that caused plenty of argument in her time was the *Liberty*. When electric launches became popular means had to be found for charging their batteries, and this gave Benjamin Barber, of Oulton Broad, the idea of converting a wherry into a floating, self-propelled power-station. So he bought the *Liberty*, took the gear out of her, and installed a steam plant made for him by Elliott & Garrood. This, and the electrical equipment, was placed in the hold and cased over, with a small funnel projecting through the deckhead. There was an ingenious method by which the propeller worked in an orbit off the rudder.

For a small charge launches could come alongside for the night, have their batteries replenished, and be ready for their owners again in the morning. But the *Liberty*'s span of usefulness was comparatively short-lived because electric launches proved more trouble than they were worth and soon gave place to steam or internal combustion engines. But there was quite a pioneering spirit about her and it is not surprising her owner should afterwards have founded the firm of Barber & Croft which, in 1902, provided Oulton village with its first electricity supply.

The battery-charging activities of the *Liberty*, however, were soon overshadowed by the doings of the little *Gipsy*. She holds a unique place in wherrying history as she crossed the North Sea, cruised the length and breadth of the Dutch waterways, and sailed on eastwards to Berlin and up the Elbe through Saxony to within a few miles of Prague. Henry Montagu Doughty, her owner and skipper, has left a record of her voyagings in two delightful books *Friesland Meres and through the Netherlands in a Norfolk Wherry*, and *Our Wherry in Wendish Lands*. Both appeared in the early nineties and the story they told of the new trails blazed by the *Gipsy* set tongues a-wagging up and down the rivers.

No wherry had ever before gone foreign and the idea of one sailing on the Zuider Zee, on the Ijssel and Rhine, and up the Weser and Elbe, was something to argue about over many pints and into the early hours. Everyone, naturally, knew her history, how she had been built by Eliza Wright at Aylsham, and launched in 1875; how she had traded for about ten years till Doughty bought her and turned her into a pleasure wherry; and how, round about midnight on 18 August, 1888, she had left Yarmouth, bound for Stavoren, behind a tug. They knew she arrived safely because the tug's crew often talked about the trip when they got back, but only when these books came out did the full extent of the *Gipsy*'s wanderings become known. I commend them to those interested in reading about yachting in the grand manner towards the close of last century.

The following quotation, after the *Gipsy* had reached her 'furthest south', gives an idea of what she accomplished: 'The *Gipsy* had now voyaged through the entire length, from north to south, of the German Empire. The Elbe flowed north from us nearly five hundred miles to the German Ocean, and southwards, only ten miles of its course were between us and the frontier of Austria.

'We might have been towed some way further up, to the confluence of the Moldau, and had the Moldau been higher, past Prague to a place called Budweis, nearly across Bohemia. But there were only twenty inches of water in the Moldau.'

As the years rolled by and the wherry fleets thinned there was less and less to gossip about; and fewer craft meant fewer crews who sought the warmth and comradeship of the tap-room. Soon only veterans like Slushy were left to spin a yarn about the old days because, when commercial life on the rivers at last came to an end, there was no one to draw in after a quart pot and with a cheery nod all round say, "Do you hear about old so-and-so?" or "What price the little old what's-her-name?"

The last time anything like it happened was on the evening of 8 August, 1951, when news got round that the *Albion* had revived yet another tradition and sailed from Yarmouth to Lowestoft by sea. I had always hoped she might make this trip but the day before, when Jack Cates and I went down to the harbour mouth, conditions were as bad as they could be. An easterly gale was blowing with broken water everywhere, especially over the bar, and when we went into the Lifeboat for a pint we both agreed we should have to call it off. But during the night it fell a flat calm and the morning broke warm and sunny with a light air from the south-east. Conditions were, in fact, almost perfect and at midday I gave the *Albion* a pluck down the harbour against the young flood and half an hour later she was tasting salt water for the first time.

She made a beautiful and unforgettable picture dipping gracefully into the gentle swell, with the sun shining down out of an almost cloudless sky turning the waters round her into a sea of sparkling diamonds.

Few who watched her progress had ever seen a wherry at sea before as the last time one made the trip was in 1907. Like all the hundreds who gathered on the foreshore I found it really exciting to see her black sail spread over open water though Jack, who was never a one for heroics, said laconically "It was just like a trip over Breydon." But that night, when the pubs opened and the regulars began rolling in, you might have heard many a greeting begin with the familiar words "What price the old *Albion*, eh?"

I doubt if we shall ever hear them again for she is now sixty-two and her working-life is drawing to a close. There are no other black-sailed traders left, and apart from holiday traffic, the Yare, the Bure and the Waveney are deserted. The navigations to Halesworth, Bungay, Aylsham and North Walsham are derelict, their locks broken and in ruins. The country staithes have crumbled away and the red brick coal-houses are empty. Lorries supply the maltings and the riverside taverns cater solely for the tripper trade.

They are very different places from what they used to be. Gone are the pink and blue beer mugs, and the giant pike in glass cases. Enclosed stoves have replaced the cheerful, crackling log fires. The warm, mellow timbering and wooden benches have been discarded in favour of chromium plate and plastic upholstery. The Slusheys, the Walters and the Martins, what few are left, have been banished to small back rooms where they will be out of the way and free to spin their yarns and dream their dreams without interfering with the new-style customers from the motor cruisers.

But for me, wherrying will always be alive so long as I can go into the back room, and in response to my modest invitation, hear the familiar, friendly words: "Thank you, I'll try a pint of mild."

Appendices

APPENDIX ONE

List of Keels and Wherries

THESE lists have been compiled from many sources: official registers, where they exist; wills; building yard account books; newspaper advertisements during the eighteenth and nineteenth centuries; various pamphlets; and the notes of Harry Beale Johnson. These latter contain many useful details which he took down in Yarmouth from wherrymen still alive there between about 1920 and 1930.

I cannot hope that every keel and wherry built is recorded here; many a one, I know, was launched and paid for, used for fifty or sixty years, and then broken up, without her name ever once being put on paper. In other cases, the very papers where they would have been found, like yard ledgers and bills for work done, have been lost or destroyed.

The period up to 1795 contains the biggest gaps, but it is now probably too late ever to fill them. From then on, however, down to our own times, I believe they are substantially complete, though there may well be the odd name which has escaped me.

The keel list is only fragmentary and sets down mainly those craft which were working at the end of the eighteenth century, the period when they were being ousted by the wherries. Only a handful were subsequently built and as records of them before that date are almost non-existent the list, inevitably, represents only a fraction of the hundreds that were in use during the preceding centuries. If it does nothing else, however, it shows that in their final development Norfolk keels were appreciably bigger than has hitherto been supposed.

Towards the end when owners were selling their wherries and going over to other forms of transport, many were bought up by Hobrough of Norwich, stripped of their gear and turned into lighters. All of these, so far as I have been able to trace them, are indicated by an asterisk(*).

In one or two cases where it has not been possible to discover who the last owners or last skippers were, I have entered the names of those who, at one time, did own and sail them.

A date in the *Remarks* column shows that the particular keel or wherry is known to have been working in that year. P.W. means converted to a pleasure wherry.

KEELS

Name	Tons burden	Date built	Where owned	Last owner	Last skipper	Remarks
AUGUSTUS	50	—	Norwich	—	—	1775
AUGUSTUS	70	—	Norwich	—	John Roper	1795-8
BEEHIVE	80	—	Yarmouth	—	William Lewis	1795-8
BLAKENEY	50	—	Norwich	—	Mathias Royal	1758
CONCLUSION	59	—	Reedham	—	William Albrow	1795-8
CONCLUSION	70	—	Yarmouth	—	James Gates	1795-8
CONSTITUTION	70	—	Norwich	—	William Thompson	1795-8
CONSTITUTION	56	—	Norwich	—	Thomas Clarke	1768
DEBORAH AND ANN	43	—	Yarmouth	William Neal	William Neal	1769
DOLPHIN	50	—	Yarmouth	—	Robert Kett	1795-8
DOVE	—	—	Norwich	Foster	—	1756
DUCK	30	—	Yarmouth	—	John Reeve	1795-8
EDMUND	90	—	Yarmouth	—	John Harvey	1795-8
ELIZABETH	60	—	Carrow	—	Robert Kett	1795-8
ELIZABETH AND ANN	80	—	Yarmouth	—	Henry Hastings	1795-8
FLORA	57	—	Yarmouth	—	Roger Page	1795-8
FLORA	70	—	Yarmouth	—	James Wakefield	1795-8
FRIENDSHIP	42	—	Yarmouth	—	John Reeve	1777-80
FRIENDSHIP	60	—	Yarmouth	—	Godfrey Seaman	1795-8
GEORGE AND CHARLOTTE	50	—	Yarmouth	—	—	1776

APPENDIX ONE

GOOD INTENT	—	—	—	—	1773
HAND IN HAND	50	—	Norwich	John Aggs	1758–68
INDUSTRY	70	—	Norwich	Thomas Pile	1795–8
JAMES AND SUSANNAH	—	—	Norwich	John Dye	1756
JOHN AND ELIZABETH	45	—	Yarmouth	William Fisher	1771–80
JOHN AND GEORGE	47	—	Norwich	Robert Osborn	1768
JULY FLOWER	80	—	Yarmouth	Stephen Godfrey	1795–8
LONDON LADY	27	—	Yarmouth	Samuel Botts	1769
LONDON LADY	35	—	Norwich	Dixon	1795–8
MARLBOROUGH	80	—	Yarmouth	James Kemp	1795–8
MORRIS	48	—	Norwich	James Hutson	1756
NORWICH COLLIER	50	—	Norwich	Foster	1756
POLLY	80	—	Yarmouth	Samuel Dye	1795–8
QUICK DISPATCH	45	—	Yarmouth	Permeter Ansell	1795–8
RECOVERY	85	—	Yarmouth	William Thomas	1795–8
RESOLUTION	—	—	—	William Thomas	1795–8
RESOLUTION	60	—	Norwich	Edward George	1763
ROBERT AND MARY	60	—	—	Robert Osborn	1795–8
ROBERT AND SUSANNAH	53	—	Norwich	John Rudram	1765
ROYAL GEORGE	—	—	—	Thomas Wickham	1768
ROYAL OAK	58	—	Bungay		1781
ROYAL OAK	70	—	Yarmouth	William Goldsmith	1795–8
SPEEDWELL	28	—	Norwich	John Starkey	1795–8
SUCCESS	53	—	Norwich	Simon Watts	1768
SUCCESS	97	—	Yarmouth	Robert Osborn	1768–80
				John Rant	1795–8

Largest recorded keel.

Name	Tons burden	Date built	Where owned	Last owner	Last skipper	Remarks
SUPPLY	95	—	Yarmouth	—	William Empson	1795–8 Second largest recorded keel.
SUSANNA	30	—	Yarmouth	—	William Eldridge	1795–8
SUSANNA	80	—	Norwich	—	Robert George	1795–8
TRIAL	40	—	Panxworth	—	William Ebbage	1795–8
TRINITY	—	—	—	—	William Harding	1603 The first keel whose name is known.
TWO FRIENDS	28	—	Coltishall	—	Elisha Royal	1795–8
UNION	70	—	Norwich	—	William Paston	1795–8
VENTURE	20	—	Panxworth	—	William Noughton	1795–8
WILLIAM	60	—	Norwich	—	John Crancher	1795–8
WILLIAM	70	—	Yarmouth	—	Henry Wells	1795–8
WILLIAM AND ANN	—	—	—	—	John Antell	1763
WILLIAM AND MARY	40	—	Yarmouth	—	John Ward	1795–8
WILLIAM AND MARY	75	—	Norwich	—	Richard Thorning	1795–8

WHERRIES

Name	Tons burden	Date built	Where owned	Last owner	Last skipper	Remarks
ACCOMMODATION	21	—	Norwich	Boardman & Harmer	—	1838
ACCOMMODATION	30	—	Norwich	Clarke & Reeve	Bob Crowe	Lugsail rigged.

APPENDIX ONE

Name			Location			Notes
ACCOMMODATION	36	—	Norwich	Smith	—	Went to Portsmouth, wrecked on I.O.W.
ACTIVE	16	—	Dilham	—	John Gunnell	1795–8
ACTIVE	16	—	Sutton	—	James Francis	1795–8
ACTIVE	19	—	Norwich	Dowson	—	1838
ACTIVE	20	—	Norwich	—	John England	1795–8
ACTIVE	28	—	Yarmouth	—	Barnard Stephens	1795–8
ACTIVE	35	—	Geldeston	—	Samuel Mayhew	1795–8
ADAM AND EVE*	24	—	Norwich	Mrs. Howes	John Watts	Mrs. Howes kept the inn of the same name in Norwich.
ADELAIDE	22	—	Norwich	Norwich Gas Co.	Jack Lowe	—
ADEONA	37	—	Horning	—	Edward Wright	1795–8
ADONIA	18	—	Norwich	Sykes	—	1838
ADVENTURE	20	—	Hoveton	—	—	1795–8
AGENORA*	—	—	Norwich	J. Ecclestone	John Benton	Had a cockerel vane.
AGENORIA	23	—	Norwich	Osbourn	J. Ecclestone	1838
ALABAMA	24	—	Sutton	Tom Worts	George Mayes	Had the nickname 'Gouge'.
ALARM	30	—	Coltishall	Mrs. Wright	Jack Barnes	Mrs. Wright kept the Rising Sun Inn, Coltishall.
ALASKA	30	—	—	—	Tom Kerrison	—
ALBERT	—	—	Aylsham	Tom Shreeve	Bircham	—
ALBERT*	—	—	Langley	John Rudd	—	—
ALBERT	24	—	Bungay	Butcher	Rodney Holmes	—

Name	Tons burden	Date built	Where owned	Last owner	Last skipper	Remarks
ALBERT	24	—	Sutton	Bailey	Ben Norgate	—
ALBERT	30	—	Norwich	Mrs. Warnes	William Jay	Mrs. Warnes kept the Foundry Bridge Tavern, Norwich.
ALBERT AND ALEXANDRA	18	—	Tunstall	Joseph Powley	Joseph Powley	Last wherry to use Tunstall Dyke, 1897.
ALBION	30	—	Norwich	Tom Mace	George Mace	1880
ALBION, then PLANE, then ALBION	40	1898	Bungay	W. D. & A. E. Walker	Jack Powley	The only carvel-built trading wherry.
ALBION, see PLANE, see ALBION	40	1898	Norwich	Norfolk Wherry Trust	Nat Bircham	Restored by the Norfolk Wherry Trust 1949. Now the last trading wherry.
ALERT	33	—	Norwich	—	James Minns	1795–8
ALERT	22	—	Norwich	Dawburn	—	—
ALERT	22	—	Norwich	Mace	—	1838
ALERT	24	—	Reedham	Mutton	—	—
ALERT	33	—	Geldeston	—	William Holland	1795–8
ALEXANDRA	22	—	Aylsham	Stanley Bullock	'Sink' Collier	—
ALICE	—	—	Antingham	Hammond	Jack Dugdale	Hammond kept the Barge Tavern, Antingham.

APPENDIX ONE 207

ALMA*	—	—	—	—	—	—
ALPHA*	28	—	Palling	Yaxley	William Hawes	—
AMELIA, see TWO BROTHERS	24	—	Oulton Broad	Bull	—	—
			Yarmouth	John Mann	John Mann	—
AMETHYST, see ENA MAY	40	1895	—	General Steam Navigation Co.	—	—
AMPHION	30	—	Norwich	Richard Buttle	Gurney Read	Buttle kept the Evening Star Tavern, Quayside, Norwich.
AMPHION	32	—	Norwich	Hawkes	—	1838
ANCHOR	24	—	Norwich	Philip Head	Bob Goulden	—
ANN	—	—	Oulton Broad	Jimmy Gibbs	Jimmy Gibbs	—
ANN	26	—	Norwich	Mealing & Mills	—	1838
ANN	32	—	Norwich	Betts	—	1838
ANSON	22	—	Wroxham	—	John Crane	1795-8
ANTELOPE	29	—	Norwich	Read & Co.	—	1838
ARIADNE	19	—	Norwich	Gibbs	—	1838
ARTHUR*	—	—	N. Walsham	Cubitt & Walker	David Scott	—
ASLACTON	—	—	Aylsham	—	Ted Brown	—
ATALANTA	24	—	Acle	Porter	Bob Harris	—
ATALANTA	33	—	Norwich	—	Edward Philips	1795-8
ATLAS	37	—	Yarmouth	—	—	1838
AYLSHAM	25	—	Aylsham	Stanley Bullock	B. Wright	—
BALDWICH	24	—	Aylsham	Barber & Ingram	—	Square stern.
BARLEYCORN	20	—	Coltishall	—	Samuel Parson	1795-8
BARLEYCORN	30	—	Horning	—	James Bowering	1795-8

Name	Tons burden	Date built	Where owned	Last owner	Last skipper	Remarks
BARLEY CORN	36	—	Coltishall	—	Gazeley Kettle	1795–8
BEACONSFIELD, then GOODWILL	30	—	Yarmouth	Bacon	Walter Hurrell	—
BEATRICE	24	—	Berney Arms	Carver	George Knights	Carver kept the Berney Arms Inn and his wherry worked for the Cement Co.
BEESTON	19	—	Barton	—	Robert Adkins	1795–8
BELL*	35	1895	Yarmouth	Walter Bunn	Albert Powley	Fastenings were all copper.
BENJAMIN	18	—	Geldeston	—	Stephen Darby	1795–8
BENJAMIN	18	—	Norwich	Dowson	—	1838
BENJAMIN	24	—	Loddon	Woods, Sadd & Moore	—	—
BERTHA	20	189—	N. Walsham	Press Bros.	Bob Brackenbury	—
BESSIE	—	—	Norwich	Robert Hipperson	—	—
BESSIE, then LEISURE HOUR	20	—	Reedham	Charles Hall	—	1880
BESSIE	22	—	Trowse	Tom Read	Dick Palmer	Only wherry owned at Trowse, Norwich.
BETSY	13	—	Yarmouth	—	John Gibbs	—
BETSEY	25	—	Beccles	—	John Mayhew	1795–8

APPENDIX ONE

Name			Place			Notes
BLANCHE	22	—	Acle	Shreeve	'Brewer' Rivett	—
BLANCHE	24	1863	Somerleyton	Leonard Welton	Leonard Welton	—
BRITANNIA	16	—	Stalham	—	William Neave	1795–8
BRITANNIA	20	—	Stokesby	—	John Harrison	1795–8
BRITANNIA	20	—	Norwich	Wm. Tooley	—	Tooley kept the Cock and Pie Tavern, Quayside, Norwich.
BRITANNIA	22	—	Burgh Castle	Burgh Castle Cement Co.	W. H. Thaxter	Square stern, 100 years old when broken up at Southwold, 1929.
BRITISH OAK	20	—	Yarmouth	Rodney Holmes	—	—
BRITISH OAK	30	—	Norwich	Mealing & Mills	Barnes	—
BRITISH QUEEN	—	—	Norwich	Gurney Read	Gurney Read	—
BRITISH QUEEN	26	1873	Reedham	Wales	Richard Goffin	—
BROTHERS	18	—	Aylsham	—	John Maidstone	1795–8
BROTHERS, then FIVE BROTHERS	30	—	Rockland	Watson	William Porter	Watson kept the New Inn, Rockland.
BROTHERS	32	—	Norwich	Saxtin	Edward Roofe	1838
BUCKENHAM	12	1780	Aylsham	—	—	—
BURE, then LAURA, then RACHEL	—	—	Rockland	Stanley	Jack Woodrow	Square stern. Had red eyes on nosing 'to see where she was going'.
CAMBRIA*	20	—	N. Walsham	Cubitt & Walker	—	—
CAROLINE*	34	1860	Norwich	J. Porter & Son	Bygrave	—

Name	Tons burden	Date built	Where owned	Last owner	Last skipper	Remarks
CARROW	35	—	Norwich	Bessey	—	Went to Portsmouth, sold there and may have gone afterwards to the Thames.
CERES, then DOROTHY	14	—	Stalham	Harry Burton	'Shoddy' Clarke	—
CHARITY	13	—	Yarmouth	Valentine Gibbs	Gibbs	—
CHARLES AND HENRY	30	—	—	—	George Palmer	—
CHIEFTAIN	—	—	Yarmouth	Bessey & Palmer	Sid Bussey	—
CHIEFTAIN*	34	—	Oulton Broad	Johnson	Oldman	—
COLTISHALL	42	—	Coltishall	—	Samuel Thaxter	1795–8
COMMERCE	47	—	Bungay	—	John Mills	1795–8
CONCORD	18	—	Dilham	—	James Willimite	1795–8
CORNUCOPIA	20	1893	Stalham	Harry Burton	Joe Bircham	Built very narrow to go through old Wayford bridge.
COURIER*	30	—	Oulton Broad	Everitt	Patterson	—
CROSTWICK	21	—	Horstead	—	Edmund Reynolds	1795–8
CROWHURST, then FIR	40	1912	Yarmouth	John Bass	John Bass	Last wherry built in Yarmouth.
CRYSTAL	—	—	Yarmouth	General Steam Navigation Co.	George Spinks	—

APPENDIX ONE

CYGNET	40	—	Norwich	William England	John England	—
CYGNUS, then DIAMOND	—	189–	Yarmouth	—	Rodney Holmes	An iron wherry.
CYPRUS	24	—	Aylsham	A. R. Amies	Joe Bircham	—
DAHLIA	30	—	Norwich	Martin Wigg	Martin Wigg	—
DART	25	—	Norwich	Holmes	'Piper' Hawes	Went to Portsmouth.
DAUNTLESS,* see WOODMAN	23	—	Yarmouth	Harry Barber	Harry Barber	—
DAUNTLESS	26	—	Reedham	Mutton	David Thompson	—
DEFIANCE	23	—	Norwich	Culley	—	1838
DEFIANCE	42	—	Aylsham	—	George Tuck	1795–8
DIAMOND,* see CYGNUS	—	189–	Yarmouth	General Steam Navigation Co.		An iron wherry.
DILHAM TRADER	20	—	Dilham	Mathison	Sam Dugdale	—
DILHAM TRADER	20	—	Dilham	R. Cooke	Bob Brackenbury	—
DILIGENT*	18	1896	N. Walsham	Press Bros.	George Gedge	—
DISPATCH*	—	—	Stalham	Harry Burton	George Rump	—
DORA	40	1897	Yarmouth	W. C. Bunn	'Ophir' Powley	One of the fastest wherries built.
DOROTHY, see CERES	14	—	Dilham	Skinner Taylor	—	—
DOUGLAS	40	—	Norwich	—	Christopher Royall	1795–8
DOVE*	24	—	Yarmouth	Liffen	—	Square stern.
DREADNOUGHT	—	—	Norwich	John Kitton	—	—
ECLIPSE	12	—	Norwich	John Gibbs	John Gibbs	—
ECLIPSE	23	—	Norwich	Jay	—	1838
EDWARD	16	—	S. Walsham	—	Ishmael Waterton	1795–8
EDWARD, then PREMIER	23	—	Norwich	Edwards	—	—

Name	Tons burden	Date built	Where owned	Last owner	Last skipper	Remarks
EDWARD	23	—	Norwich	Harper	—	1838
EDWARD AND EMILY	22	—	Norwich	Edward Crowe	Billy Crowe	—
EDWIN	30	—	Norwich	Kitton	Dick Kersey	1880
ELDER, see IOLANTHE	33	—	Yarmouth	General Steam Navigation Co.	—	—
ELEANOR	24	—	Norwich	Holmes	Ted Carr	—
ELEPHANT*	44	—	Norwich	Dawburn	—	—
ELIZA	20	—	Norwich	Ned Osborne	Ned Osborne	—
ELIZABETH	27	—	N. Walsham	Press Bros.	George Gedge	—
ELIZABETH	28	—	Norwich	Osbourn	—	1838
ELIZABETH	29	—	S. Walsham	—	Benjamin Porter	1795–8
ELIZABETH	32	—	Norwich	Kett	—	1838
ELIZABETH	34	—	Norwich	Holmes	—	—
ELLA	24	1912	Wroxham	Nat Bircham	Nat Bircham	Last wherry ever built.
ELLEN	24	—	Loddon	J. J. Goff	Harry Deacon	In collision racing at Lowestoft, 1884, beached.
ELSIE, see LILY	18	—	N. Walsham	Press & Pallett	—	Lost at sea crossing to Holland.
ELSIE, then MIZPAH, P.W., see STALHAM TRADER	20	—	Horning	Martin Gedge, jun.	Martin Gedge, jun.	—

APPENDIX ONE

Name	Length	Year	Place	Builder/Owner	Skipper	Notes
EMERALD	35	—	Beccles	Crisp	'Duckie' Pleasance	—
EMILY*	—	1880	Hickling	George Beales	—	—
EMILY	28	—	Norwich	Potter	—	1838
EMMA, see INTREPID	20	—	Burgh Castle	Burgh Castle Cement Co.	George Knights	A very old wherry, square stern.
EMMA	24	—	Norwich	Tom Read	'Tebby' Martins	1852
EMMA JANE	40	—	Norwich	Ranson	Valentine Gibbs	—
EMMANUEL	22	—	Yarmouth	James Pumphry	George Knights	Square stern.
EMPRESS*	48	—	Lowestoft	Goldsmith	R. Kemp	Intended for steam wherry but converted to sail.
ENA MAY, then AMETHYST	40	1895	Yarmouth	Jay	Jack Mann	Last wherry built east side of Yarmouth harbour. Only one to set foresail regularly.
ENCHANTRESS	34	—	Yarmouth	Bessey & Palmer	—	—
ENCHANTRESS*	40	—	Norwich	Lawrie	Ben Smith	Fitted tanks for carrying tar in bulk.
ENDEAVOUR	16	—	Irstead	—	John Balls	1795-8
ENDEAVOUR	16	—	Aylsham Burgh	—	Matthew Bidney	1795-8
ENDEAVOUR	20	—	Norwich	Dowsing	'Kangaroo' Thetford	—
ENDEAVOUR	22	—	Geldeston	—	Thomas Hunt	1795-8
ENDEAVOUR	37	—	Norwich	—	William Lefever	1795-8
ENDEAVOUR	50	—	Bungay	—	Benjamin Ward	1795-8
ENFIELD	18	—	Bungay	Walker	—	—

Name	Tons burden	Date built	Where owned	Last owner	Last skipper	Remarks
ENTERPRISE	—	—	Dilham	Mallet	Colby	—
ENTERPRISE	24	—	Salhouse	William Nicholson	William Nicholson	—
ENTERPRISE	24	—	Yarmouth	James Pumphrey	Harry Neave	—
ENTERPRIZE	30	—	Bungay	—	Thomas Luster	1795–8
ERNEST	—	—	Aylsham	Stanley Bullock	—	—
ETHEL	24	—	Beccles	Darby Bros.	Dan Underwood	—
ETHEL	30	—	Ludham	George Newton	James Cooper	—
ETHELBERT	—	—	Coltishall	Ling	Bob Bates	—
ETHNIE	22	1894	N. Walsham	Press Bros.	John Loynes	—
EUDORA	30	—	Bungay	W.D. & A.E. Walker	'Charger' Salmon	—
EVA ROSA, see WAVENEY	22	—	Somerton	Di Thain, sen.	Di Thain, sen.	—
EVE	23	—	Norwich	Briggs	—	1838
EVENING STAR	26	—	Norwich	Reeds	William Corbett	—
EXCHANGE	30	—	Norwich	Richard Buttle	Jimmy Seago	1838
EXCHANGE	36	—	Norwich	Cousins	—	—
EXPERIMENT, then GARNET, P.W.	—	—	—	—	Tom Lodge	—
EXPRESS	20	—	Lowestoft	East Anglian Ice Co.	A. Baldry	—
FAIR TRADER	16	—	Acle	—	Edward Shingles	1795–8
FAIR TRADER	24	—	Dilham	—	Thomas Purdy	1795–8
FAIRY QUEEN	—	—	—	William Tooley	William Tooley	1876

APPENDIX ONE

FAIRY QUEEN	22	—	Salhouse	Nickerson	Bob Grimes	—
FAITH, see PARAGON						
FANCY	24	—	Reedham	Mutton	Joe Powley, jun.	—
FANCY	25	—	Horstead	—	Robert Blyth	1795–8
FANNY	—	—	Halesworth	Robert Burleigh	—	1883
FANNY	—	—	Norwich	Jex	John Mann, sen.	—
FANNY	30	—	Burgh Castle	Burgh Castle Cement Co.	George Knights	—
FARMER	25	—	Bungay	—	Benjamin Chase	1795–8
FAWN	26	1875	Reedham	Wales	Harry Bunn	Probably the fastest wherry ever built.
FIR, see CROWHURST	40	1912	Yarmouth	General Steam Navigation Co.	Jack Cates	Last wherry built in Yarmouth.
FIREFLY	42	—	Yarmouth	Bessey & Palmer	—	—
FIVE BROTHERS, see BROTHERS	30	—	Yarmouth	Bacon	S. Holmes	—
FLORA	34	—	Oulton	—	Charles Bull	1795–8
FLORDEN	39	—	Norwich	Brandford	—	1838
FLORENCE	48	—	Norwich	Ranson	—	—
FORGET ME NOT	33	—	Norwich	Royall	Royall	—
FORTITUDE	17	—	Norwich	—	William Lefever	1795–8
FORTITUDE	37	—	Norwich	Mealing & Mills	Charles Rumbold	1838
FOUNTAIN	30	—	Norwich	Mealing & Mills	'Trombone' Larkman	1838
FOX	30	—	Salhouse	—	Joseph Tooley	1795–8
FRANK	—	—	Burgh Castle	Burgh Castle Cement Co.	—	—
FREDERICK*	34	—	Norwich	Norwich Gas Co.	Tom Tooley	—

Name	Tons burden	Date built	Where owned	Last owner	Last skipper	Remarks
FRIENDS' ADVENTURE	14	—	Stalham	—	Thomas Staff	1795–8
FRIENDS' ADVENTURE	35	—	Coltishall	—	William Horn	1795–8
FRIENDSHIP	21	—	S. Walsham	—	John Newstead	1795–8
FRIENDSHIP	22	—	Norwich	Dawburn	Joe Jay	—
FRIENDSHIP	24	—	Potter Heigham	—	Robert Newstead	1795–8
FRIENDSHIP	30	1779	Norwich	—	John Leeds	—
FRIENDSHIP	30	—	Belaugh	—	William Martin	1795–8
FRIENDS' INCREASE	20	—	Sutton	—	John Ward	1795–8
FRIENDS' INCREASE	24	—	Potter Heigham	—	John Bowering	1795–8
FRIENDS' INCREASE	28	—	Somerton	—	John Dawson	1795–8
FRIENDS' INCREASE	30	—	Repps	—	Thomas Crane	1795–8
GARNET	34	—	Oulton Broad	Smith	A. Baldry	—
GELDESTON	28	—	Norwich	Howes	—	1838
GELDESTON	35	—	Geldeston	—	Stephen Darby	1795–8
GEM	28	—	Norwich	England	—	1876
GEORGE	18	—	Norwich	Juniper	Harry Royall	—
GERTRUDE*	40	—	Norwich	Ranson	Mayes	—
GLANCE, then HAZEL, see TWO FRIENDS	26	—	Stokesby	E. G. Trett	E. G. Trett	—
GLEANER	—	—	Aylsham	George Bircham	—	—
GLEANER	24	—	Norwich	Robert Steward	Edmund Royall	—

APPENDIX ONE

Name	No.	Year built	Place built	Builder	Owner	Notes
GLEANER, see ORION	25	1894	Horning	Gedge	Gedge	—
GLEANER	29	—	Yarmouth	Clark	—	1838
GO FORWARD*	27	1898	Yarmouth	Lee Barber	William Barber	—
GOOD INTENTION	20	—	Lowestoft	Harry Bunn	—	1795–8
GOODWILL,* see BEACONSFIELD	30	—	Yarmouth	—	—	—
GRATITUDE	23	—	Norwich	Boardman & Harmer	—	1838
GRATITUDE	32	—	Norwich	Clarke & Reeve	Jonas Buttle	—
GREAT EASTERN	12	—	—	—	—	Worked in Horstead marl pits.
HALESWORTH	34	1772	Halesworth	—	William Forman	The only wherry built at Halesworth.
HALESWORTH TRADER	32	1799	Halesworth	—	William Blanden	The first wherry built at Southwold.
HAND OF PROVIDENCE	28	—	Lowestoft	Anthony Brookes	—	1883
HANKEY	—	—	Halesworth	Robert Burleigh	—	The only one of Clarke & Reeve's fleet not lugsail rigged.
HANNAH	18	—	Norwich	Clarke & Reeve	'Rattler' Kemp	—
HAPPY RETURN	20	—	Norwich	—	George Carey	1838
HAPPY RETURN	25	—	Norwich	Richard Buttle	Harry Buttle	—
HARRIET*	18	—	Ludham	Hall	—	1838
HARRIET	22	—	Norwich	John Clark	William Holmes	1860
HARRIET	23	—	Norwich	Davy	'Spuddy' Osborne	1838
HARRIET	24	—	Norwich	Bessey	James Hunt	—
HARRIET	26	—	Norwich	Tidman	—	1838
HARRIET				Edwards		

Name	Tons burden	Date built	Where owned	Last owner	Last skipper	Remarks
HARRIET	28	—	Norwich	Manthorp	—	1838
HARRIET	28	—	Lowestoft	East Anglian Ice Co.	Jimmy Farrow	—
HARRY AND ETHEL*	30	1879	Yarmouth	Pratt	Jimmy Knights	1852
HARVEST	—	—	Salhouse	—	—	1795–8
HARVEST HOME	20	—	Coltishall	—	John Fox	1838
HARWICH	32	—	Norwich	Merry	—	—
HAZEL, see GLANCE, see TWO FRIENDS	26	—	—	—	—	—
HELEN, then PETREL, then MYSTERY, then LEANDER, P.W.	—	—	Horning	R. C. Locket	—	—
HELEN	32	—	Yarmouth	George Osborne	George Osborne	Skipper would never work on Sundays.
HENRY	19	—	Norwich	Brinded	—	1838
HENRY	20	—	N. Walsham	Frank Brackenbury, jun.	Frank Brackenbury, jun.	—
HERALD	20	—	Yarmouth	Brown	—	—
HERALD	24	—	Yarmouth	Deacon	'Ophir' Powley	—
HERALD, see MORNING STAR	26	—	Surlingham	Barnes	—	—

APPENDIX ONE

HERALD, then ROBERT AND EMMA	34	—	Norwich	Hipperson	—	—
HERBERT	—	—	Burgh Castle	Burgh Castle Cement Co.	George Thaxter	Lugsail rigged.
HERO	27	—	Norwich	Harry Hobrough	—	—
HERO	30	—	Norwich	J. & J. Colman	Danny Annison	—
HERO	37	—	Norwich	Wilde	—	1838
HEROIC	20	—	Norwich	Hobrough	—	1838
HETTY	—	—	Tunstall	—	—	—
HILDA	22	1898	Horning	Charles Rump	Charles Rump	—
HOPE	—	—	Halesworth	Robert Burleigh	—	1883
HOPE	17	—	Horning	—	John Hotson	1795–8
HOPE	18	—	N. Walsham	Frank Brackenbury, sen.	Frank Brackenbury, sen.	—
HOPE	19	—	Norwich	Dresser	—	1838
HOPE	21	—	Norwich	John Kitton	C. Hurrell	—
HOPE	22	—	Yarmouth	Newhouse	Christopher Royall	—
HOPE	24	—	Loddon	Bates	'Slant' Helsdon	—
HOPE	26	—	Norwich	J. & J. Colman	William Holmes	—
HOPE	29	—	Bungay	W.D. & A.E. Walker	Jimmy Lacey	1795–8
HOPE	40	—	Bungay	—	Saul Smith	1795–8
HOPEWELL	16	—	Sutton	—	Benjamin Mayes	1838
HOPEWELL	18	—	Norwich	Bessey	—	—
HOPEWELL	20	—	Catfield	—	Richard Salmon	1795–8
IDA, then BLACK PRINCE, P.W.	30	—	Yarmouth	Bessey & Palmer	Billy Bartram	—

Name	Tons burden	Date built	Where owned	Last owner	Last skipper	Remarks
I'LL TRY*	20	—	Somerton	John Squire	Di Thain, sen.	—
I'LL TRY, see OUR BOYS	30	—	Somerton	Di Thain, jun.	Di Thain, jun.	—
INDUSTRY	—	—	Loddon	Tom Beeching	Dick England, jun.	—
INDUSTRY	17	—	Cantley	—	Charles Hall	1795–8
INDUSTRY	20	—	Hickling	—	James Thaine, jun.	1795–8
INDUSTRY	24	—	Barton	John Gilding	John Gilding, jun.	—
INDUSTRY	25	—	Wroxham	—	Thomas Williams	1795–8
INDUSTRY	26	—	Norwich	Osbourn	—	1838
INDUSTRY	32	—	Norwich	Cook	—	1838
INDUSTRY	34	—	Norton	—	James Hunt	1795–8
INDUSTRY	37	—	Coltishall	—	James Willins	1795–8
INDUSTRY	40	—	Norwich	Brown	Gill Lanham	1838
INTEGRITY	34	—	Norwich	Norwich Provident Society	—	—
INTEGRITY	37	—	Norwich	George	—	1838
INTREPID	20	—	Wainford	—	Richard Darby	1795–8
INTREPID, then EMMA	20	—	—	—	—	—
IOLANTHE, then ELDER	33	—	Bungay	W.D. & A.E. Walker	J. Patrick	—
IRON DUKE, then	40	—	Southwold	Harvey	—	First iron wherry built at Southwold.
JAMES AND JESSIE						
ISAIAH	26	—	Norwich	Wilde	—	1838

APPENDIX ONE

Name			Place	Builder	Owner	Date
JAMES	50	—	Norwich	Clarke & Reeve	—	Lugsail rigged.
JAMES AND ELIZABETH	15	—	Reedham	—	Barzella Gosling	1795–8
JAMES AND ELIZABETH	17	—	Sutton	—	Benjamin Mayes	1795–8
JAMES AND JESSIE, see IRON DUKE	40	—	Yarmouth	Prentice Bros.	Harry Barber	—
JAMES AND ROBERT	32	—	Norwich	Dun	—	—
JANE	30	—	Norwich	Bullard	—	—
JEANETTE	18	—	Norwich	Dowsing	—	—
JENNY JONES	20	—	Yarmouth	James Pumphrey	Platten	1838
JENNY LIND	32	—	Norwich	Harry Hobrough	James Southgate	—
JENNY MORGAN, then NAIDE, P.W.	—	—	Yarmouth	Bacon	'Ophir' Powley	—
JESSIE	28	—	Norwich	William Bygrave, sen.	William Bygrave, sen.	—
JOHN	18	—	Herringfleet	—	John Woods	1795–8
JOHN	22	—	Beccles	—	Robert Barcham	1795–8
JOHN	30	—	Norwich	Orfeur & Bellin	Benjamin Smith	—
JOHN AND ANN	15	—	Yarmouth	—	George Bowering	1795–8
JOHN AND ELIZABETH	34	—	Norwich	Kitton	Jepha Dunn	1860
JOHN AND HENRY*	24	—	N. Walsham	Cubitt & Walker	Waters	—
JOHN HENRY	31	—	Norwich	Hobrough	Stephen Field	—
JOHN AND JAMES	35	—	Norwich	Brinded	—	1838
JOHN AND MARY	38	—	Coltishall	—	Joseph Chamberlain	1795–8
JOHN AND SARAH	24	—	Yarmouth	—	Valentine Reeve	1795–8
JOY	30	—	Dilham	—	Edward Livock	1795–8
JUMBO	—	—	Yarmouth	James Pumphrey	—	—
KATE	20	—	N. Walsham	Press & Pallett	—	Used for dydling.

Name	Tons burden	Date built	Where owned	Last owner	Last skipper	Remarks
KATE	22	—	Aylsham	Ben Cooke	'Shiner' Wright	Once did eight trips Aylsham–Yarmouth and back in one month.
KEARSAGE	20	—	Sutton	Tom Worts	Wright	—
KATHLEEN*	50	—	Norwich	J. & J. Colman	Dick Palmer	Ended in the Norwich refuse trade.
KATHLEEN	34	—	Norwich	J. Lee Barber	Stephen Wright	1860
KING EDWARD, see WONDER	90	1878	Yarmouth	Press Bros.	—	—
LADY VIOLET	27	—	Loddon	Case & Steward	George Rump	—
LAND PROVIDER	24	—	Hickling	—	James Moore	1795–8
LAND PROVIDER	26	—	Salhouse	—	John Riches	1795–8
LARK	14	—	Irstead	—	John Richardson	1795–8
LAURA, then RACHEL, see BURE	—	—	—	—	—	—
LEANDER	28	—	Coltishall	Mrs. Wright	George Kerrison	Mrs. Wright kept the Rising Sun Inn, Coltishall.
LESURE HOUR, see BESSIE						
	20	—	Reedham	G. Grimsell	—	—

APPENDIX ONE

Name		Place	Owner	Master	Notes
LEONARD	20	Beccles	Darby Bros.	Rodney Holmes	—
LEVERET*	40	Norwich	William England	Billy Royall	Once did ninety-four trips in a year.
LIBERTY	18	Bungay	—	—	1795–8
LIBERTY	24	—	Electric Boat Co.	John Knights	This was a floating electric power station.
LIBERTY	40	Yarmouth	—	—	—
LILY, then ELSIE	18	Antingham	William Horsfield	David Mason	1795–8
LITTLE BEE	23	Norwich	Thompson	Bob Bates	—
LITTLE GEORGIE	—	Ludham	George Griffen	—	1838 Used often for smuggling.
LITTLE MARGARET	28	Lowestoft	Saul	—	—
LITTLE MARY	20	Burgh St. Peter	—	Tom Seago	1795–8
LITTLE MARY	25	Norwich	Shaw	James Fish	1838
LITTLE SPARK, then MAID OF THE MIST, P.W.	12	Horstead	—	—	Worked in Horstead marl pits.
LODDON	30	Langley	—	Richard Ecclestone	1795–8
LORD EXMOUTH	28	Coltishall	Mealing & Mills	'Flea' Wright	—
LORD KITCHENER,* see METEOR	27	Yarmouth	S. Holmes	—	—
LORD ROBERTS	40	Somerton	Di Thain, sen.	Di Thain, sen.	—
LORELEI, see LUCY	20	Loddon	Case & Steward	Teddy Dean	—
LOUISA	—	Acle	James Benns	—	—
LOUISA	—	Martham	William Bracey	—	—
LOUISA*	—	Rockland	Sayer	Sayer	Sayer kept the New Inn, Rockland.

Name	Tons burden	Date built	Where owned	Last owner	Last skipper	Remarks
LOWESTOFT TRADER	26	—	Yarmouth	Warner	R. Pearson	—
LUCY, then LORELEI	20	—	N. Walsham	Press Bros.	—	—
LUCY*	42	—	Norwich	J. & J. Colman	—	—
LUDLOW	32	—	Norwich	Juby	—	1838
MACADAM,* see UNKNOWN	32	—	Norwich	Edwards	—	—
MADGE*	—	—	Yarmouth	Press Bros.	—	—
MAHALA	24	—	Yarmouth	Bessey & Palmer	Edward Farrow	Went to Portsmouth.
MAID	14	—	Tunstall	—	William Powley	1795–8
MALVE, see OLGA	34	1896	Yarmouth	General Steam Navigation Co.	George Farrow	—
MARBLE, see OLIVE	28	—	Yarmouth	General Steam Navigation Co.	Henry Andrews	—
MARGARET	—	—	Yarmouth	Hudson Barber	George Cooper	—
MARIA	24	—	Norwich	Tom Read	Jack Wright	—
MARIA	25	187–	Bungay	W.D. & A.E. Walker	Harry Bunn	Lugsail rigged.
MARIA	32	—	Norwich	Clarke & Reeve	Balden	1838
MARIA	37	—	Norwich	Butter	—	1838
MARIA	40	—	Norwich	Boardman & Harmer	—	—
MARIE	22	—	Horning	Gedge	Gedge	—
MARTHA	32	—	Norwich	Cope	—	1838
MARTHAM TRADER	—	—	Martham	William Bracey	—	—

APPENDIX ONE

MARTIN	32	—	Norwich	Cross	—	1838
MARY	—	—	Burgh Castle	Burgh Castle Cement Co.	James Halesworth	—
MARY	42	—	Norwich	—	John Taylor	1795–8
MARY ANN	—	—	Horning	—	—	1852
MARY AND ELIZABETH	25	—	Norwich	C. Smith	—	1838
MARY AND ELIZABETH	27	—	Beccles	—	John Cox	1795–8
MARY ANN, see ROYAL GEORGE	—					
MARY ANN, then SWALLOW	24	—	Cantley	A. J. Goldspink	Horace Hurrell	Goldspink kept the Red House Inn, Cantley.
MARY ANN	32	—	Norwich	Roger Moughton	Goulden	1860
MATILDA	26	—	Cantley	Walter Crowe	—	—
MAUD*	—	1900	Yarmouth	W. C. Bunn	'Shiner' Wright	—
MAYFLOWER	—	—	Aylsham	Isaac Helsdon	—	—
MAYFLOWER	14	—	Martham	—	James Myhill	1795–8
MAYFLOWER	20	—	Norwich	—	James Briggs	1795–8
MAYFLOWER	20	—	Beccles	W. Knights	W. Knights	—
MAYFLOWER	30	—	Bungay	W. D. & A. E. Walker	—	Reputed to be the phantom wherry.
MAYFLOWER	40	—	Norwich	—	Gilbert Crane	1795–8
MAYFLOWER	50	—	Norwich	—	Edward Fuller	1795–8
MAY FLOWER	16	—	Aylsham	—	William Sago	1795–8
MAY FLOWER	20	—	Ranworth	—	Charles Rumble	1795–8

P

Name	Tons burden	Date built	Where owned	Last owner	Last skipper	Remarks
MERMAID	34	—	Norwich	Mrs. Warnes	'Piper' Hawes	Mrs. Warnes kept the Foundry Bridge Tavern, Norwich.
METEOR, then LORD KITCHENER	27	—	Surlingham	Barnes	Jimmy Amis	—
METEOR	32	—	Norwich	Gurney Read	—	1838
MILDRED	29	—	Norwich	Bygrave	—	—
MONARCH	—	—	Acle	John Benns	—	—
MONARCH	30	—	Yarmouth	Newhouse	Bob Mann	—
MORNING STAR	18	—	Yarmouth	Tom Barber	—	—
MORNING STAR, see HERALD	26	—	Norwich	Reeds	William Corbett	—
MORTON	24	—	Burgh Castle	Burgh Castle Cement Co.	George Knights	—
MUTFORD	20	—	Yarmouth	—	William Callow	1795–8
MYSTERY, then LEANDER, P.W. See HELEN, see PETREL	—	—	Somerleyton	—	—	—
MYSTIC*	38	—	—	—	—	—
MYTH*	40	—	Norwich	Lee Barber	Jimmy Mulliner	—
NANCY	35	—	Norwich	Bullard	—	1838

APPENDIX ONE

NAUTILUS	18	—	Ludham	—	George Bowering	1795–8
NELSON	16	—	Reedham	Goffin	—	1860
NELSON	29	—	Norwich	Thomas Hearnass	—	1838
NELSON	29	—	Norwich	Cornelius Brown	—	1838
NIL DESPERANDUM	24	—	Yarmouth	James Pumphrey	—	Turned into dredger.
NORFOLK FARMER	30	—	Aylsham	—	John Rous	1795–8
NORFOLK HERO	40	—	—	—	—	Went to Portsmouth.
NORFOLK HERO	48	1860	Yarmouth	W. Bacon	Fred Crane	Had Nelson vane.
NORWICH TRADER	23	—	Norwich	Boardman and Harmer	—	1838
NORWICH TRADER	32	—	Norwich	Clarke & Reeve	'Shiner' Howard	Lugsail rigged.
NUMBER ONE*	45	1850	Lowestoft	Lucas Bros.	—	Went to Portsmouth.
NYMPH	32	—	Norwich	William England	'Nolly' Farrow	—
ODDFELLOW*	28	—	Lowestoft	East Anglian Ice Co.	—	—
OLGA, then MALVE	34	1896	Reedham	Wales	'Ophir' Powley	—
OLIVE, then MARBLE	28	—	Oulton Broad	Everitt	Tom Lodge	1888
OLIVE BRANCH	—	—	Potter Heigham	George Applegate	—	—
OLIVE BRANCH	20	—	Norwich	—	John Burgess	1795–8
OLIVE BRANCH	36	—	Aylsham	—	Clement Cook	1795–8
ONWARD	22	—	Somerton	Di Thain, sen.	Jimmy Betts	—
ORION, then GLEANER	25	1894	Loddon	Woods, Sadd & Moore	'Pintail' Thomas	—
OXNEAD	18	—	Oxnead	—	William Spinks	1795–8
OUR BOYS, then I'LL TRY	30	—	Oulton Broad	Rounce	Charlie Sayer	—
PALMERSTON	—	1898	Aylsham	Stanley Bullock	—	—
PAMELA	—	—	Barton	Jacob Cox	—	1888
PARAGON,* then FAITH	24	—	—	B. Barwood	—	—

Name	Tons burden	Date built	Where owned	Last owner	Last skipper	Remarks
PEARL	18	—	Norwich	Dowsing	Billy Helsdon	Helsdon kept the Barge Tavern, Yarmouth.
PEARL	24	—	Yarmouth	Tom Southey	S. Holmes	1876
PEARL	30	—	Beccles	Crisp	'Rattler' Kemp	—
PERSEVERANCE, then RUDDER GRANGE, P.W.	22	—	Yarmouth	Prentice Bros.	Billy Benns	—
PERSEVERANCE	24	—	Wainford	—	Stephen Darby	1795–8
PETREL, then MYSTERY, then LEANDER, P.W., see HELEN	—	—	—	—	—	—
PHAROS	16	—	Somerton	Di Thain, sen.	William Thain	1870
PHEONIX	—	—	Barton	William Hewitt	—	1888
PILOT	40	—	Norwich	Boardman & Harmer	—	1838
PLANE, then ALBION. See ALBION	40	1898	Norwich	J. & J. Colman	Farrow	—
PREMIER, see EDWARD	23	—	Norwich	Holmes	'Nolly' Farrow	—
PRIMUS	—	1896	Yarmouth	George Rumbold	Wright	—
PRINCE,* see WANDERER	70	—	Yarmouth	Press Bros.	—	Next largest wherry after the *Wonder*.
PRINCE OF WALES	—	—	—	—	Chris. Royall	1880

APPENDIX ONE

PROFIT	22	—	Whitlingham	—	William Brinded	1795-8
PROGRESS	36	—	Norwich	Jay	—	1838
PROGRESS	36	—	Norwich	Pope	Gosling	—
PROSPECT	13	—	Aylsham	Bircham	Parsons	—
PROSPECT	34	—	Norwich	Pope	'Cropper' Parsons	1838
PROSPEROUS	32	—	Norwich	Jay	—	—
PROVIDENCE	18	—	Langley	Rudd	—	1838
PROVIDENCE	19	—	Norwich	Hart	—	—
PROVIDENCE	20	—	Acle	—	Daniel Shingles	1795-8
PROVIDENCE	22	—	Norwich	Man	—	1838
PROVIDENCE	22	—	Horning	Horace Gedge	Horace Gedge	1795-8
PROVIDENCE	30	—	Upton	—	Benjamin Munford	—
PROVIDENCE*	30	—	Catfield	Riches	Jack Starling	1795-8
PROVIDENCE	32	—	Bungay	—	George Browne	1838
PROVIDENCE	36	—	Norwich	Davidson	—	1795-8
PROVIDENCE	40	—	Horning	—	John Kirk	1795-8
PYTHOE	23	—	Woodbastwick	—	John Macky	1795-8
QUEEN*	—	—	—	—	—	Used by Commissioners for ballasting in harbour.
QUEEN ALEXANDRA*	—	—	Yarmouth	Press Bros.	—	
QUEEN OF THE YARE, see WAVENEY QUEEN	32	—	Norwich	Steward & Patteson	—	—
RACHEL, see BURE, see LAURA	—	—	Norwich	Edward J. Edwards	—	—
RAMBLER	—	189—	Horning	Crowe	Jack Mann, jun.	—

Name	Tons burden	Date built	Where owned	Last owner	Last skipper	Remarks
RAMONA*	23	—	Yarmouth	Harry Barber	Joe High	—
RANSON*	34	—	Yarmouth	Bessey & Palmer	Jimmy Mulliner	—
RED ROVER	34	—	Yarmouth	Sidney Lacon	—	—
REED BIRD	20	—	Lowestoft	East Anglian Ice Co.	—	—
RHODA*	45	—	Norwich	William England	Bob England	—
RIGBY	—	—	—	—	—	Two men killed aboard 1863.
ROBERT	29	—	Norwich	Merry	—	1838
ROBERT ALFRED*	30	1882	Yarmouth	R. Pratt	William Hurrell	—
ROBERT AND CHARLOTTE	20	—	Reedham	George Porter	George Porter	—
ROBERT AND EMMA, see HERALD	34	—	Yarmouth	Bessey & Palmer	—	—
ROBERT AND FRANCES	43	—	Yarmouth	—	John Thomas	1795–8
ROBERT AND HENRY*	22	—	Yarmouth	Horace Hurrell	'Dorry' Hurrell	1838
ROBERT AND MARY	32	—	Norwich	Knobbs	Robert Nobbs	1795–8
ROBERT AND MARY	45	—	Norwich	John Anderson	John Anderson	Known as the 'Market Wherry'.
ROB ROY	20	—	Reedham	—	—	
ROCKLAND TRADER	—	—	Norwich	Lacey & Lincoln	—	—
ROVER	20	—	Norwich	—	Michael Jay	1795–8

APPENDIX ONE   231

Name				Place	Owner	Skipper	Notes
ROYAL CHARLOTTE	—	—	—	Norwich	—	John Sidel	1762. One of the passenger wherries between Norwich and Yarmouth.
ROYAL CHARLIE	—	—	—	Oxnead	Charles Browne	—	—
ROYAL GEORGE, then MARY ANN	—	—	—	—	Sacret	Sam Holmes	1888 Square stern.
ROYAL GEORGE	16	—	—	Yarmouth	—	William Lilly	1795–8
ROYAL GEORGE	20	—	—	Flixton	—	James Mingay	1795–8
RUBY	17	—	—	Loddon	Woods, Sadd & Moore	Jimmy Waterson Clarke	—
RUBY	40	—	—	Beccles	Crisp	—	—
SAGAMORE	26	—	—	Norwich	Squirrel & Utting	Sam Gutteridge	—
SALLY	36	—	—	Yarmouth	Bessey & Palmer	—	—
SAMUEL	—	—	—	Ludham	S. Clarke	—	—
SAMUEL AND HARRIET	29	—	—	Norwich	Gurney Read	—	1838
SARAH	14	—	—	Barton	—	James Amis	1795–8
SARAH	18	—	—	Rockland	Stanley	—	Square stern.
SARAH ANN	25	—	—	Norwich	Utting	William Appleby	Square stern.
SECUNDA*	20	1902	—	Yarmouth	James Pumphrey	—	—
SELINA	—	—	—	Yarmouth	George Rumbold	Jack Goodrich	—
SEVEN BROTHERS	—	1902	—	Horning	J. Ecclestone	J. Ecclestone	—
SHAMROCK*	35	—	—	Yarmouth	Robert Crowe	—	—
SHANNON	24	—	—	Yarmouth	W. C. Bunn	Albert Powley	—
SHEPHERD, then BRITANNIA, P.W.	—	—	—	Coltishall	Bailey & Sutton Ling	Sam Wenn	—

Name	Tons burden	Date built	Where owned	Last owner	Last skipper	Remarks
SHIP	20	—	Reedham	Richard Mutton	'Piper' Hawes	Mutton kept the Ship Tavern, Reedham.
SIRIUS	30	1896	Loddon	Woods, Sadd & Moore	Bob Bailey	—
SISTERS	30	—	Oulton Broad	Joe Powley	—	—
SNIPE	28	—	Norwich	Cook & Wright	—	1838
SNIPE	30	—	Norwich	Collier	Ben Atkins	—
SPRAY	36	—	Norwich	Billy Royall	Billy Royall	—
SPREAD EAGLE	—	—	Yarmouth	James Smythe	—	1610 The first wherry whose name is known.
SPRING	30	—	Norwich	Holmes	Dick Palmer	1880
SPRING	42	—	Norwich	Palmer	—	1838
STALHAM TRADER, then ELSIE, then MIZPAH, P.W.	20	—	Stalham	Robert Cooke	Bob Brackenbury	—
STAR	18	—	Halesworth	Lambert	Lambert	Last wherry on Blyth Navigation.
STAR	20	—	Norwich	Holmes	Arthur Baldry	—
STAR	24	—	Reedham	Wales	Charles Calver	—
STAR	24	—	Acle	Squires	Ben Bessey	—
STAR	28	—	Norwich	Ecclestone		Went to Portsmouth.

APPENDIX ONE 233

STAR OF HOPE*	44	—	Norwich	J. & J. Colman	Bob Hovell	—
STELLA	20	—	Rockland	Stanley	—	—
STOKESBY TRADER	30	—	—	—	—	—
SUCCESS	40	—	Norwich	—	Joshua Jay	1795-8
SURPRISE	—	—	Yarmouth	—	—	—
SURPRISE	28	—	Norwich	Howes	—	1838
SUSIE AND ROSA, see URSA MINOR	26	—	Somerleyton	Somerleyton Brick Co. 'Rattler' Kemp		
SWALLOW, see MARY ANN	24	—	Yarmouth	Newhouse	'Deaf' Durrant	—
SWIFT	24	—	Yarmouth	Newhouse	—	—
SWIFT	29	—	Norwich	Squire	—	1838
THEOBALD	28	—	Norwich	Norwich Provident Society	Gill Lanham	—
THEODORE	18	—	Lowestoft	R. J. Latten	—	—
THERESA	42	—	Yarmouth	Bessey & Palmer	—	—
THERESA	44	—	Norwich	Fred Brown	William Parker	—
THISTLE	20	—	Oulton Broad	East Anglian Ice Co.	—	—
THOMAS	16	—	Norwich	Crane	—	1838
THOMAS	30	—	Norwich	Bygrave	—	—
THOMAS	34	—	Norwich	Tom Read	John Bullard	—
THOMAS AND MARIA	37	—	Norwich	Jay	—	1838
THOMAS AND MARIA	34	—	Yarmouth	Martin Barber	Wright	Lugsail rigged.
THOMAS THE FRIEND-SHIP	40	—	Salhouse	—	Robert Dingle	1795-8
THORN*	22	—	Reedham	Mutton	—	—
THREE SISTERS	18	—	Aylsham	—	John Lovorick	1795-8

Name	Tons burden	Date built	Where owned	Last owner	Last skipper	Remarks
THREE BROTHERS	25	—	Norwich	Wells	—	1838
TIGER*	38	—	Norwich	Clarke & Reeve	Jimmy Lambert	Ended in Norwich refuse trade.
TRADER	—	—	Hautbois	Girling	—	1888
TRAFALGAR	40	—	Norwich	Hawkes	—	1838
TRIXIE	—	—	—	E. J. Larner	—	1888
TUNSTALL TRADER	—	—	Tunstall	Roger Powley	Roger Powley	—
TWO BROTHERS	24	—	Yarmouth	W. C. Bunn	Harry Brinded	—
TWO BROTHERS, then AMELIA	24	—	Yarmouth	Crowe	—	—
TWO BROTHERS	29	—	Langley	—	William Porter	1795–8
TWO BROTHERS	30	—	Yarmouth	—	Isaac Cheeper	1795–8
TWO BROTHERS	40	—	Norwich	Knobbs	—	1838
TWO FRIENDS, then GLANCE, then HAZEL	26	—	Langley	John Rudd	—	—
TWO WILLIAMS	29	—	Beccles	—	Robert Mayhew	1795–8
TWO WILLIAMS	32	—	Norwich	Thompson	—	1838
UNEXPECTED*	30	—	Yarmouth	James Pumphrey	Rodney Holmes	—
UNION	—	—	Aylsham	—	—	—
UNION	28	—	Horstead	—	John Reynolds	1795–8

APPENDIX ONE

UNKNOWN, then MACADAM	32	—	Norwich	Mrs. Dawson	Sukie Dawson	—
URANUS	35	1895	Loddon	Woods, Sadd & Moore	Bob Barnes	—
URSA MINOR, then SUSIE AND ROSA	26	—	Loddon	Woods, Sadd & Moore	—	—
VALENTINE	32	—	Norwich	Rose	—	1838
VEGA	29	1896	Loddon	Woods, Sadd & Moore	Jimmy Porter	—
VENUS	15	—	Dilham	—	Robert Chase	1795–8
VENUS	20	—	Norwich	Wm. Tooley	Philip Hollis	1860 Tooley kept the Cock and Pie Tavern, Quayside, Norwich.
VENUS	23	—	Norwich	Thompson	—	1838
VICTOR	28	—	Oulton	T. Johnson	—	—
VICTORIA	18	—	Norwich	J. Porter & Sons	—	—
VICTORIA, then CHLOE, P.W.	24	—	Bungay	W.D. & A.E. Walker	—	—
VICTORIA	25	—	Norwich	Riches	—	1838
VICTORY	—	—	Antingham	Mrs. Larner	—	—
VICTORY	21	—	Yarmouth	William Carr, sen.	William Carr, sen.	1872
VICTORY	32	—	Norwich	Edwards	—	1838
VIOLET	20	—	Yarmouth	Tom Barber	—	—
VIOLET	—	—	Catfield	Riches	—	—
VIRGIN	22	—	Wroxham	—	Thomas Swan	—
VIVID	—	—	Norwich	John Anderson	John Anderson	1795–8
VOLUNTEER	26	—	Aylsham	Tom Shreeve	Rivett	—

Name	Tons burden	Date built	Where owned	Last owner	Last skipper	Remarks
WALBERSWICK	24	—	Norwich	J. & J. Colman	Joe Jay	—
WANDERER, then PRINCE	70	—	Yarmouth	Lee Barber	Dan Watts	Next largest wherry after the *Wonder*.
WARHAWK	—	—	—	Bon Edwards	—	—
WARRIOR	30	—	Oulton Broad	H. Johnson	—	1838
WATERLOO	26	—	Norwich	Boardman & Harmer	—	1795–8
WAVENEY	20	—	Geldeston	—	William Holland, jun.	—
WAVENEY, then EVA ROSA	22	—	—	—	—	—
WAVENEY QUEEN, then QUEEN OF THE YARE	32	—	—	—	—	—
WELCOME HOME	18	—	N. Walsham	Cubitt & Walker	Richard Buttle	—
WELCOME HOME	22	—	Norwich	Richard Buttle	John Mann	Went to Portsmouth.
WELLINGTON	36	—	Norwich	—	'Friday' Wright	—
WENSUM*	36	—	Norwich	William England	—	1838
WENSUM	36	—	Norwich	Cousins	—	—
WENSUM	60	—	Norwich	Hobrough	—	—
WHEATSHEAF	42	—	Coltishall	—	Gould Scott	—
WIDGEON	28	1897	Norwich	Billy Tooley	Billy Tooley	1795–8
WILLIAM	20	—	Norwich	J. & J. Colman	William Clark	Ended in Norwich refuse trade.

APPENDIX ONE 237

Name	Tons	Built	Port	Owner	Skipper	Notes
WILLIAM	20	—	Stalham	Robert Cooke	Harry Powley	—
WILLIAM	30	—	Norwich	Clarke & Reeve	Albert Gutteridge	Lugsail rigged.
WILLIAM	32	—	Norwich	Boardman & Harmer	—	1838
WILLIAM	38	—	Norwich	Kitton	'Jacko' Scarles	1860
WILLIAM IV	32	—	Norwich	Squire	—	1838
WILLIAM AND BETSEY	43	—	Coltishall	—	Edward Smith	1795–8
WILLIAM AND ELIZABETH	29	—	Norwich	William Wickham	—	1838
WILLIAM AND MARIA	23	—	Norwich	Crow	—	1838
WILLIAM AND MARY	15	1777	—	—	—	—
WILLIAM AND MARY	15	—	Norwich	Bell	—	1838
WILLIAM AND MARY	25	—	Norwich	Clear	—	1838
WILLOCK	16	—	Sutton	—	—	1795–8
WODEHOUSE	25	—	Norwich	Hawkes	—	1838
WONDER,* then KING EDWARD	90	1878	Yarmouth	T. M. Reed	George Copling	Largest wherry ever built.
WOODMAN, then DAUNTLESS	23	—	N. Walsham	Cubitt & Walker	George Roper, jun.	—
YARE	37	—	Norwich	Bean	—	1838
ZEPHYR	20	—	Beccles	J. Barber	John Thomas	—
ZEPHYR	30	—	Acle	James Benns	Walter Tyrell	—
ZEPHYR*	40	—	Yarmouth	T. M. Read	—	Last wherry to have peak halliard.
ZOE	20	—	Rockland	Stanley	Bob Hovell	—
ZULU	20	—	Catfield	Riches	Jimmy Wright	—

APPENDIX TWO

List of Pleasure Wherries

THE first pleasure wherries were traders with their holds swept out and a few pieces of rough furniture installed such as beds, tables, chairs and chests-of-drawers. Cooking for the passengers was done by the crew on the cabin stove. After serving in this way for a month or two in summer they reverted to normal working for the rest of the year.

The *Blanche*, in 1863, started the fashion and from then on holidays of this kind became so popular that a number of craft were permanently converted for pleasuring, the hold being decked over and the space divided up into saloon, bedrooms, lavatory, galley and so on.

The success of these conversions led to pleasure wherries being specially designed and built and they were never used for trading. All these, together with the permanent conversions, are included in this list, but not the traders which were only used temporarily.

An asterisk (*) indicates those built as pleasure wherries.

*Alma**	*Darkie**	*Fawn*
*Arcadia**	*Diligent*	*Flora**
*Ardea**	*Dragon**	*Florence**
Bertha	*Ecila**	*Garnet*
*Black Prince**	*Elizabeth*	*Gaviota**
*Bramble**	*Elsie*	*Gipsy**
Britannia	*Endeavour**	*Gladys*
British Queen	*Enterprise*	
	*Empress of India**	
	Ethnie	*Hathor**
Chloe		*Hautbois*
*Claudian**		*Herald*
*Corinne**	*Fairy Queen**	*Heron*
*Cyclops**		

APPENDIX TWO

Idler*
Industry*
Iolanthe*

Kate

Leander
Liberty*
Lion*
Lorelei
Lorna Doone

Maid of the Mist
Mizpah

Naide
Natal*

Olive May*

Rambler*
Red Rover
Reindeer*
Rose*
Rudder Grange

Samuel
Silver Cloud
Solace*
Sunbeam*
Sun Dog*
Surprise*

Sydney
Sylvia

Toad
Triumph

Vera*
Victor
Victoria
Victory*
Volunteer

Warrior

Zenobia
Zoe

APPENDIX THREE

Glossary of Wherrymen's Terms

BILLET WOOD: oak branches for smoking bloaters.
BIN IRON: half-round iron, 2½ inches wide, extending round the sheer strake to form a rubber.
BOKE: to load cargo above the level of the shifting right-ups, with the hatches resting on top: equivalent to deck cargo.
BONNET: extra canvas added to the foot of the sail in light airs: sometimes called the 'Irishman's topsail'.
BOTT: knob on the shoulder end of the quant, similar to the truck on a mast.
BRIDGE HOLE: space for a craft to go through after a bridge has swung or lifted.
BROAD: fresh water lake, i.e. broad water, in distinction to narrow water, or river.
BUNCH OF PEARS: decorative device, much favoured at one time, drawn entirely with a compass.
BUTT: large section of tree trunk weighing a ton or more.
CABIN SLIP: sliding hatch in cabin top, found only in wherries with high sternsheets.
CARLING BOARD: small hatch covering the space in foredeck in which the foot of the mast swings.
COBURG: wooden fairing round the protrusion of the stove-pipe through the cabin top: the chimney, un-shipped when sailing, fits on to this protrusion.
DROPPING CHAINS: chains thrown over from the bows for negotiating Yarmouth Haven bridge stern first: comparable with dredging an anchor, but more easily controlled.
DOWN TO HER BINS: heavily-laden wherry with bin irons submerged.
DYDLE: to dredge, or clean out, rivers and dykes.
FATHOM OF REEDS: number of bundles a man can get both arms round, usually five or six.
FOOT: piece of wood at the bottom end of the quant to prevent it sinking too deeply into the river bed.
FOREPEAK: forecastle.
GAFF LINE: rope from gaff-end to sternsheets for use when gybing with the sail goosewinged, i.e. scandalized.
HAIRPIN IRON: bin iron where it goes round the stem.

HARPENS: overhangs of the covering board fore and aft: probably derived from 'hairpins', which shape they resemble.
HERRING HOLE; sheeve-hole at the mast head.
HORSA: horse.
HOVES: roots of riverside vegetation growing out into stream: unless regularly 'drawn' choke the navigation.
JENNY MORGAN: wind-vane depicting Welsh girl: all other devices are simply vanes.
KILLER: small wooden washtub or hand-basin.
KINDLE: wind is said to kindle up when it starts to freshen.
LAID: water just frozen over.
MARDLE: to chat or gossip.
NOGG: strong beer, hence noggin.
PARREL LASHING: cord threaded through trolleys, or wooden balls, to keep gaff-jaws to mast.
PINPATCHES: winkles.
PLANCEA: covering board, from just aft of the forward timber head to just forward of the after one.
PLANKWAY: deck, made of a single plank, on either side of the hold.
PLEASURING: taking holiday parties instead of trading.
QUANT: wooden pole, 24 feet long, for pushing wherry when wind is unfavourable or when there is no wind.
REED ROND: bed of reeds: swamp where reeds grow.
RIGHT-UPS: fixed coamings: no doubt a Norfolk inversion of 'up-rights'.
ROND ANCHOR: anchor with only one arm which is driven into the rond or marsh for a mooring.
ROOT: tendency of a heavily laden wherry to sail her nose under.
SHIFTING RIGHT-UPS: portable coamings above the fixed ones.
SHOE: bottom end of the quant is shod with an iron shoe tapering to a point.
SHRUFF: sawdust and shavings for smoking kippers.
SINGLE LOADED: all cargo below hatches.
SLIPPING KEEL: false keel attached or removed while afloat with two, sometimes three, bolts.
SPENS: inner and outer spens distribute the weight of hoisting over the length of the gaff.
SWIPE: pump: to have a swipe is to try the pump.
TIMBER HEAD: bollard.
TROLLEYS: parrel balls.
WALING: method of loading with deals by stacking over plankways to increase carrying capacity.

APPENDIX FOUR

Some Owners' Masthead Colours

I HAVE had to compile these lists of masthead colours from what old wherrymen have been able to remember of them because such details were never recorded on paper. Although far from complete they do include most of the prominent owners of the last sixty or seventy years and serve to show the variety and combinations of colours that were used.

When it is recalled that all this display was surmounted by a gaudily-painted vane with a fathom of crimson bunting streaming from it, the expression of one writer will be appreciated that the top of a wherry's mast makes a picture of 'barbaric splendour'.

The order of the colours is from the top downward.

Bessey & Palmer, Yarmouth	Blue masthead; white and red bands.
H. Burton, Stalham	Green masthead; red, white and blue bands.
J. & J. Colman, Norwich	Blue masthead; white band.
Crisp, Beccles	Black masthead; white band.
Cubitt & Walker, N. Walsham	Green masthead; yellow band.
General Steam Navigation Company, Yarmouth	Red masthead; yellow and black bands.
Hobrough, Norwich	Red masthead; black band.
Mutton, Reedham	Green masthead; yellow and blue bands.
Press Bros., N. Walsham	Blue masthead; yellow, white, yellow and red bands.
Ranson, Norwich	White masthead; red, white, red and white bands.
T. M. Read, Norwich	Black masthead; red and yellow bands.
G. Rumbold, Yarmouth	Blue masthead; gold band.
W. Royall, Norwich	Blue masthead; red band.
I. J. Wales, Reedham	Blue masthead; yellow and blue bands.
W. D. & A. E. Walker, Bungay	Light green masthead; yellow and blue bands.
Woods, Sadd & Moore, Loddon	Blue masthead; red, white, red and white bands.

MASTHEAD COLOURS OF INDIVIDUAL WHERRIES MOSTLY SKIPPER-OWNED

ALBION, ex Norfolk Blue masthead; red, white and blue bands.
PLANE, ex Wherry Trust
ALBION
BLANCHE, Leonard Welton Blue masthead; two brass bands.
ELLA, Barclay & Pallett Blue masthead; yellow, white, yellow and red bands.
GLEANER, ex Jack Gedge Green masthead; red, white and blue bands.
ORION
GO FORWARD, W. H. Thaxter Green masthead; red, white and blue bands.
GOODWILL, ex R. J. Read Bright blue masthead; two gold bands.
BEACONSFIELD
HILDA, Martin Gedge Blue masthead; red, white and blue bands.
LORD ROBERTS, Di Thain, snr. White masthead; black, white, metal, white and metal bands.
METEOR, Barnes Black masthead; two white bands.
MYSTERY, Somerleyton Brick Co. Green masthead; red, gold and blue bands.
OUR BOYS, Rounce Blue masthead; yellow and blue bands.
THOMAS, Holmes Red masthead; yellow band.
WIDGEON, W. Tooley White masthead; red, gold and blue bands.
ZULU, J. C. Riches White masthead; red, white and gold bands.

APPENDIX FIVE

List of Southwold Ships

A LIST of vessels owned at Southwold from shortly after the opening of the Blyth Navigation up to 1845.

Out of a total of 164, 18 were built at Southwold, on the north side of the river, and 4 at Walberswick, on the south side.

Yarmouth heads the list with 38, followed by Lowestoft with 26, while 11 came from Ipswich.

It will be noted that a number of places now derelict, such as Aldeburgh, Dunwich, Woodbridge and Wells, were then building seagoing ships.

APPENDIX FIVE

Vessel's name	Tonnage	Last Master	No. of crew	When and where built	Remarks
ABEONA	19	William Bokenham	5	1824, Aldeburgh	A Pilot Cutter; draft 8 feet. Sold to Yarmouth, 1845.
ACTIVE	80	William Palmer	4	1789, Yarmouth	Lost on Hasbro' Sand, 29 November, 1814.
ACTIVE	81	William Aldrich	4	1815, Ipswich	In Coasting Trade; draft 10 feet. Sold to N. Shields, 1844.
ADVENTURE (New)	40	James Gauntlett	4	1799, A Prize	Confiscated in Holland, 1801.
ALBION	80	Daniel Forman	5	1831, Woodbridge	In Coasting Trade; draft, 10 feet.
ALERT	80	Joseph Pyett	4	1802, Yarmouth	Wrecked at Blakeney, 16 July, 1817. B. Crickmer and F. Stannard drowned.
ALERT	16	Edward Palmer	10	1821, Southwold	Broken up at Southwold, 1834.
AMICITIA	27	William Easy	6	1805, Yarmouth	A Pilot Cutter; draft, 8 feet. Broken up and sold, 1845.
APOLLO	132	Thomas Calver	6	1802, Southwold	Sold to Sunderland, 1818.
BETSY	46	Robert Woolage	4	1788, Southwold	Lost, 19 May, 1791.
BETSY	17	George Elmy	3	1811, Greenwich	Sold to Aldeburgh, 1827.
BETSY	17	Richard Kerridge	4	1811, Greenwich	Sold to Colchester, 1832.
BETSY	60	James Holly	4	1812, A Prize	Sold to Aldbrough, 1821.
BLUCHER	16	William Smith	4	1811, A Prize	Lost, 1822.
BLYTH	42	Robert Gallant	11	1815, Lowestoft	Sold to Yarmouth, 1834.

Vessel's name	Tonnage	Last master	No. of crew	When and where built	Remarks
BOREAS	30	James Magub	11	1806, South Town	Sold to Yarmouth, 1835.
BRITISH LAUREL	131	Edmund Bardwell	8	1785, Yarmouth	Sold to London, 1793.
BRITISH TAR	30	Thomas Penny	10	1830, Yarmouth	Pilot Boat.
BROTHERS	72	Edward Palmer	4	1822, Yarmouth	Lost on Cornish Coast, 8 December, 1830.
BROTHERS' FRIEND	68	Samuel Wayth	4	1827, Yarmouth	In Coasting Trade; draft, 10 feet.
CAMPION	70	Thomas Calver	4	1800, Wells	Sold to Wisbech, 1809.
CERES	65	David Carman	5	1778, Ipswich	Sold to Aldeburgh, 1801.
CHARLES	78	Richard Sones	5	1802, Yarmouth	Sold to Yarmouth, 1819.
CHARLES	71	John Simpson	5	1835, Southwold	In Coasting Trade; draft, 9 feet.
CHARLOTTE	90	James May	5	1818, Ipswich	Lost on Goodwin Sands, 31 August, 1833.
COMMERCE	73	Timothy Church	4	1818, Lowestoft	In Coasting Trade; draft, 8 feet 6 inches. Lost Robin Hood's Bay, 12 March, 1843.
CONQUEROR	132	Peter Palmer	6	1800, Yarmouth	Wrecked on Southwold Bar, 1817.
CYNTHIA	131	Thomas Simpson	7	1800, Lowestoft	Sold to London, 1821.
DEPENDANCE	93	John Edgar	6	1799, Yarmouth	Wrecked, Deal Beach, 10 November, 1807.
DE WITTE	36	Thomas Smith	4	1797, A Prize	Lost, 1799.
DIANA	67	Mesbach Lilly	4	1806, Sweden	Lost on Lincolnshire Coast, 11 October, 1824.
				1818, Bought from Cley	

APPENDIX FIVE

DISPATCH	74	Robert C. Magub	5	1839, Newcastle	In Foreign Trade; draft, 10 feet.
DOLPHIN	120	James Atkins	7	1792, Yarmouth	Sold to Sunderland, 1820.
DOLPHIN	24	Thomas Jarvis	6	— Rye	A Pilot Cutter; draft, 8 feet.
DUNWICH	86	David Archer	5	1803, Walberswick	Lost with all hands, 4 April, 1815.
DUNWICH	60	Thomas Archer	4	1778, Ipswich	Sold to Lynn, 1803.
EBENEZER	60	James Welch	4	1829, Yarmouth	In Coasting Trade; draft, 9 feet. Wrecked on beach Herne Bay, 15 April, 1845. Sold by auction, repaired and sent to sea.
EDWARD	27	Thomas Shepperd	5	1786, Colchester	Taken by the French, 1796.
EDWARD AND ANN	26	John Hunting	11	1799, Walberswick	Sold to Yarmouth, 1814.
EFFORT	19	James Easy	3	1801, Southwold	Sold to Government, 1803.
ELLEN	51	John Gayford	3	1829, Aldeburgh	Sold to Woodbridge, 1837.
ENTERPRIZE	107	Edward Kilwick	7	1788, Yarmouth	Lost in the Bay of Dundrum, 1795. Iron-clench built.
ENTERPRIZE	20	Benjamin Howard	2	1841, Ipswich	Sold to London, 1833. Lost, 1836.
EXMOUTH, LORD	149	William Carter	7	1816, Blyth	Sold to Yarmouth, 1792.
FARMERS' ADVENTURE	73	David Burwood	5	1750, Harwich	Wrecked Yarmouth Beach, 12 October, 1836.
FARMERS' ADVENTURE	63	Thomas Calver	4	1793, Lowestoft	In Coasting Trade; draft, 9 feet.
FLY	73	William Wright	4	1808, Yarmouth	Lost off Dunwich, 22 March, 1836.
FLY	17	Barnes Hill	3	1823, South Town	Sold to Cork, 1793.
FOUNTAIN	85	Robert Mills	6	1783, Yarmouth	Taken by the French, 5 August, 1810.
FOUNTAIN	113	Robert Mills	8	1796, Lowestoft	Sold to London, 1832.
FOUNTAIN	132	Thomas Gull	8	1814, Ipswich	In Coasting Trade; draft, 9 feet.
FOUR FRIENDS	61	Henry Waters	4	1831, Yarmouth	

Vessel's name	Tonnage	Last Master	No. of crew	When and where built	Remarks
FRIENDS	39	John Saunders	4	1814, Woodbridge	Sold to Yarmouth, 1824.
FRIENDSHIP	80	Edward Duke	5	1782, Yarmouth	Sold to London, 1792.
FRIENDSHIP	79	Robert J. Archer	4	1793, Yarmouth	Sold to Sunderland, 1817.
FRIENDSHIP	34	Edward Gillings	3	1821, Sunderland	In Coasting Trade; draft, 7 feet.
FRIENDSHIP	87	Robert Bugg	4	1800, South Town	Sold to Aldeburgh, 1809.
FRIENDS' GOOD WILL	13	Edward Garrard	3	1785, Colchester	Sold to Emden, 1787.
FRIENDS' INCREASE	130	Francis Everrard	7	1794, Lowestoft	Wrecked at Winterton, 1804.
FRIENDS' INCREASE	96	Simon Spicer	4	1811, Lowestoft	Sold to Ipswich, 1836.
GENEROUS FRIENDS	148	David Brown	6	1800, Lowestoft	Sold to London, 1823.
GLENMORISON	66	Francis Stannard	4	1820, Invermoris	In Coasting Trade; draft, 8½ feet.
GLEANER	80	James May	5	1815, Ipswich	In Coasting Trade; draft, 10 feet.
GOOD INTENT	50	Joseph Montague	3	1776, Folkestone	Sold for a Fire Ship, 1804.
GOOD INTENT	49	Thompson Swan	4	1776, Folkestone	Sold to Yarmouth, 1787.
GOOD INTENT	36	Joseph Wells	7	1780, Colchester	Taken by the French, 1797.
GOOD INTENT	25	John Collett	3	1782, Faversham	Sold to Bremen, 1803.
GOOD INTENT	46	Thomas Penny	4	1790, Yarmouth	Sold for Ballast Lighter, 1815.
GOOD WILL	100	Rowland Twaddell	6	1765, Ipswich	Sold to Sunderland, 1815.
GREYHOUND	107	Rowland Twaddell	8	1819, Yarmouth	Lost, Goree Island, 18 January, 1832.
HALESWORTH	34	William Forman	3	1772, Halesworth	Broken up, 1818.
HALESWORTH TRADER	95	James Curdy	5	1789, Lowestoft	Wrecked St. Andrew's Bay, 21 March, 1812.

APPENDIX FIVE

HALESWORTH TRADER	32	William Blanden	3	1799, Southwold	River Craft; draft, 4 feet.
HAMBLETONIAN	112	James Bardwell	6	1799, Southwold	Sold to Sunderland, 1813.
HARMONY	92	John Bokenham	5	1803, Lowestoft	Broken up, 1834.
HAWK	66	John Laws	4	1809, Selby	Lost in the Tees, 24 October, 1822.
HEART OF OAK	56	David Green	4	1835, Southwold	In Coasting Trade; draft, 8 feet.
HENRY AND ANN	61	John Blanden	4	1806, A Prize	Sold to Wells, 1815.
HERRING	69	John Benstead	4	1784, Yarmouth	Wrecked on Yarmouth Beach, 1825.
HOPE	16	James Easy	3	1768, Southwold	Condemned in the Exchequer, 1777.
HOPE	116	Joseph Elmy	6	1798, Lowestoft	Taken by the French, 1799.
HOPE	49	Henry Sayer	4	1819, Lowestoft	In Coasting Trade; draft, 7 feet.
HOPEWELL	65	John Simpson	4	1803, West Ferry, Lincs.	Lost within the Cocket Island, Coast of Northumberland, 13 August, 1832. Crew saved.
INDUSTRY	48	John Laws	4	1823, Walberswick	In Coasting Trade; draft, 8 feet 6 inches. Lost 18 April, 1845, on the East Burrows. Crew saved.
JAMES AND ELIZABETH	41	Thomas Waters	4	1817, Yarmouth	In Coasting Trade; draft, 8 feet.
JOHN	20	Alexander Scott	3	1773, Lowestoft	Condemned in Exchequer, 30 July, 1800.
JOHN AND ELIZABETH	9	Robert English	2	1788, Gillingham	Wrecked on Walberswick beach, crew saved, 8 September, 1842.
JOHN AND SARAH	78	David Brown	5	1767, Southwold	Sold to London, 1788.
JOHNSON	76	James Welch	4	1787, Lowestoft	Sold to Sunderland, 1811.
JUBILEE	25	John Rogers	10	1810, Lowestoft	Pilot Boat; 24 October, 1844, wrecked on Southwold Beach, Edward Palmer drowned.

Vessel's name	Tonnage	Last master	No. of crew	When and where built	Remarks
KING GEORGE	6	James Gauntlett	3	1793, Ipswich	Condemned in Exchqeuer, 1800.
LAPWING	114	Robert John Archer	7	1792, Yarmouth	Sold to Yarmouth, 1813.
LAUREL	34	Timothy Church	3	1813, A Prize	Lost, Mouth of Thames, 2 March, 1820.
LIBERTY	61	Mesbach Lilly	4	1790, Lowestoft	In Coasting Trade; draft, 8 feet. Lost with crew on Yorkshire coast, 2 February, 1843.
LION	141	John A. Kilwick	7	1800, Yarmouth	Taken by the French, 1805.
LOUISA ELIZABETH	70	John Bokenham	5	1836, North Shields	In Coasting Trade; draft, 10 feet.
LOWESTOFT	24	William Aldrich	6	1781, A Prize	Lost, Coast of Holland, 14 December, 1792.
MARIA	77	Edward Palmer	5	1817, Gateshead	In Coasting Trade; draft, 9 feet 6 inches. Foundered off Cromer, Crew saved, 2 October, 1843.
MARY	118	Edward Coleman	7	1798, Yarmouth	Lost at Carrickfergus, 1805, with all hands but William Lanchester.
MARY	11	George Elmy	2	1826, Woodbridge	Broken up, 1834.
MARY ANN	48	John Chittleburgh	3	1812, A Prize	In Coasting Trade; draft, 7 feet.
MARY AND ELIZABETH	44	John Laws	4	1802, Humstill	Broken up, 1810.
MAY FLOWER	45	William M'Cowan	3	1783, Lowestoft	Sold to Lowestoft, 1813.
MINERVA	63	John Harman	5	1772, Yarmouth	Sold to Sunderland, 1789.

APPENDIX FIVE

MONTEFIORE	29	William Wright	7	1793, Southwold	Broken up, 1818.
MOORE	30	John Williams	6	1802, Cowes	Sold to Lowestoft, 1836.
NELSON	127	John Laws	7	1800, Selby	Sold to London, 1808.
NELSON, LADY	79	James Sterry	5	1803, Lowestoft	Lost on the Coast of Kent with all hands, December 1836.
NELSON, LORD	164	John Gardiner	7	1802, Lowestoft	Sold to London, 1805.
NEW PROSPEROUS	61	George Day	4	1805, Aylesford	In Coasting Trade; draft, 6 feet.
NORFOLK	75	John Sones	4	1826, Walberswick	In Coasting Trade; draft, 8 feet 6 inches.
PEGASUS	130	John Magub	7	1841, Yarmouth	In Foreign Trade; draft, 11 feet.
PERMANENT	59	Francis Wayth	4	1790, South Town	In Coasting Trade; draft, 8 feet. Wrecked on Bacton Beach, 9 March, 1842, crew saved.
PERSEVERANCE	44	John Burwood	4	1800, A Prize	Foundered in Humber, 26 December, 1801.
PERSEVERANCE	95	John Magub, sen.	6	1818, Lowestoft	In Coasting Trade; draft, 10 feet. Wrecked on Cardigan Bar, S. Wales, 5 February, 1840, crew saved.
PRIME	20	John Wells	3	1777, Ipswich	Taken by the French, 1795.
PRINCE REGENT	26	Balantine Brown	10	1818, Lowestoft	Sold to Yarmouth, 1824.
PRINCE OF WALES	110	Edmund Bardwell	6	1768, Unknown	Sold to Sunderland, 1793.
PRINCESS CHARLOTTE	49	Timothy Church	4	1815, A Prize	Broken up, 1832.
PROVIDENCE	25	John Bint	4	—, A Prize	Taken by *Agressor* Gun Brig, 1805.
PROVIDENCE	113	William Carman	7	1762, Ipswich	Sold to Sunderland, 1793.
PROVIDENCE	53	William M'Cowan	4	1780, Lowestoft	Sold to Yarmouth, 1826.
PROVIDENCE	27	Malachi Block	3	1795, Queenborough	Wrecked on Southwold Beach, 1810.

Vessel's name	Tonnage	Last master	No. of crew	When and where built	Remarks
PROVIDENCE	47	John Crisp	3	1798, Yarmouth	Wrecked Lowestoft Beach, 22 November, 1829.
PROVIDENCE	34	George Elmy	6	1802, Lowestoft	Pilot Cutter; draft, 7 feet.
RAMBLER	13	James Galer	4	1815, Woodbridge	Sold to Colchester, 1822.
REINDEER (New)	17	Henry Waters	5	1807, Lowestoft	Sold to Yarmouth, 1815.
REWARD	13	Thomas Penny	3	1817, Southwold	Sold to Yarmouth, 1819.
ROBERT AND SARAH	150	Robert Teasdell	7	1800, Yarmouth	Sold to London, 1810.
ROBERT AND SARAH	256	Robert Teasdell	8	—, A Prize	Sold to London, broken up, 1817.
ROBERT AND WILLIAM	64	Benjamin Baxter	4	1836, Dundee	In Coasting Trade; draft, 9 feet. Sold to Woodbridge, 1844.
ROSE AND JUNE	123	John Edgar	7	1801, Lowestoft	Wrecked on Spanish Coast, 15 February, 1814.
SALLY	34	John Murrells	4	1787, Bridport	Sold to Antona, 1788.
SALMON	49	William Dean	4	1770, Yarmouth	Sold to Sunderland, 1783.
SAMUEL	33	William Easy	6	1796, Yarmouth	Pilot Cutter, broken up 1831.
SAMUEL AND JOHN	65	William Carman	5	1772, Yarmouth	Lost, 1795.
SARAH AND ANN	56	Rowland Twaddell	4	1828, Portrack	In Coasting Trade; draft, 8 feet 6 inches. Lost 10 April, 1845, with crew.
SOLE BAY	94	James Sterry	5	1798, Southwold	Sold to Sunderland, 1807. Lost 6 September, 1837.

APPENDIX FIVE 253

SOLE BAY	63	J. D. Strowger	4	1844, Southwold	In Coasting Trade; draft, 8 feet.
SOPHIA	67	James Holly	4	1808, A Prize	Lost on the Lincolnshire Coast with all hands, 13 October, 1822.
SOPHIA	72	Marshall Twaddell	4	1833, Southwold	In Coasting Trade; draft, 8 feet.
SOUTHWICK	50	William Crisp	4	1815, Sunderland	In Coasting Trade; draft, 8 feet.
SUCCESS	65	Marshall Twaddell	4	1786, Wells	Broken up, 1832.
SUFFOLK	75	John Palmer	5	1818, Wells	In Coasting Trade; draft 9 feet 6 inches.
SWAN	44	William Hurr	4	1764, Yarmouth	Taken by the French, 1793.
THOMAS AND BETSY	53	Samuel Sayer	4	1813, A Prize	Wrecked Southwold Beach, 9 August, 1828.
THREE FRIENDS	44	Henry Waters	4	1814, A Prize	Broken up, 1830.
THREE FRIENDS	45	Henry Smith	4	1818, South Town	In Coasting Trade; draft, 7 feet 6 inches.
THREE SISTERS	14	Edmund Salter	3	1789, Rowhedge	Sold to Woodbridge, 1802.
TRIMMER	166	D. B. Gardiner	9	1801, Southwold	Lost, Etaples, all hands, 13 November, 1803.
TRUE BLUE	97	Thomas Calver	5	1818, Boston	Sold to Yarmouth, 1831.
TRUE FRIENDS	125	William Peacock	9	1801, Lowestoft	Taken by the French, 1803.
TWO BROTHERS	4	Joseph Garrard	3	1793, Sunderland	Broken up, 1806.
TWO BROTHERS	62	Malachi Block	4	1800, A Prize	Broken up, 1805.
TYNE	87	William Wayth	6	1823, Newcastle	In Coasting Trade; draft, 9 feet.
VIGILANT	75	John Magub	5	1834, Southwold	In Coasting Trade; draft, 9 feet.
UNION	84	Benjamin Spicer	5	1784, Yarmouth	Sold to Sunderland, 1817.
UNION	91	Benjamin Spicer	5	1817, Fellingshore	Lost off Cromer, 2 March, 1823.
UNITY	78	William Woodard	5	1777, Yarmouth	Sold for Fire Ship, 1805.

Vessel's name	Tonnage	Last master	No. of crew	When and where built	Remarks
VICTORIA	88	Simon Spicer	5	1839, Southwold	In Coasting Trade; draft, 10 feet.
WILLIAM'S ADVENTURE	55	Robert Moss	4	1763, Lowestoft	Sold for Fire Ship, 1805.
WILLIAM AND MARY	59	Henry Wright	4	1819, Dunwich	In Coasting Trade; draft, 8 feet.
WILLIAM AND MARY	—	—	—	1845, Aldeburgh	Pilot Cutter; draft, 8 feet.

BIBLIOGRAPHY

AMONG the many books and documents consulted I would especially mention the following:

BAYNE: Industry and Trade of Norwich and Norfolk, 1858.
BRAUN AND HOGENBERG: Atlas of the Cities of the World, 1572.
BRØGGER AND SHETELIG: Viking Ships, 1953.
CROSBY: Complete Pocket Gazetteer of England and Wales, 1815.
DEFOE: Tour through the Eastern Counties, 1724.
DOUGHTY: Friesland Meres and Through the Netherlands in a Norfolk Wherry, 1889.
    Our Wherry in Wendish Lands, 1890.
EMERSON: On English Lagoons, 1893.
HAKLUYT: Principal English Voyages, 1599.
MAGGS: Handbook to the Port and Shipping of Southwold, 1842.
MARSHALL: Rural Economy of Norfolk, 1787.
MILLICAN: History of Stanninghall and Horstead, 1937.
PRIESTLY: Navigable Rivers, Canals, and Railways of Great Birtain, 1831.
STARK: Scenery of the Rivers of Norfolk, 1834.
STEVENSON: English Lighthouse Tours, 1946.

Registry of Keels, Great Yarmouth Records.
Report of Evidence given before the Harbour Commissioners at Southwold, 1839.
Files of the *Norwich Gazette*, *Norwich Mercury* and *Eastern Daily Press*.

INDEX

A

Accidents, 90, 95, 111, 140, 155-6, 190-1, 192-4
Accommodation (Wherry/Lugger), 85, 135, 139-40, 195
Active, S.S., 192
Adam and Eve (Wherry), 91
Albert (Wherry), 80
Albion (Wherry), 8, 11-33, 34, 43, 51, 57, 59, 66, 68, 70, 72, 74, 78, 80-1, 83, 86, 88, 109, 154, 158, 165, 167, 197-8
Aldeburgh, 124, 126
Allen, Messrs., 58, 76
Alma (Wherry), 151
Amelia (Wherry), 131
Anderson, John, 24
Annie (Steam Wherry), 83
Ardea (Wherry), 158
Atlas of the Cities of the World, 38, 39
Augustus (Keel), 49
Aylsham, 70, 107, 198

B

Barber, Benjamin, 195
  „   , H., 90
  „   , Messrs., 78
  „   , Tom, 129
  „   and Croft, Messrs.., 196
Barnard, Messrs., 68
Barton, 52, 73, 77, 108, 148, 158, 159, 160, 163, 189
Batley, Thomas, 79, 80
Beaconsfield (Wherry), 144, 149, 151, 158, 161-2, 164

Beccles, 7, 11, 12, 14, 17, 18, 21, 25, 32, 72, 76, 78, 82, 108, 125, 166
Beccles-Bungay Canal, 57
Beehive (Keel), 49
Bell (Wherry), 74, 75, 104, 108-9, 154, 192
Bell, William, 191
Benjamin (Wherry), 58
Benns, Ben, 73, 77
  „   , Jack, 164
Berney Arms, 88-9, 91
Bertha (Wherry), 52, 57, 58, 162
Bessey and Palmer, Messrs., 78
Bessie (Wherry), 104
Bexfield, Joseph, 191
Black Horse Reach, 17, 107
Blackshore, 114, 115
Blanche (Wherry), 73, 86
Blanden, William, 114, 122-3
Blyth Canal and River, 57, 112-29, 176
Bramble (Wherry), 158
Braun and Hogenberg, 38, 39
Breydon Water, 19, 20, 24, 28, 34, 48, 50, 66, 72, 82, 88, 89, 94, 106, 131, 164, 165, 180, 189, 190
Brighton, Billy, 72-4, 77, 83, 106, 115, 162
Britannia (Wherry), 89, 90, 91
British Laurel, 123
British Queen (Wherry), 74, 116, 151, 155, 156, 159, 163, 164
Brittania (Wherry), 161, 163
Buckenham Halt, 7, 10, 11, 20, 104
Bullen (of Oulton), 162
Bunaway, Alice and Christopher, 177-8

INDEX

Bungay, 72, 73, 78, 125, 128, 198
Bunn, Cecil, 96
„ , W. C., 152, 153
Bure, River, 48, 57, 76, 107, 176, 198
Burgh Castle, 89, 91, 94, 148, 164–5, 189
„ „ Cement Co., 89, 91
Burleigh, Robert, 114–5
Burton, Benjamin, 24
Butcher, George, 115
Bygrave, Billy, 104

C

Calver, Capt. E. K., 120
Cambria (Wherry), 80
Canals, 11, 18, 19, 25, 57, 123, 185, 190
Capulet (Steamship), 105
Cargoes—Carried by wherries, 7, 28, 47, 49–50, 58, 82, 83, 88–90, 91–3, 97–101, 102–9, 111–2, 113,
Carrow (Wherry), 135, 139, 141
Cates, George, 12, 18
Cates, Jack, 7–33, 78, 158, 197–8
„ , Walter, 18
Cement Factories on Broads, 89–93
Ceres (Wherry), 77, 96
Chapman, Mrs., 115
Charles and Henry (Wherry), 91
Cheeper, Anthony, 49
Chet, River, 58, 96
Chieftan (Wherry), 77, 80
Chittleburgh, John, 122
City of Norwich, 18, 79, 136–8
Clarke (of Ludham), 159
Clarke, Charlie, 131
Clarke and Reeve, Messrs., 85, 91
Claudian (Wherry), 158, 163
Coldham Hall, 74, 77, 191
Coltishall, 58, 76, 92, 107

Coltishall–Aylsham Canal, 57
Complete Pocket Gazateer of England and Wales, 97
Conclusion (Keel), 49
Constitution (Keel), 49
Cornelius, John, 42
Cornucopia (Wherry), 76
Cossey, Messrs., 78
Courier (Wherry), 76, 155
Cox, Jacob, 52–7, 58
Crisp, John & Sons, 76, 82, 83
Crowhurst (Wherry)—See *Fir*
Crystal (Wherry), 193
Cubitt, William, 120
Cumberland, 135
Cygnet (Wherry), 76

D

Dahlia (Wherry), 141
Dancing—by wherrymen, 188
Dauntless (Wherry), 78, 160, 163, 164
Davies, G. Christopher, 128
Defoe, Daniel, 97–9, 101, 104
Dilham–Antingham Canal, 53, 57, 77, 106, 176
Dilham Trader (Wherry), 159, 166
Diligent (Wherry), 80
Dora (Wherry), 74, 112, 152, 153, 154, 158, 162
Dorothy (Wherry)—See *Ceres*
Doughty, H. M., 196
Dove (Brig), 101
Dragon (Wherry), 158
Dress—of wherrymen and women, 186, 187–8
Drownings, 160–1, 191, 193
Dunwich, 113, 139
Dutchmen, Flee to East Anglia, 39

E

Earl of Beaconsfield (Wherry), 78, 85
Ecila (Wherry), 74
Edmund (Keel), 49
Edward (Wherry), 91
Elizabeth (Wherry), 151, 155, 158, 159, 160, 161-2, 164, 166
Elizabeth and Ann (Keel), 49
Ella (Wherry), 76
Ellen (Wherry), 151, 155, 164
Ellen and Mary (Brig), 101
Ellett, Messrs., 66
Ellis, Edward, 80
Ellis, Lt., R.N., 121
Emerald (Wherry), 76, 131
Emerson, Dr., 93-5
Emma (Wherry), 89, 90, 91, 159
Emperor (Steamship), 79
Empress (Wherry), 80, 82
Ena May (Wherry), 78
Endeavour (Brig), 101
Enfield (Wherry), 86, 157
Ethel (Wherry), 155
Etheridge, Frank, 186
Ethnie (Wherry), 52, 57, 58, 161
Eudora (Wherry), 51, 78, 86, 96, 153, 176
Eva Rosa (Wherry), 73, 106, 160, 161-2. See also *Waveney*

F

Faith (Wherry), 78
Fair Trader (Brig), 101
Fairy Queen (Wherry), 91
Fancy (Wherry), 147-8
Fanny (Wherry), 89, 90, 114, 115
Farmers' Liberty (Brig), 113
Fawn (Wherry), 74, 85, 143-5, 149-50, 151-7, 158, 159, 160, 161-4

Fellow's (of Yarmouth), 83, 115
Field, Stephen, 80, 81
Fir (Wherry), 78
Firefly (Wherry), 84
FitzGerald, Edward, 76-7
Five Brothers (Wherry), 192
Flora (Keel), 49
Florence (Wherry), 84
Fore-and-Aft Rigging, 37-41
Forget-Me-Not (Wherry), 78
Forman, William, 114
Frank (Wherry), 89
Free British Herring Society, 112
Friesland Meres and through the Netherlands in a Norfolk Wherry, 196
Frobisher, Sir Martin, 42

G

Gaff-Rigging, 40, 41
Gallant, Harry, 80
Geldeston, 78, 95, 176
Gelly, Anne, 191
Gem (Wherry), 91
George, Thompson, 115
Gibbs, Sam, 129
Gibbs, Valentine, 78
Gipsy (Wherry), 196-7
Gleaner (Wherry), 58, 59, 80. See also *Orion*
Go Forward (Wherry), 131, 132-3
Godison, Billy, 131
Good Intent (Lighter), 116, 119
Goodwill (Wherry), 96
Gorleston, 148, 151, 154
Gosport Barracks—wherries part in building of, 133-141
Gratitude (Wherry/Lugger), 85
Great Yarmouth, 23-4, 29, 41, 43-4, 45, 47, 49, 50, 58, 66, 68, 70, 78,

Great Yarmouth (contd.)
  81, 84, 90, 96, 97–101, 106, 110–12, 113, 116, 124, 125, 126, 131, 148–9, 151–2, 154, 164
Great Yarmouth Shipping Company, 82
Griffin, George, 179
Grubb's Haven, 179–80

H

Haddiscoe, 11, 18–19, 20, 57, 96, 129
Haddiscoe Cut, 22, 23
Hakluyt, Richard, 42
Halesworth, 57, 112, 113, 114, 115, 118, 120–1, 124, 127, 128, 131, 176, 198
Halesworth (Wherry), 114
Halesworth Trader (Wherry), 114, 122
Hall, Charles, 74, 146
  „ , Dan, 74
  „ , James, 74
  „ , Messrs., 76, 77, 81, 90
Hamburg, 135
Hand of Providence (Wherry), 80
Hankey (Wherry), 114
Hannah (Wherry/Lugger), 85
Happy Return (Brig), 101
Hardley Cross, 164–5
Harrod, George, 20–1
Harry and Ethel (Wherry), 156
Harvest (Wherry), 159
Harvey's Academy, 115
Harwich, 41, 126, 138, 139
Hathor (Wherry), 74
Hawes, "Piper", 91
Hawk, 125
Helen (Wherry/Yacht), 115, 160
Henry (Wherry), 159
Herbert (Wherry), 89, 91

Heron (Wherry), 162
Hilda (Wherry), 76, 160
History of Horstead and Stanninghall, 92
Hobrough, William, 77, 80
Holland, Revolt in (1568), 39
Holmes, Rodney, 91
Holt, "Times", 112
Hope (Wherry), 86, 114
Hopewell (Brig), 101
Horse Packet, The, 81–2
Horsey Mere, 166, 176, 185
Houghton (of Norwich), 79
Howes, Mrs., 91

I

Illustrated Guide Book to Lowestoft, 136
Industry (Keel), 49, 158, 163
Ingram, Ben, 129
Inn Signs—wherry used as symbol, 175–6
Integrity (Wherry), 189
Intrepid (Wherry)—See *Emma*
Iolanthe (Wherry), 86
Ipswich, 41, 79, 98, 124, 125, 126, 176
Iron Duke (Wherry), 115, 128
  See also *James and Jessie*

J

James (Wherry/Lugger), 85
James and Jessie (Wherry), 91
  See also *Iron Duke*
Jay, Joe, 129
Jekyll, Cornelius, 105
Jenny Lind (Steamer), 74
Jenny Morgan (Wherry), 80, 156, 157, 159
"Jenny Morgans", 68, 86

July Flower (Keel), 49
Jupiter, 135

K

Kathleen (Wherry), 84
Keels (Vessels), 36–41, 45, 48–50, 79, 111, 112, 114, 193
Kemp (of Oulton), 77
Kemp, "Rattler", 131, 132–3
King Henry, 21
Kings Lynn, 124, 126
Knights, George, 90, 91
„ , James, 91
„ , Thomas, 113

L

Lacey, Jimmy, 154
Lady Violet (Wherry), 78, 151
Lambert, Fred G., 129
Langley, 14, 176
Lanham, Gill, 189
Leipsig, 135
Leonard (Wherry), 151, 155, 157
Leveret (Wherry), 80
Liberty (Wherry), 122, 195–6
Lifton, Richard, 147
Lilly, Meshac, 122
Little Georgie (Wherry), 73, 77, 179
Little Spark (Wherry), 93–5
Longships, Viking, 35–6
Lord Roberts (Wherry), 74, 77
Louisa (Wherry), 77
Lowestoft, 18, 21, 25, 57, 76, 77, 82, 112, 120, 124, 125, 129, 131, 135–8, 142, 148–9, 151–6
Lowestoft Trader (Wherry), 58, 78, 85, 131, 151, 155
Lowestoft, Beccles and Norwich Shipping Co., 79

Lowestoft–Norwich Canal, 57, 79
„ „ Navigation Act (1927), 79
Lucas Bros., Mrssrs., 131, 133, 140, 141
Lucy (Wherry), 84
Ludham Bridge, 96, 160

M

Madge (Wherry), 80
Magub, John, Jnr., 122
Maid of the Mist (Wherry)—See *Little Spark*
Maid of the Yare (Brig), 66
Mahala (Wherry), 135, 139–40, 141, 142
Mann, John, 131, 141
Maria (Wherry/Lugger), 85, 86, 157, 159
Marlborough (Keel), 49
Martham Broad, 107, 177
Martham Trader (Wherry), 149, 151, 160
Mary (Wherry), 89, 90, 91
Mary Ann, 122, 159
Matilda (Wherry), 76
Maud (Wherry), 74, 154
Mayflower (Wherry), 50, 86, 159
Mayland (Ketch/Barge), 115
Mermaid (Wherry), 68, 89, 91
Meteor (Wherry), 96
Microphone, S.S., 192
Morgan's Brewery, 68
Morton (Wherry), 89, 90, 91, 131
Myth (Wherry), 80, 151, 155

N

New Cut, 11, 18, 19, 25, 57, 123, 185, 190

Nightingale, Samuel, 90
Nil Desperandum (Wherry), 131-2
Norfolk Hero (Wherry), 68, 84, 108, 141
Norfolk Wherry Trust, 15, 72
North of Europe Steam Navigation Company, 135
"North River" Wherries, 57
North Walsham, 106, 198
Norwich, 18, 36, 43-4, 45, 47, 49-50, 51, 57, 78-80, 81, 82, 91-2, 96, 97-105, 108, 175-6, 189
   „ , Prosperity of, 99-105
   „ , Shipbuilding in, 78-80
   „ , Weaving industry, 99
Norwich Corporation, 37, 43, 164
Norwich Gazette, 45
Norwich Mercury, 46
Norwich Rivers and Streets Book, 42
Norwich Soup and Provident Coal Society, 189
Norwich Trader (Wherry/Lugger), 85
Norwich, Lowestoft & London Shipping Company, 18
Norwich-Lowestoft Navigation—See New Cut
Number One (Wherry), 77, 135, 139, 141, 142
Nymph (Wherry), 192

O

Olga (Wherry), 146, 149, 152-3, 158, 162
Olive (Wherry), 76
On English Lagoons, 93
Onward (Wherry), 107
Opal (Steam Wherry), 82, 83, 87
Orion (Wherry), 58. See also *Gleaner*

Oulton Broad, 58, 72, 73, 77, 89, 90, 95, 115, 131, 148, 156, 157, 158, 159, 176
Our Boys (Wherry), 74
Our Wherry in Wendish Lands, 196

P

Palmer, John, 122
Patch, William, 80
Pearl (Wherry), 91
Perseverance, 122, 125
Peto, Samuel Morton, 135, 136
Phantom Wherry—Legend of, 28-30
Pharos (Wherry), 106, 107
Phoenician (Barge), 58
Pike, Messrs., 68
Plane (Wherry)—See *Albion*
Playford, Benjamin, 191
Polly (Keel), 49
Pondere, John, 78-9
Poole, "Guinea", 90, 131
Powley, Albert, 145, 150-1, 154, 157, 162, 166-7, 192
   „ , Jack, 66, 154
   „ , Ophir, 74, 144-6, 152-3, 156, 157, 161
Pratt, Robert, 156
Press Bros., Messrs., 159
Prince of Wales (Wherry), 159
Princess (Wherry), 112
Providence (Brig), 101, 123
Providence (Wherry), 80

R

Raleigh, Sir Walter, 42
Rambler (Wherry), 78, 163
Recovery (Keel), 49
Red Rover (Wherry), 67

Reedham, 10, 11, 17–18, 22, 23, 24, 25, 57, 74, 76, 77, 81, 90, 103, 146, 149
Regattas, 85, 146–50, 151–67, 189
Rennie, John, 119
Reynolds, Charles, 77
Riches (of Catfield), 77
Rigby (Wherry), 193
Rob Roy, 23–4
Robert (Brig), 101
Robert Alfred (Wherry), 151, 155
Robert and Frances (Wherry), 50
Robert and Henry (Wherry), 160
Robert and Mary (Wherry), 50
Royal Oak (Keel), 49
Royal Sovereign (Steamship), 79, 81
Royal Victoria, 135
Royall, Christopher, 180
  „ , Edmund, 91
  „ , Family, 180–3
Ruby (Wherry), 131
Rural Economy of Norfolk, 92
Russell, Harry, 91

S

Sailor's Word Book, The, 42
Samuel (Wherry), 156, 158–9
Sarah (Brig), 101
Sarah Ann (Wherry), 122, 166
Scandal (Yacht), 76
Scenery of the Rivers of Norfolk, 111
Secunda (Wherry), 96
Shepherd, Jimmy, 131
Sirius (Wherry), 58, 83, 112
Smith, Henry, 122
Smith, Len, 90
Smuggling, 176–83
Smyth, Admiral, 42
Smythe, James, 42
Solace (Wherry), 74

Somerleyton, 25, 73, 86, 103, 131, 132
Somerton, 73, 77, 107
Sophia, 122
Southwold, 57, 112–29, 131, 132, 139, 186
Southwold (Sloop), 113
Spalding, Frederick, 76
Spred Eagle, 42
Spring (Brig), 79
Sprit-Sails, 37, 38, 40, 41
Square Sails, 35, 26, 37, 38, 40
Squire (Steamship), 18, 79
Stalham, 77, 107, 160
Star (Wherry), 129, 141, 189
Star of Hope (Wherry), 80
Stark, James, 111
Stead, Patrick, 120–8
Stevenson, Robert, 81
Steward and Patteson, Messrs., 83
Stradbroke, Lord, 118, 121
Success (Brig), 101
Success (Keel), 49
Suffolk, 122
Supply (Keel), 49
Surprise (Wherry), 160
Susanna (Keel), 49
Swift (Wherry), 85, 158

T

Teasdel, Joe, 77
Test, 20
Thain, Dionysius, 73, 106
  „ , William, 106
Thaxter, George, 91
  „ W. H., 90, 131
Theobald (Wherry), 189
Theodore (Wherry), 157
Thomas, Gaby, 93
Thomas, William, 49

Thomas and Mary (Brig), 101
Three Friends, 122
Thurgar, Billy, 20-1
Thurne, River, 107, 176
Tidal Harbours Inquiry (1845), 120
Tiger (Wherry), 80, 84, 85
Tooley, Billy, 168-9, 171-5
Topaz (Steam Wherry), 83
Tour through the Eastern Counties, 97-9
Turnpike Acts, 47
Twaddle, Marshall, 122
    „   , Rowland, 122
Two Brothers (Wherry), 159
Tyrrell, "Skeweye", 77

U

Unexpected (Wherry), 77, 80
Union (Keel), 49
United (Tug), 112
Uranus (Wherry), 58, 83, 112, 115
Ursa Minor (Wherry), 58, 192

V

"Vanes", 67-8, 91
Vega (Wherry), 58, 83, 192
Vigilant, 122
Viking Longships, 35-6
Violet (Wherry), 166
Volunteer (Wherry), 85, 131, 151, 156

W

Walberswick (Wherry), 128, 129
Wales, I. J., 146, 149, 152, 153, 156, 162
Walker, James, 120, 127
Walker, Messrs., W. D. & A. E., 72, 78, 83, 86, 153

Wanderer (Wherry), 77-8, 112
Warnes, Mrs., 91
Watts, J., 79
Waveney, River, 11, 19, 21, 25, 28, 30, 48, 57, 78, 131, 166, 190, 198
Waveney (Wherry)—See *Eva Rosa*
Wellington (Wherry), 141
Welton, Leonard, 86
Wherries, Name of first known, 42
    „   , Name of last made, 76
    „   , Probable origin of word, 41-2
    „   , Register of, 48
    „   , Specification, early, 45-6
White Heather, 192
Whiteside, John, 112
Whitlingham, 7, 11, 42, 91, 103
Widgeon (Wherry), 168, 172-3
Wigg, Martin, 139, 141
William (Keel), 49
William (Wherry/Lugger), 84, 85, 125
William and Mary (Keel), 49
Winter (of Bungay), 78
Wonder (Wherry), 77, 78, 84, 85, 154
Woodbridge, 124, 125, 126
Wooden, Richard, 78
Woodland Lass (Wherry), 115
Woods, Sadd & Moore, Messrs., 58, 83, 86, 192
Wright (of Beccles), 76-7, 86
Wright, Eliza, 196
Wroxham, 76, 96, 148, 160-3, 176, 189

Y

Yare, River, 11, 18, 21, 47, 48, 57, 96, 97, 104, 164, 180, 189, 191, 198
Zephyr (Wherry), 77, 156

www.ingramcontent.com/pod-product-compliance
Lightning Source LLC
Chambersburg PA
CBHW082053230426
43670CB00016B/2875